How It Works®

Science and Technology

Third Edition

Marshall Cavendish
99 White Plains Road
Tarrytown, NY 10591

Website: www.marshallcavendish.com

Third edition updated by Brown Reference Group plc.

Library of Congress Cataloging-in-Publication Data
How it works: science and technology.—3rd ed.
p. cm.
Includes index.
ISBN 0-7614-7314-9 (set)   ISBN 0-7614-7316-5 (Vol. 2)
1. Technology—Encyclopedias. 2. Science—Encyclopedias.
[1. Technology—Encyclopedias. 2. Science—Encyclopedias.]
T9 .H738 2003
603—dc21   2001028771

Consultant: Donald R. Franceschetti, Ph.D., University of Memphis

Brown Reference Group
Editor: Wendy Horobin
Associate Editors: Paul Thompson, Martin Clowes, Lis Stedman
Managing Editor: Tim Cooke
Design: Alison Gardner
Picture Research: Becky Cox
Illustrations: Mark Walker

Marshall Cavendish
Project Editor: Peter Mavrikis
Production Manager: Alan Tsai
Editorial Director: Paul Bernabeo

Printed in Malaysia
Bound in the United States of America
08 07 06 05 04   6 5 4 3 2

Title picture: The Eskimo nebula, see *Astronomy*

How It Works®

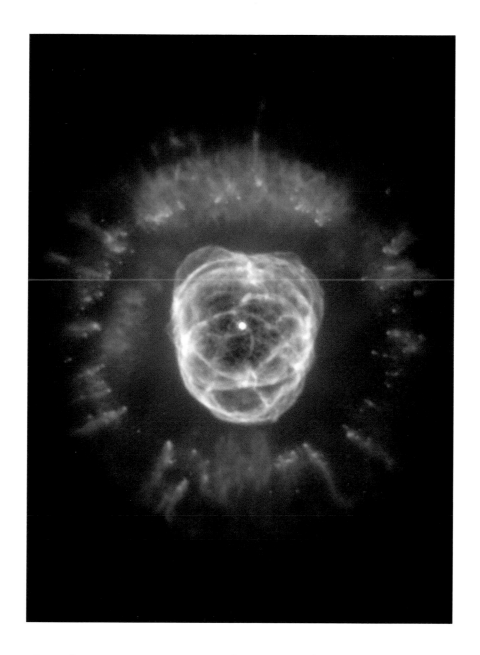

Science and Technology

Volume 2

Antifouling Techniques

Bomb-Aiming Device

Marshall Cavendish

New York • London • Toronto • Sydney

Contents

Volume 2

Antifouling Techniques

Antifouling techniques are used to prevent the buildup of aquatic animals and vegetation that foul or obstruct the underwater surfaces of structures and vessels. The most common fouling species are barnacles and green algae; in some parts of the world, tube worms, hydroids, sea squirts, mussels, and various red and brown algae also cause fouling problems.

Antifouling coatings for ships

The main reason for using antifouling techniques on a ship's hull is economic. A ship whose hull is encrusted in barnacles gains weight and encounters more resistance as it moves through water, reducing the maximum speed of a vessel and increasing the rate of fuel consumption at its cruising speed. The drag factor of a ship that is allowed to encrust for six months in temperate water will increase by ¼ percent. The increased drag can reduce the ship's top speed by 2 knots (2.3 mph, 3.7 km/h) and increase its fuel consumption at cruising speed by 40 percent. Further costs, such as docking fees and cleaning costs, arise if a ship is docked to have fouling removed.

The most efficient means of keeping a ship's hull free of barnacles and other buildup is with the use of antifouling paints. The first antifouling paints contained a biocide, such as copper (II) oxide (CuO), which prevented organisms from becoming attached to the hull. The biocide was mixed into the paint, and it would seep out during the life of the coating. The concentration of biocide around the hull would diminish rapidly as the biocide content of the coating dropped. After two to three years, the coating would no longer be effective, and the ship would have to be repainted. This technique compared with semiannual defoulings for ships without antifouling.

By the late 1980s, a new type of biocidal coating had replaced the original antifouling coatings: the self-polishing copolymer, or SPC. The biocide in SPC is tributyltin oxide, or TBTO, which was used as a booster for copper (II) oxide in earlier antifouling coatings. Unlike copper (II) oxide, TBTO is chemically bonded to the copolymer molecules that are the basis of the paint. The copolymer "self-polishes" by dissolving into the seawater around it. The rate of release is constant, and the coating always presents a fresh biocidal surface to the water around it, which means that an SPC can provide the same protection as an earlier antifouling coating while using less bio-

▲ The red cuprous oxide used in antifouling paint contrasts vividly with the incrustation of barnacles and algae on untreated steel.

cide. Thicker coats of SPC can be applied to increase the time between dockings to between five and seven years.

Ecological impact of TBTO

In the late 1980s, marine biologists reported that tributyltin oxide from antifouling coatings was damaging certain species of marine life, particularly bivalves and mollusks. By the early 1990s, many countries had restricted the use of TBTO-based antifoulings to ships longer than 27.3 yds. (25 m).

Alternatives to TBTO coatings are original copper-based antifouling coatings or coatings based on epoxy-silicone resins, which rely on nonstick properties to minimize fouling and assist cleaning with pressure hoses.

Antifouling for fixed structures

In general, increased drag caused by fouling is not a problem for fixed structures, although floating oilrigs can experience a stronger pull from waves if they become encrusted. Nevertheless, there are cases where fixed structures need protection from fouling: when the presence of fouling blocks water intake pipes or when it quickens the rate of corrosion of the underlying metal. One way to remove fouling from water intakes is to periodically pump hot water out through the pipes. Ultrasound generators provide some protection against fouling, as do regular sandblasting or steam cleaning.

SEE ALSO: Corrosion prevention • Metal • Ship • Warship

Antimatter

The existence of antimatter was first proposed by the British physicist Paul Dirac. In the late 1920s, Dirac was developing quantum mechanics as a mathematical description of the behavior of matter that conformed to Einstein's special theory of relativity. In 1928, Dirac formulated a successful description of the electron. To his surprise, he found that his description predicted that each type of particle should be matched by a similar particle of equal mass but opposite charge. Dirac called these shadowy partners antimatter. In 1933, Dirac shared with the Austrian physicist Erwin Schrödinger the Nobel Prize in Physics for their respective achievements in quantum mechanics.

Detection of the positron

In 1932, four years after Dirac's proposal, a U.S. physicist, Carl Anderson, was observing the effects of electric and magnetic fields on cosmic rays—high-energy charged particles that burst into Earth's atmosphere from space. The particles traced paths in a cloud chamber as the fields deflected them. Anderson detected particles whose paths curved to the same extent as the paths of electrons but in the opposite direction. This indicated positively charged particles whose charge-to-mass ratio was identical to that of the electron. He guessed that he had found an example of antimatter and named it the positron.

Annihilation and pair production

In his Special Theory of Relativity of 1905, the German-born physicist Albert Einstein proposed that mass and energy are simply two different aspects of the same thing—a property he called mass–energy. Interactions between matter and antimatter provide one of the ways in which mass can be converted into energy and vice versa.

When a particle meets an antiparticle, they can annihilate each other and produce an amount of energy, E, given by the formula $E = mc^2$, where m is the combined mass of the particle and antiparticle and c is the speed of light. The mass of the particle and antiparticle disappears, and the energy is released as two photons of light.

▼ Smashing high-speed protons from a particle accelerator into a target of metal atoms produces a variety of particles and antiparticles. A magnetic field then separates the different particles according to mass and charge, forming a beam of antiprotons that can be held in a storage ring or accelerated in another particle accelerator for further collisions.

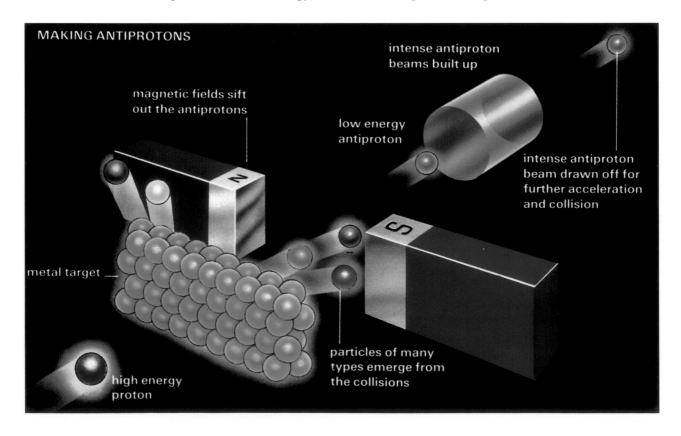

MAKING ANTIPROTONS

magnetic fields sift out the antiprotons

intense antiproton beams built up

low energy antiproton

intense antiproton beam drawn off for further acceleration and collision

metal target

particles of many types emerge from the collisions

high energy proton

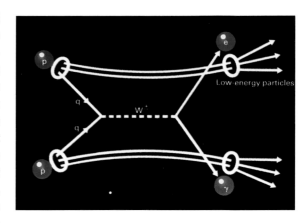

The reverse of annihilation is a process called pair production, in which energy—often as the kinetic energy of fast-moving particles—gets converted into mass. The formula $E = mc^2$ applies to this process as it does to annihilation. In 1955, a team led by a U.S. physicist, Owen Chamberlain, and an Italian-U.S. physicist, Emilio Segrè, used the Bevatron particle accelerator at Berkeley, California, to accelerate protons to a kinetic energy of 5.6 GeV, or 9×10^{-10} joules per proton. When these protons struck target protons, their kinetic energy became converted into the mass of proton–antiproton pairs. Physicists have since discovered a number of antiparticles and other subatomic particles. Some particles are their own antiparticles: the photon is an example.

▲ This type of diagram is used to map the interactions between subatomic particles and antiparticles. Here, a proton and an antiproton (p and p̄) form an electron (e) and a gamma ray (γ) via formation of a quark–antiquark pair (q and q̄) and W bosons (W±). The mass of the single electron that results from this interaction is around ¼₀₀₀ the mass of the original proton–antiproton pair: the remaining mass is converted into a gamma ray.

Positron emission

Cosmic rays and particle accelerators are not the only sources of antimatter. Certain radioactive nuclei emit positrons as they decay: positron emission happens as a proton transmutes into a neutron in a decaying nucleus.

Artificial positron-emitting radionuclides of carbon, nitrogen, oxygen, and fluorine can be made in nuclear reactors. By injecting compounds of these radionuclides into the bloodstream of a patient, a radiologist can monitor the progress of the compound through the patient's body. Each time a positron is emitted, it self-destructs as soon as it meets an electron. The two photons emitted in this process can be detected and their origin traced. A technique called positron-emission tomography uses a computer to form three-dimensional images from the detector signals.

▲ These are two views of a proton–antiproton collision (center right). A shower of subatomic fragments leaves traces of condensation in a cloud chamber, and the shapes of these traces can be studied to identify the particles and antiparticles that formed by collision.

Antiatoms

Once positrons and antiprotons had been proven to exist, it was clear that antihydrogen atoms could be made by combining an antiproton and a positron. The practical problems are immense, however, since both antiparticles are prone to self-destruct before they can meet one another.

In 1995, a team led by Walter Oelert of the Jülich Research Center in Germany managed to create nine antihydrogen atoms in the CERN European Laboratory for Particle Physics in Switzerland. They first created a number of antiprotons in a particle accelerator and kept them circulating in a magnetic storage ring—an enormous hollow ring in which a magnetic field exerts a force on moving charged particles that keeps them moving in a circle. Squirting xenon gas into the path of the antiprotons then produced a few electron–positron pairs in the stream. Each time an antiproton and a positron paired, the uncharged antihydrogen atom that resulted would no longer be held by the magnetic field in the ring. Instead, it would fly to the wall of the ring where its annihilation would be detected.

The next challenge in antiatom research will be to trap an antiatom long enough to observe its properties. It is unlikely that anyone will ever be able to make enough antiatoms to observe chemical reactions between them, but it might be possible to examine single atoms by spectroscope.

◄ A technician inspects a section of a particle accelerator at CERN in Switzerland. The curved surface is the wall of the particle path; the red structures are powerful electromagnets.

SEE ALSO: ATOMIC STRUCTURE • BUBBLE AND CLOUD CHAMBER • PARTICLE ACCELERATOR • PARTICLE DETECTOR

Aquaculture

Aquaculture is the farming of fish, mollusks, and crustaceans, which are stocked, fed, and protected much as livestock is on land. The cultured animals are in individual or corporate ownership; aquaculture is therefore sharply distinguished from the traditional "capture" fisheries. Although aquaculture has a long history, it was only in the 1980s that scientific and technical advances began to boost production. The global fisheries catch reached over 120 million tons in 1997, while world production of cultivated aquatic organisms rose to 28.8 million tons—three times as much as in 1990. A key factor in the rise has been the increase in cultivation of aquatic plants such as kelp, which accounted for a quarter of aquaculture production in 1997. Most of the remaining increase has come from filter-feeders like mussels, scallops, cockles, and other mollusks.

Aquaculture now accounts for more than half of world production of freshwater and brackish-water fish. These fish are predominantly various species of carp, tilapia, and milkfish reared in traditional fishponds in Asia for local consumption at low cost. By contrast, Japan, the United States, and Europe rear salmon, trout, and catfish and marine fish such as yellowtail and sea bream in intensive systems for diversified and distant markets.

New technologies supply seed

Aquaculture relies increasingly on artificially propagating eggs and "seed," or fry (recently hatched fish), rather than on collecting wild fry, the supply of which is both limited and seasonal. The aim is to control the sexual cycle of the fish, which include species of carp, catfish, and marine fish. This is now largely done with injections of

◀ Fish fry used in aquaculture tend to be raised artificially, often using hormones and genetic engineering to produce the required quality of stock. These carp fry are from a factory in Java, Indonesia.

▼ A salmon farm in Scotland. When fish are farmed in close confinement, disease can spread rapidly. Scottish farms were badly hit by disease in the early 1990s. Building pens in fast-flowing currents ensures good water quality and makes the fish fight the current, which develops their muscle flesh.

modern synthetic hormones, which are more reliable than traditional pituitary extracts.

Trout, sea bass, and turbot are controlled by alternating light and darkness to simulate the changes of the seasons and trick the fishes' "biological clocks" into advancing or delaying spawning. Many hatcheries maintain several separate brood-stocks with different "day" and "night" patterns to ensure year-round egg supplies.

Fish sperm can be preserved as a gene bank for several weeks at 25°F (–4°C) and can be preserved indefinitely in liquid nitrogen at –321°F (–196°C). In the case of salmon or trout, it is now commonplace to manipulate the chromosome number. To do this, eggs are subjected to heat or pressure soon after fertilization, which results in triplets of chromosomes rather than the usual pairs. These fish grow rapidly to market size but do not become sexually mature and cannot interbreed with wild populations. By using sperm that have been treated with ultraviolet light, only the female chromosomes are active, and all the offspring are genetically identical.

Advances in feeding

Much of the recent expansion in marine fish and shrimp culture has been triggered by the development of improved feeds in the form of suitable live plankton and "microencapsulated" food pellets. Many hatcheries enrich these foods with HUFA (higher unsaturated fatty acids), derived from fish or squid oil, which is vital for normal development.

Fish require approximately 30 to 50 percent animal protein in their diet. Aquaculture consumes one-seventh of the world's fish meal; this may ultimately limit production from intensive aquaculture unless cost-effective substitute protein sources are developed.

New dietary formulations have a higher energy content and more digestible proteins and carbohydrates, which minimize the production of

feces and thus pollution from the animals' wastes. Modern extrusion and expansion processes yield food pellets that do not break up so readily in water and are designed to have the right buoyancy: demersal fish such as turbot will only eat pellets that sink to the bottom, while salmon, for example, prefer slow-sinking pellets.

Rearing sites

Fish farming has been practiced for centuries, usually of freshwater species, which were kept in large ponds to supply a family or small community. This is still the case in much of India, Southeast Asia, and China, where carp and tilapia are grown as subsidiary crops in flooded rice-paddy fields. They are low-value fish in export terms, but provide a valuable source of protein for local people. Shrimp, on the other hand, are in great demand all over the world and fetch good prices. Special ponds are built for shrimp, and these ponds often form part of a water reuse scheme, with the water being used for irrigation afterward.

Trout farms can be very elaborate, incorporating pumps, aerators, and specialist equipment to keep the water chemistry constant. Mollusks are grown in beds on the seashore. Often they need little more than a supporting structure to attach themselves to, as they feed on microscopic plant life and filter contaminants from the surrounding water. Mollusks are not always bred as a food crop—Australia and Japan rear oysters to supply a thriving trade in cultivated pearls.

Moving to deeper waters

Most marine fishes are reared in cages in sheltered inshore sites. Further expansion depends on moving farther offshore, where there is better water quality and waste dispersal and where nets can be larger and deeper. With such expansion the fish would not have to be stocked as densely, resulting in less disease and faster growth. Offshore systems need to be strong to withstand the wind and waves. They also present problems for monitoring and harvesting the stock.

Some nets enclose nearly a million cubic feet (25,000 m³) of water and 400 tons (360 tonnes) of fish. Possible alternatives to nets are "curtains" of air bubbles or of cold water, pumped from the depths and allowed to descend around the enclosed area. The latter technique is currently being tested with tuna, which do not like to enter cold water.

Disease control

In 1991, more than one in three Scottish salmon died from disease, mainly caused by bacteria and parasitic sea lice. Bacterial and viral epidemics have caused serious losses of marine shrimp. Antibiotics are increasingly used against bacteria, but the appearance of drug resistance, and even cross-resistance to more than one drug, calls for a wider range of measures. One alternative is to use vaccines. The problem of injecting large numbers of fish has led to the development of oral vaccines against the major diseases of salmon and catfish.

In the past, sea lice have been controlled with organophosphate pesticides, but these threaten the natural balance of marine life and have become less effective as resistance has developed. Alternative natural compounds are under test— one from a fungus, another from a chrysanthemum. Biological control with wrasse, fish that are natural "cleaners," looks promising.

The best method of disease control is good husbandry: ensuring good water quality, preventing excessive densities of stock, and avoiding feed wastage. Marine farms increasingly rotate their sites and allow each to lie fallow for a season, to give it a chance to recover from the pollution and parasites that will inevitably have built up. Neighboring enterprises synchronize their disease treatments to avoid a cycle of reinfection.

▲ Harvesting oysters by hand. The oysters are grown on a substructure in shallow water and are harvested at low tide. The large metal collection cages are hauled up the beach, where the oysters are washed in tanks of clean water before being sent all over the world.

 SEE ALSO: FISHING INDUSTRY • MARINE BIOLOGY

Aqualung

The aqualung or SCUBA (Self-Contained Underwater Breathing Apparatus) is a life support system that supplies air to a diver without the need for safety lines to the surface or for cumbersome protective bells. The development of the aqualung has led to the growth of diving as a sport throughout the world. More important, though, the aqualung has become invaluable in offshore oil and gas operations, marine engineering, and search-and-rescue work.

Essentially, the aqualung consists of three main units: a demand valve, a cylinder filled with compressed air, and a harness. Two important functions of the demand valve are to provide air only on demand (when the diver inhales) and to exhaust exhaled air, but its vital role is to regulate the pressure of air supplied to the diver. Typically, the cylinder is pressurized to 2,800 psi (200 bar)—more than sufficient to explode the lungs and entire chest cavity if applied to the respiratory tract, which is accustomed to breathe at only 14.5 psi (1 bar).

Moreover, the deeper the diver descends, the greater is the pressure owing to the weight of the water above. At 30 ft. (10 m), the water exerts a pressure of 29 psi (2 bar), and 14.5 psi (1 bar) for every additional 30 ft. (10 m) of depth. The body consists largely of solids and liquids that, unlike air, are virtually incompressible, even under great pressures. It also contains air-filled cavities—the lungs, sinuses, inner ear, and stomach—all of which connect with the respiratory system. If the air being inhaled is not at the same pressure as the water around the body, these cavities are forced to contract. Even at shallow depths, the contraction can compress the air, making breathing extremely difficult. In fact, at sufficient depths, the pressure crushes the cavities flat and kills the diver. The demand valve regulates the supply pressure from the cylinder and matches it with the pressure at the various depths to which the diver descends without the need for manual adjustment.

The demand valve

In its simplest form, the demand valve is a circular box consisting of two chambers, each separated by a flexible diaphragm. One chamber is open to the sea, so the diaphragm is at the same pressure as the surrounding water. The other chamber is connected to the diver's mouth by a flexible tube. Inside the second chamber is a tilt valve, which seals off the high-pressure air supply from the cylinder. When the diver inhales, the pressure in the second chamber is reduced, and the diaphragm is pushed in by the water pressure so it presses on the tilt valve. By making the diaphragm large, the tilt-valve lever long, and the high-pressure-valve seat small, the small pressure change is amplified to open the high-pressure valve against the pressure of the spring.

As the tilt valve opens, high-pressure air rushes into the second chamber, raising the pressure and pushing the diaphragm back until the pressure in both chambers is the same as the water pressure. The tilt valve closes and no more air enters until the diver inhales again or descends with the valve. Exhaled air is vented into the first chamber to balance the unit.

This type of valve is called a single-stage valve, but it is more usual to reduce the cylinder pressure in two stages to provide smoother air flow. The first stage is on the cylinder, and the second forms part of the mouthpiece. Some demand valves can be connected to a low-pressure air supply from a large cylinder or compressor at the surface, enabling the diver to stay submerged for long periods.

The cylinder

The cylinders containing the air supply are deceptively simple. They are made from steel or aluminum and are strictly controlled in manufacture and maintenance to ensure that they are safe to use. The development of a reliable high-pres-

▼ The modern aqualung is a development of the sports equipment used by swimmers just before World War II. The first self-contained system, which freed the diver from the air hose and surface pump, was designed by an Englishman, H. A. Fleuss, in 1878. The rebreather suit, in which the exhaled gases were circulated through a container of chemicals to scrub out the carbon dioxide, formed the basis of self-contained suits from the turn of the 19th century until 1943, when Emil Gagnan developed the fully automatic valve.

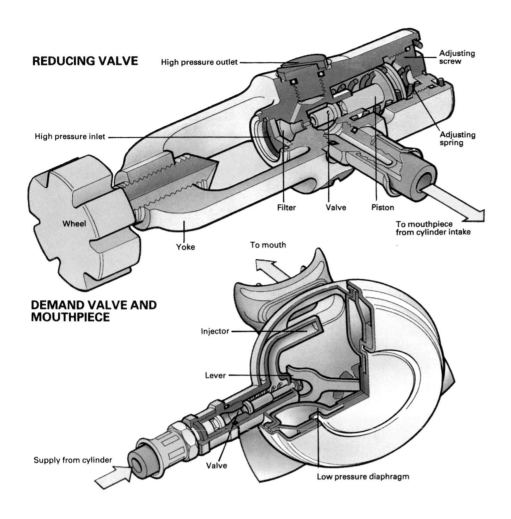

REDUCING VALVE

High pressure outlet

Adjusting screw

High pressure inlet

Adjusting spring

Wheel

Filter   Valve   Piston

Yoke

To mouthpiece from cylinder intake

DEMAND VALVE AND MOUTHPIECE

To mouth

Injector

Lever

Supply from cylinder

Valve

Low pressure diaphragm

◄ The first stage of a piston-type demand valve (top) serves to reduce the pressure of the charged-air cylinder from 2,800 psi to 108 psi (200–7.5 bar). The second stage of the demand valve (bottom) incorporates the diver's mouthpiece. Both the diaphragm and the exhaust valve are made from soft, flexible silicone. During exhalation the valve spring holds the valve shut and spent air is exhausted through the rubber-sealed valve at the side. When the diver breathes in, a slight suction is created in the injector tube, causing the inlet valve to open and thus provide air on demand. The first stage of the demand valve is attached to the top of the compressed-air cylinder and is joined by a flexible tube to the second stage.

sure cylinder has enabled divers to carry sufficient compressed air, which is healthier to breathe than pure oxygen, which becomes toxic at depths greater than about 30 ft. (10 m). A 23 in. (60 cm) long cylinder having a diameter of 7 in. (17.5 cm) might contain about 1.7 mm³ of air, compressed at a pressure of around 2,800 psi (200 bar). On the surface, this air should last an adult about 100 minutes; at a depth of 30 ft. (10 m), it lasts about 50 minutes and at 90 ft. (30 m) about 25 minutes.

Birth of the aqualung

The aqualung is a refinement of diving equipment that had remained relatively unchanged for nearly 100 years, until just prior to World War II. At about this time, swimmers started using the new goggles, fins, and snorkels in the Mediterranean for sport fishing and fun. Among them was a young naval gunner, Jacques Cousteau. In 1943, a French engineer, Emil Gagnan, developed a fully automatic demand valve for Cousteau, and the modern aqualung was effectively born.

Dangers of diving

It is not just the downward part of a dive that poses a threat to divers from the effects of air pressure. If a diver comes back up to the surface

too quickly, he can suffer from decompression sickness, also known as "the bends." This happens because compressed air contains a large proportion of nitrogen gas, which gets absorbed into the blood. This is usually exhaled, but if the diver ascends at too fast a rate, bubbles form, which block the flow of blood and can kill the diver. Divers use a decompression table to tell them how long they can stay at a particular depth without absorbing too much nitrogen. If a diver suffers the bends, he or she must go immediately into a decompression chamber, which is set according to the depth at which the diver was working, and gradually returned to surface pressure over a number of hours or days.

Working at depths of over 250 ft. (83 m) also poses the danger of nitrogen narcosis, which makes divers feel drugged and confused. To counteract this, many deep-sea divers breathe a mixture that replaces nitrogen with helium. Similarly, breathing pure oxygen or high-oxygen-content air at depth can cause dizziness, vomiting, and convulsions.

SEE ALSO: Breathing apparatus • Diving suit • Gas laws • Lung • Undersea habitat

Archaeological Technologies

Archaeology is the study of the human past from its material remains. These remains range from fragile traces of campsites nearly two million years old in East Africa to early villages in the Near East where the first farmers lived to more recent historical settlements such as the colonial town of Williamsburg in Virginia.

While modern archaeology is not an experimental science itself, it utilizes many recently developed scientific methods to help find, excavate, and analyze material from ancient sites.

Discovering sites

The first stage in any archaeological investigation is to locate the sites where people once lived. Archaeologists are always on the lookout for traces of former human habitation in the landscape, from pieces of broken ceramics to coins. While many sites are still found by chance, many

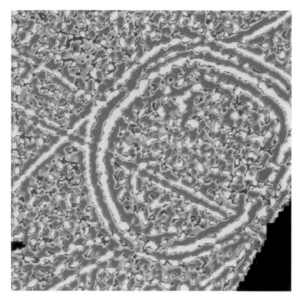

▲ An Iron Age settlement in Cornwall, Britain, discovered using a magnetometer. The large enclosure is about 23 ft. (70 m) in diameter.

◄ Ancient ditches discovered beneath Georgian buildings in Bath, Britain, by means of a portable proton magnetometer—a device that can detect where top soil has sifted into different strata.

potential areas have now been surveyed. Rather than examine a whole area in minute detail, small areas are studied intensively either by looking for surface remains or by digging small trenches.

Statistical techniques then help archaeologists to work out the total number and distribution of sites. Samples of as little as 4 percent of the total area have been used to draw conclusions about both the settlement patterns within a region and the internal structures of individual sites.

Aerial photography has been used for many years to look for such things as ancient earthworks. Although it is usually carried out from airplanes, airplanes cannot fly low enough. In recent years, cameras, using a radio signal to trigger the shutter, have been hoisted aloft on tethered blimps or balloons and kites.

Close-up views of buildings such as the palace of Knossos in Crete allow every stone to be plotted on highly accurate plans. These are vertical views, but airplanes can also take oblique pictures, which give better perspective and place a site in its environmental context. Some sites are totally invisible from the ground but, under suitable conditions of climate and crop growth, may be seen from the air by means of crop marks.

At the other extreme, satellite images can show vegetation differences through false-color imagery, thus revealing overgrown ruins. Equally useful is airborne radar, which penetrates vegetation and thus is helpful in forested regions such as the tropics. It was used by NASA to map extensive networks of canal-like features in Belize and northern Guatemala. Some of these networks were ancient Mayan drained fields, once used for intensive agriculture; others were merely natural joints in the bedrock. In Costa Rica, ancient footpaths were found, documenting a web of communications several thousand years old.

Mapping sites

Once an archaeological site has been pinpointed, both buried and surface features need to be plotted as accurately as possible before excavation begins. For many years, archaeologists have used such tools as resistivity meters, proton magne-

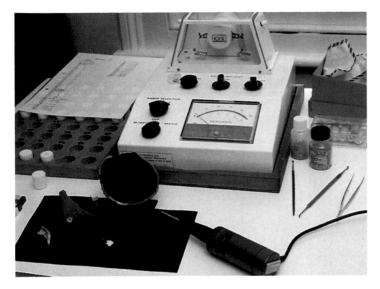

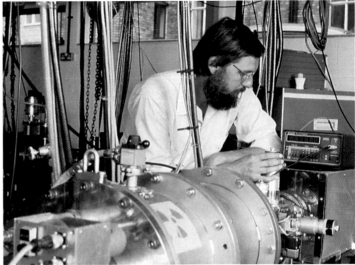

tometers, and metal detectors to build up a picture of the site. However, these archaeological tools are now being supplemented by a range of new techniques also used in geophysics. For example, a subsurface radar scanner mounted on a trolley and dragged across the site on transects sends rapid pulses into the soil to a depth of 10 ft. (3 m). Different echoes return from solid features, such as walls, compared with softer ones, such as grave fill.

Geo-radar equipment, mounted on a slow-moving vehicle, assesses time and energy differences between transmitted and reflected pulses to locate layers of contrasting density, while the seismic "standing wave technique" sends sound waves through the soil by striking it repeatedly and measuring the time that the waves take to reach a detector—they will move more slowly through soft deposits. This is similar to sonar, long used by ships as an echo sounder to detect navigational hazards and now by maritime archaeologists to find wrecks on the sea floor. Sonar has been used also on dry land to detect tombs in the Valley of the Kings in Egypt.

All of these methods measure anomalies or irregularities below ground. Natural features, as well as archaeological remains, will give signals, so it is necessary to define the general area of investigation as closely as possible.

New instruments have greatly speeded up the process of mapping on the surface and in the excavation of trenches. While the traditional plane table and alidade, or surveyor's level and staff, are still widely used by archaeologists, the electronics revolution has produced the electronic distance-measuring theodolite. In this, a standard optical telescope is used to locate the target staff, up to 1.24 miles (2 km) away, and then an ultrasound signal is sent to it and reflected by retroprisms attached to the staff. The distance

▲ Left: Roman pottery being prepared for analysis by atomic absorption—one of the techniques used to determine the elemental composition of archaeological samples. By determining the composition of ceramic containers researchers have been able to trace ancient trade routes. Right: A purpose-built accelerator mass spectrometer at a leading dating laboratory in the U.K. The sample is ionized and the ion beam is separated into a spectrum of particles by means of an electric field.

can be measured to within a few centimeters, and the instrument can be set to display the horizontal and vertical angles.

Dating sites

Radiocarbon dating is still the most widely used scientific method of deciding on the age of a sample. Carbon is present in all living things, and where it has been protected from burning, waterlogging, or desiccation, it is one of the most common constituents of ancient structures, burial sites, and trash heaps. Measuring the rate of decay of the isotope carbon-14 yields the ratio of carbon-14 to the more common isotopes carbon-12 and carbon-13, which do not decay. From this, the age of the organic material can be calculated.

Radiocarbon dating has become more precise with the development of accelerator mass spectrometry (AMS): instead of counting the decay events of carbon-14, the numbers of atoms are counted directly and compared to those of the stable isotopes carbon-12 and carbon-13.

Because far smaller samples are needed with the AMS method, single seeds or tiny fragments of important objects can be dated. Among the results has been the exposure of the Turin Shroud as a 14th-century fake. In a less well publicized investigation, it was discovered that cultivated barley found on a 17,000-year-old site at Wadi Kubbaniya in Egypt actually belonged to much later layers on the site. If the older date had been confirmed, it would have meant that the practice of farming was almost twice as old as had originally been thought. Dates have even been obtained from blood used as a binder in Pleistocene cave paintings in both Europe and Australia, while other analytical methods have been used to identify the blood as human or otherwise.

Thermoluminescent dating, first demonstrated at Oxford in 1968, has proved valuable in assessing the age of fired materials, such as pottery. Energetic particles given off by the decay of the naturally occurring radioisotopes tend to knock off electrons from the atoms of materials through which they pass. In many crystalline minerals, some of these electrons become trapped, creating imperfections in the structure of the crystal.

When the crystalline matter is heated, the electrons are released and energy is given off in the form of light. The intensity of the glow is related to the age of the crystal or to the time that has elapsed since the material was heated by ancient people: each period of heating drives off the geologically accumulated glow, and the buildup begins again. Particles of quartz are present in almost all ceramics, and these quartz crystals are commonly used in dating.

Analyzing finds

One important archaeological technique is used to establish exactly where a particular artifact was made or where its materials originated. For example, thin sections of stone axes or Mayan jades can be placed by matching them with existing rock samples, and minerals in pottery can be used to help identify where trade wares come from. Neolithic ceramics were transported over distances up to 60 miles (100 km) before 3000 B.C.E., while Roman amphorae were distributed throughout the empire.

While many materials have a basically similar composition, with the same major elements occurring everywhere, trace elements present only in a few parts per million often vary between one source and another. The volcanic glass obsidian has been successfully traced from many sources to its final destination in ancient trash heaps by several methods.

Chemical analysis of artifacts is usually done by optical emission spectroscopy. A small sample is burnt between carbon rods carrying an electric current, the light is separated by prisms, and the resulting spectrum recorded. The position of

▲ The analysis of DNA extracted from once-living tissue has become an important tool in archaeology. Just two grams of bone can provide enough DNA to give genetic information about the ancestry of its former owner, and population movements over time.

bright lines in the spectrum indicates what chemical elements are present and in what quantities. This has made it possible to distinguish groups of artifacts with similar compositions and hence, quite probably, similar origins.

Optical emission spectroscopy is increasingly being replaced by neutron activation analysis, which can be nondestructive and more accurate. Neutron activation analysis uses slow neutrons in a reactor to excite the atoms in the sample and convert them to unstable isotopes, which emit gamma rays of a characteristic frequency as they decay, producing a series of lines in a spectrum. The intensity of each spectral line indicates how much of each element is present. Proton-induced X-ray emission (PIXE) produces similar results, using an accelerator instead of a nuclear reactor. X-ray fluorescence spectrometry uses a beam of X rays to excite secondary X rays in the sample, with wavelengths and energies indicating how much of each element is present. The electron microprobe focuses a fine beam on a small area of the sample, again exciting electrons to emit characteristic X rays.

Atomic emission spectrometry uses the principle that a material at high temperature will release light of a particular wavelength or color for each element present. In another method, known as inductively coupled plasma emission spectrometry (ICPS), the sample is excited in a plasma arc at much higher temperatures, with less overlap between the responses from each element. These methods are accurate within 5 percent; most results are plotted with a 95 percent confidence limit. The particular combination and concentration of trace elements will characterize most sources of obsidian and other useful minerals such as flint or chert, enabling the archaeologist to make maps of ancient trade routes.

The study of biological remains from archaeological sites does not usually require elaborate equipment. A sample of soil can be agitated in water, using a flotation machine. Small seeds, charcoal fragments, bones, snails, and insect remains float to the surface. These can give information about diet, vegetation, and climate.

Pollen is extremely resistant and is often well preserved in lake muds, heathland soils, and particularly in peat bogs. These are important because they contain a pollen record of vegetational, and hence climatic, changes that have taken place in the region while the bog was forming. Pollen is extracted by destroying other organic and mineral matter with strong acids, then it is collected as a residue and examined under a microscope.

Conservation and preservation

Once a site has been discovered, the archaeologist has to decide how best to conserve it and prevent structures and artifacts from disintegration. Burial underground or submersion in water effects chemical changes in natural materials. Usually the artifact has survived only because it is in equilibrium with its surroundings, preventing further damage from bacteria, fungi, or chemical breakdown. Conservation is an expensive process, and the archaeologist has to consider whether it is better to rebury material after excavating the site or to employ a method of preservation that allows people to explore their cultural heritage without risk to the find.

First the archaeologist has to determine how stable the material is within the site. This often begins with monitoring hydrological conditions long before excavation starts. The type of soil, height of the water table, and even drainage activities several miles away can affect how the site will respond to exposure. A number of urban sites explored in the 1960s and reburied under buildings are having to be reexamined after it was discovered that engineering solutions used at the time have not been effective in preventing damage to the artifacts.

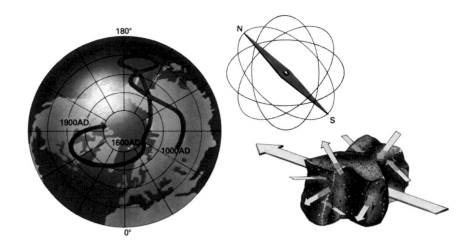

▲ Pottery can be dated through magnetic measurements. The location of the Earth's magnetic poles has changed over time (globe, left). When pottery is fired and then cools, the iron oxide particles in the clay become oriented with regard to the magnetic pole at the time. This orientation can be compared with the data stored in the national archaeomagnetic data file to determine the approximate date that the pottery was made.

Wood can be preserved for long periods of time in the anoxic conditions common to waterlogged sites. Initial decay processes cause it to lose much of its cellulose, leaving only a lignin skeleton that retains the original features of the item, but in a considerably weakened state. Reexposure to air causes the wood to shrink, destroying the artifact. Archaeologists can overcome this problem by maintaining the artifact under controlled temperature and humidity or replacing the interstitial water with another substance.

The technique used by researchers on King Henry VIII of England's warship *Mary Rose* involved freeze-drying of the timbers followed by spraying of polyethylene glycol, a waxy substance commonly used as an antifreeze in cars, to replace water in the pores. The ship will have to be sprayed at regular intervals until the year 2015 before the timbers are completely impregnated and the structure becomes resistant to further degradation.

The new technique of supercritical drying replaces liquid in the wood with high-density carbon dioxide, which will not mix with water; so

◄ Two pictures showing the contours of the famed Hadrian's Wall, which stretches across northern Britain, and one of its forts. Oblique sunlight reveals more to the aerial camera than the eye on the ground can discern. Infrared cameras can show crop marks, indicating the location of Roman ditches, trackways, and enclosures.

FACT FILE

- *Most archaeological studies are concerned solely with the artifacts that people leave behind. Occasionally, the people themselves are discovered, preserved in peat. For example, 168 bodies dating from around 5500 B.C.E. were found in peat near Titusville, Florida.*

- *Although the bodies are shrunken, the skin and internal organs are often present. It is even possible to investigate the stomach contents. In the case of the body of an Iron Age woman that was recovered from a peat bog in Djursland, Holland, in 1879, the remains had been kept in a museum for over a century before investigations were carried out.*

- *Using a medical technique, computerized tomography showed the position of food residues within the body; these were then removed with minimum damage by cutting a small opening in the abdominal wall. Her last meal had been of gruel made from rye.*

- *Skin taken from a male body found in a bog at Lindow, England, was examined using an electron probe X-ray microanalyzer. The results implied that paints containing copper and zinc were present, presumably as part of body decoration.*

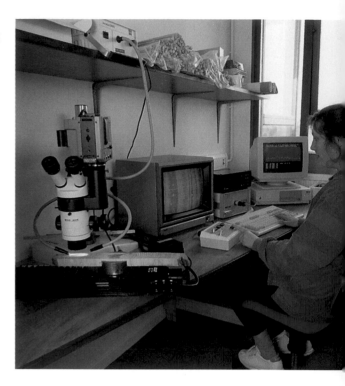

▶ Archaeologists can use tree-dating analysis to find the precise date of a site they are investigating. A TV camera is attached to the microscope to help measure the distance between growth rings, and the results are analyzed by computer. Scientists can not only date the site by this method, but can also determine much about the environmental conditions and the climate.

undergo an electrolytic process called anodic stripping/cathodic polishing to remove any blackening and stabilize the surface of the object. This process is repeated many times until the surface appears bright and any traces of blackening have vanished. After rinsing and a neutralizing bath, objects are given a light polishing with baking soda and sprayed with a clear protective coating or stored in airtight containers.

▼ Conservation of the *Mary Rose*, a 16th-century warship that lay in the English Channel for over 400 years. Its timbers have to be sprayed regularly with chemicals to prevent them drying out and disintegrating.

the water is first replaced with an organic solvent such as methanol, which readily dissolves in the carbon dioxide. This residue can then be removed by decompression without forming a liquid phase, thus preventing shrinkage.

Fabrics are fragile, and fragments often survive through minerals impregnating their woven structure. A mild acid called Aracon can be used to dissolve minerals without destroying the cloth. A weak solution of hydrochloric acid is then used to remove rust and other stains. After repeated soaking in water to remove the acid, the item is then left in polyethylene glycol for several days.

Methods of conserving metal objects vary, depending on the properties of the metal involved. Gold and silver are comparatively inert and need little more than light cleaning. Other metals such as pewter may need to be put into a weak solution of muriatic acid to remove any mineral concretions and then rinsed. They then

SEE ALSO: Corrosion prevention • Magnetometer • Metal detector • Radioisotopic dating • Salvage, marine • Spectroscopy • X-ray imaging

Armor

Armor is a protective barrier—usually in the form of clothing—that is designed to protect its user from injury in combat. The use of armor has been recorded for more than 5,000 years. In that time, armor has progressed from toughened animal-hide garments, through suits of metal chain mail and plate, to garments reinforced with high-strength polymers and composite materials. The future might bring garments reinforced with biodegradable spider's-web silk produced from the milk of genetically modified goats.

Ancient armor

The earliest records of armor date from around 3000 B.C.E. Assyrian wall carvings in northern Iraq show simple helmets, probably made of leather or bronze, with flaps to protect the ears. Around the same time, the Egyptians were using knee-length padded wraparound aprons to protect from body blows, and the Sumerians used close-fitting copper helmets. By 1400 B.C.E., Syrian soldiers had scale armor, a leather or fabric cloak covered with small overlapping plates of bronze or iron.

The ancient Greeks fashioned bronze helmets and shaped bronze plates to cover the torso and the lower legs. A handheld shield would protect the parts of the body not covered by armor. The ancient Romans used a number of combinations of armor. Some were variations on the scaled armor of Syria; others were jackets made from overlapping iron plates. In other parts of the world, notably China, armor made of multiple layers of rhinoceros or ox hides continued to be used perhaps until the 13th century C.E.

Chain mail

Chain mail is a form of fabric made by linking together small metal rings, each ring interlocking with four rings around it. The chains resisted the cutting edges of swords while padded undergarments softened the impact of blows. Flexibility was the great advantage of chain mail over previous forms of armor. The Roman legionary used chain mail as early as the third century B.C.E. During the Middle Ages, the skill of the armorer improved; before long, the entire body was protected by mail.

Early suits of armor

Although the flexibility of chain mail made it the predominant form of armor in Europe during the Middle Ages, chain mail provided little protection against penetrating weapons, which could

break open the metal rings. As stronger weapons were developed to pierce the mail, extra protection was obtained by the fitting of metal plates at the most vulnerable points. The earliest evidence for these plates appears in drawings from the mid-13th century, which show chain-mail suits with reinforcing plates fitted at the knee—a difficult area to protect with chain mail and particularly vulnerable for horse riders. Improvements in crossbows in the early 14th century made chain mail largely ineffective, and suits that protected the entire body with plate armor were in use by around 1350 C.E.

Medieval armor

During the 15th century, German and Austrian armorers made suits of fully articulated armor in a Gothic style that reflected the architecture of the era. It was characterized by straight lines and edges cut in cusps and trimmed with brass. By the start of the 16th century, German armorers developed Maximilian armor, named for Emperor Maximilian I. It was a stronger and more rounded version of the Gothic style. Maximilian armor is

▼ Foot combat armor made in 1591 for King Christian I of Saxony. The advent of firearms at the beginning of the 16th century began to render full armor obsolete, until by the middle of the 17th century, only the breastplate and helmet were still in use.

easily recognized, since the surface of all pieces—except the lower-leg armor, or greaves—were fluted to give extra strength and good glancing surfaces. The helmet enclosed the head and was known as a close helm.

The advent of firearms

The use of guns in the early 16th century brought about changes in the use and form of armor. While the best suits of armor until then had offered almost complete protection against cutting weapons such as swords and spears, bullets from even the crudest of guns could penetrate them. Some thicker suits of armor were made that could withstand bullets, but the increased weight of such suits made their use in battle impracticable.

Many troops began to discard full armor, relying instead on partial armor made of thicker plate. Some wore heavily armored cuirasses (or armor for the torso); a few wore heavier armor with long thigh pieces reaching to the knees. Mail continued to be widely used as a secondary defense until the 17th century. By the end of the 17th century, the majority of European troops had discarded armor, and only a few cavalry units

▲ Football players wear armor that protects without hindering the movement of the wearer.

◀ Armor typical of a Japanese Samurai warrior at the end of the 16th century. Unlike their European counterparts, the Japanese adopted a lightweight, flexible armor made from bamboo, cloth, and metal. Although most of the armor was made of lacquered bamboo, interlaced to provide flexibility, they used a chestplate made of one piece of metal. The arms and neck were also protected by small pieces of metal laced together with colored strings. The Samurai's two swords have been mounted on a shoulder plate.

still retained their cuirasses. In the 18th century even cavaliers abandoned cuirasses as firearms improved.

By the 19th century, armor was no longer used in Europe, and few thought that it would ever return. In the Orient, however, armor continued in use much longer. Indian, Persian, and Turkish warriors wore defenses composed of mail and plates. Japanese samurai armor differed in that it was made of small lacquered metal plates and pieces of bamboo laced together. Such armor was used until the late 19th century.

World War I

During World War I (1914–1918), troops in the trenches suffered a high proportion of head wounds caused by bullets and shrapnel (the metal fragments from ballistic shells). From 1915, most armies began to issue a form of head protection known variously as a tin hat or a steel helmet. Machine gunners, snipers, and others liable to suffer dangerous exposure were also equipped with heavy fabric and metal armor for the upper body.

Chain mail had a resurgence when tanks were introduced in 1915–1916. Tank crews were issued with face masks that consisted of metal plates that covered the eyes, cheeks, and nose. A short curtain of mail hanging from the metal plate protected the mouth and chin. These face guards protected crewmen from a phenomenon called bullet splash, which could immobilize early tanks if they came under sustained machine gun fire. Although the bullets could not pierce the tank's armor, they could knock chips of metal off its interior. Also, if a bullet struck a joint between armor plates, its nickel jacket could be ripped off while its core of molten lead squeezed through the tiny gaps between plates. This made the inside of a tank under fire a hail of tiny metal fragments that were unpleasant if rarely lethal.

Modern body armor

By World War II (1939–1945), fighting personnel on land and sea relied mainly on armored tanks, ships, and other vehicles, and buildings to provide protection. The exceptions were bomber crews, who used flak jackets to protect them from hostile fire. These jackets took their name from the abbreviation of the German word *Flieger-abwehrkanone*, meaning "antiaircraft gun." Combining padding with steel, aluminum, or glass fiber-plates and heavy nylon textile, flak jackets were found to give reasonable protection against low-velocity bullets and shrapnel without being so cumbersome as to restrict the wearer's movements. After World War II, flak jackets went on to be used by ground and air personnel during conflicts in Korea, Vietnam, and Northern Ireland.

Bulletproof jackets

The main limitation of the flak jacket was that it did not provide effective protection against high-velocity projectiles, such as those from a revolver or rifle fired at close range. During the 1960s, much research was done to improve the resistance of flak jackets to high velocity rounds. At first, scientists believed that steel plate was the most likely material to be able to provide effective body armor and the only type likely to resist high-velocity rounds. They used newly developed tempering and quenching processes to produce a low-alloy steel that was extremely tough. Incorporating layers of the new steel into a padded jacket produced a bulletproof garment that was cumbersome but not hopelessly unwieldy. Other designs used layers of boron nitride—an extremely hard ceramic—instead of steel. These designs were lighter than the steel-containing jackets. Unfortunately, they were bulkier than the steel-based jackets and also less resistant to penetration—particularly under fire from automatic weapons that can secure a number of hits in a small cluster.

The greatest advance in bulletproof jackets came when scientists changed their approach to stopping bullets. In early designs, they had sought to use materials that would be hard enough to repel a bullet strike. In the new design, they sought to dissipate the kinetic energy of a bullet by using a material that would yield slightly while still being tough enough to prevent bullets from breaking through.

At the start of the 1970s, the U.S. National Institute of Justice (NIJ) was running a research program to develop lightweight body armor that could be worn for hours by on-duty law-enforcement officers. Early trials showed that heavy-weave nylon cloth could stop a low-velocity round by causing the nose of the heat-softened bullet to spread. Some of the kinetic energy of the bullet went into making it deform in this way; the rest was spread over a larger impact area, reduc-

▲ The type of armor worn by aircrew gives protection from a crash as well as from gunfire.

ing the penetrating power of the bullet. A textile made with 16 layers of heavy weave nylon will keep out all standard handgun bullets; 24 layers will defeat magnum sizes.

In 1971, the NIJ researchers started looking at Kevlar, an aramid-type nylon that had recently been developed to replace steel belts in car tires. Being much tougher than standard nylon, Kevlar proved to be the ideal material for a new generation of bulletproof jackets. These jackets have been standard since the mid-1970s. Perhaps the strongest body armor worn today is the Explosive Ordnance Disposal suit worn by bomb-disposal experts, which weighs 48 lbs. (22 kg) and can be fitted with a cooling system.

Future developments

It is possible that the next advance in body armor will be achieved with the help of spiders and goats. The silk that a spider produces to build webs is a protein. Proteins and nylons are both variants of chemical compounds called polyamides. When a spider spins a web, it secretes a solution of protein that shrinks as it dries. The shrinkage aligns the protein molecules in such a way that they form strong attractions to one another. The result is a crystalline fiber that is much stronger than the same weight and thickness of steel or Kevlar while also being more elastic than either material.

A group of researchers in Canada has genetically engineered the mammary cells of goats to produce the silk protein in milk using genes from spiders. The next stage in the development will be to find a way to cause the dissolved protein molecules to align and crystallize in the way that they do when a spider spins its web. If they can do this, the material that results, which they intend to call biosteel, will find use in a variety of applications, including body armor and space suits. Being biodegradable, biosteel will have to be sealed from the environment for these purposes.

SEE ALSO: AMMUNITION • ARMORED VEHICLE AND TANK • POLYAMIDE

Armored Vehicle and Tank

An armored vehicle is a personnel carrier that moves on wheels and is reinforced to withstand armed attacks. Some types of armored vehicles are fitted with weapons, but the main purpose of an armored vehicle is to protect its occupants. A tank is a self-propelled armored vehicle that moves on tracks and mounts one or more weapons. Its distinguishing features—tracks for cross-country mobility and armor to protect the crew inside against attack—enable the weapons to be used more effectively.

History

The forerunners of armored vehicles were built as early as the Boer War (1899–1902), when the machine-gun-carrying four-wheel vehicle and the armored steam traction engine were devised. The first vehicles to combine weaponry and armor were built between 1902 and 1904 by Vickers, Son and Maxim Ltd. in England; Société Charron, Girardot et Voigt in France; and Austro-Daimler in Austria.

The outbreak of World War I in 1914 prompted the hasty development and construction of armored cars in Belgium, Britain, and France. Because the first models ran on wheels, they were practically useless for trench warfare. The solution lay in the tracked carriages that had recently been developed for agricultural tractors to be able to move across fields.

Tank technology began with the problem of attacking enemy trench lines that were protected by barbed wire and defended with machine guns. The solution appeared to be a machine that could surmount obstacles and that would be immune to bullets. For security reasons, the prototype tank was developed by groups who worked separately on the track and hull components. Those engaged in building the hull referred to it as a "tank," believing it to be a water carrier for desert regions. Thus the military tank acquired its name.

The earliest tanks were developed almost simultaneously in Britain and France. In Britain, their development was initiated by the Admiralty Landships Committee created by Winston Churchill, who was First Lord of the Admiralty. A prototype was built in September 1915, and one year later the first British tanks went into action near the Somme River in France.

By the end of World War I, Britain had produced 2,600 heavy tanks, while France had produced 3,870 tanks of a more lightweight type.

Between the end of World War I and the outbreak of World War II, tank design made great progress. The ponderous assault machines of World War I, which moved at no more than 5 to 6 mph (8–10 km/h), were replaced by versatile fighting vehicles capable of 30 mph (48 km/h) or more. By 1939, tanks were being produced in quantity in several countries. The British had more than 1,000 tanks, the Germans 3,000, and the Soviets 20,000.

Organized armored tank divisions became a decisive factor in all the major campaigns of World War II. Tanks were built in increasing numbers: by the end of the war, the United States and the Union of Soviet Socialist Republics had each produced around 90,000 tanks, for example. Tanks continued to be of importance in the coldwar period after World War II. In the 1980s, NATO armies maintained some 10,000 tanks in Europe to counter the 26,000 tanks of the Warsaw Pact.

Panoramic periscopes

Secondary sighting telescope

Gunsight with integrated thermal image unit

120 mm smoothbore gun

Bore evacuator

Steering column

Driver's seat

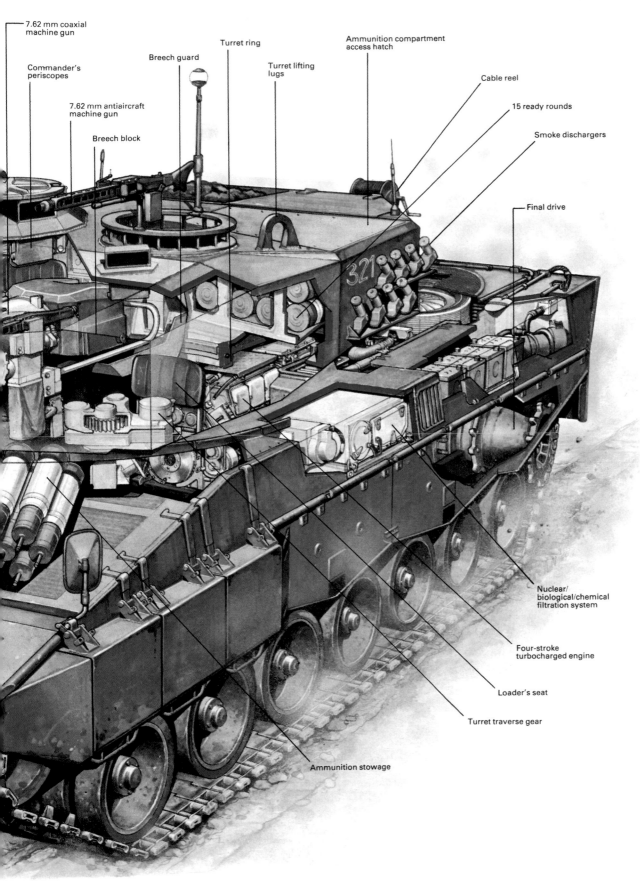

7.62 mm coaxial
machine gun

Commander's
periscopes

7.62 mm antiaircraft
machine gun

Breech block

Breech guard

Turret ring

Turret lifting
lugs

Ammunition compartment
access hatch

Cable reel

15 ready rounds

Smoke dischargers

Final drive

Nuclear/
biological/chemical
filtration system

Four-stroke
turbocharged engine

Loader's seat

Turret traverse gear

Ammunition stowage

◄ The German Leopard 2 is a typical heavily armored modern tank. Effective shock absorbers and an extremely powerful engine allow it to reach speeds as high as 42 mph (66 km/h) on firm terrain.

There are two main categories of tanks: light tanks and main battle tanks, or MBTs. Light tanks remain popular in some armies for reconnaissance duties and because they are easily transported by air, but the majority of tanks built today are MBTs. Unlike other armored vehicles, such as infantry carriers or self-propelled guns, the MBT has no other function than as a protected maneuverable weapons platform. It is designed entirely for combat. As such, MBTs are designed to be a

Big Willie (Mother) Mk 1 1916   Medium A Whippet 1917   Vickers Medium 1923   Light Tank Mk 1 1930

good compromise between protection, maneuverability, and firepower. Since effective armor and sophisticated weaponry are heavy items, maneuverability calls for powerful engines that can accelerate the weight of a battle-ready tank—up to 62 tons (56 tonnes) in some cases—at an acceptable rate. Most of the MBTs developed in the 1980s—the U.S. M1 Abrams, the British Challenger, the German Leopard 2, and the Soviet T-80—have noticeably similar resources of firepower and motive power.

Tank armament

An MBT is designed to be superior to all other vehicles in battle. Above all, this means that it must be adequately armed. The main armament must be capable of destroying enemy tanks, and its subsidiary armament, usually machine guns, must give some protection against infantry and aircraft. The main armament favored for most MBTs is a smoothbore 4.1 to 4.9 in. (105–125 mm) gun capable of firing armor-piercing ammunition and conventional high-explosive shells.

When one tank meets another in battle, it is usually the first tank to fire an accurate shot that

▲ The evolution of the British tank from 1916 to 1943. The first tank, Big Willie, had a top speed of only 3 mph (5 km/h) while the Cromwell's 600-horsepower (450-kW) engine gave it an impressive top speed of 40 mph (64 km/h).

▼ These Scimitar armored reconnaissance vehicles are snow-camouflaged for NATO maneuvers in Norway. They carry 1.30 inch (33 mm) rapid-fire guns.

survives. Modern tanks are fitted with highly accurate computerized fire-control systems. One such system is the solid-state digital computer of the U.S. M1 Abrams MBT, which gathers information about the position and motion of a target from a laser rangefinder and combines it with data about wind speed and barrel status to calculate an aim. The gunner selects a type of ammunition, puts the target in the sights of the rangefinder, and then starts the aim and firing sequences. A thermal-imaging system makes it possible to locate targets at night and in fog. Because the sights and the gun are fully stabilized by gyroscopes, the tank can fire on the move.

Tank layouts

In most cases, tank guns are mounted in turrets that cater for a 360-degree traverse. The turrets are generally crewed by three people: the gunner, who aims and fires the main gun and a machine gun using a telescopic sight; the loader, who feeds the guns with ammunition (30 to 60 rounds for the gun and 3,000 to 6,000 for the machine gun); and the commander. The commander, located behind the gunner, is usually provided with a cupola with several periscopes that enable observation of the surroundings in safety. Tanks that are equipped with automatic loading mechanisms have only two people in the turret.

The crew of a tank is completed by a driver, whose station is in the hull ahead of the turret. The driver often lies at an inclined angle, so the tank hull can have a lower profile. The engine and transmission of such a tank occupy a space in the rear portion of the hull.

The turrets in several types of light tank are crewed by only two people, and their total crews, therefore, consist of only three members. Some light tanks have their engines at the front of the hull alongside the driver's station, which makes for a more compact vehicle. The engine of the Israeli-designed Merkava MBT is an example of a tank with this type of layout.

A notable exception to the conventional designs is represented by the Swedish turretless S-tank, whose gun is fixed in the hull and elevated and lowered by altering the pitch of the hull by means of an adjustable suspension. The gun is traversed only by turning the whole vehicle.

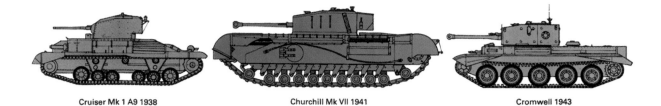

Cruiser Mk 1 A9 1938   Churchill Mk VII 1941   Cromwell 1943

Armor

The turrets and hulls of most early tanks were made of solid nickel–chrome steel, which is hard enough to resist penetration by projectiles yet sufficiently tough to absorb their energy without cracking. Since the 1970s, layered armor packed with liquid or plastic or ceramic granules replaced solid armor. The filling of this type of armor is intended to absorb the energy of high-explosive antitank (HEAT) rounds. A further development, first used in Israeli tanks in 1982, is reactive armor. This type of armor has an explosive filling that provides a counterblast to repel penetrating warheads such as armor-piercing, fin-stabilized, discarding-sabot (APFSDS) ammunition.

Armor accounts for approximately one-half of the total weight of a tank. This total weight is restricted by the allowable pressure on the ground and the carrying capacity of bridges to a maximum of around 60 tons (54 tonnes). Within this limit, the thickness of armor plating can reach 4.7 inches (120 mm) or more at the front, where a tank is most likely to be hit, and the thinnest at the rear. Wherever possible, the surfaces of turrets and hulls are inclined away from the vertical to increase their effectiveness against armor-piercing projectiles.

Turrets are of a convenient size and shape to be cast in one piece, which increases their integral strength. Most hulls are assembled by welding plates and castings together, although some hulls are cast in one piece despite their size.

Engines and transmissions

Most MBTs are equipped with diesel engines that have a low fuel consumption and a long operating range for a given fuel capacity. The latest MBTs usually carry around 317 gallons (1,200 l) of fuel, which is sufficient to cover 345 miles (550 km) on roads. The off-road range is lower because the increased resistance to motion on soft ground demands more power from the engine.

Most tank engines have 12 cylinders and produce 990 to 1240 horsepower (900–1,125 kW), which will drive a 55-ton tank at more than 40 mph (64 km/h) on a hard level surface. Some tanks are driven by gas-turbine engines, which develop more power. The gas-turbine-driven U.S. M1 Abrams, for example, has the power to

accelerate from a standstill to 20 mph (32 km/h) in seven seconds. The Swedish S-tank has a gas turbine engine that is used to boost power for short bursts of acceleration: a conventional diesel engine provides the power for normal running.

The power of a tank's engine is transmitted to the tracks by a multigeared transmission similar to that of other vehicles. The transmission system of a tank incorporates a steering mechanism. Unlike wheeled vehicles, which are steered by turning their wheels, tracked vehicles are steered by changing the relative speeds of their tracks so the track on the outside of a curve moves faster.

Running gear

Each track is driven by a toothed sprocket and is made up of 100 or so pin-jointed cast-steel or forged-steel links. In some cases, the pins run in plain holes in the sprockets, although the tracks of several tanks now have rubber-bushed pins that reduce wear by eliminating metal-to-metal contact. An increasing number of tracks are also fitted with rubber road pads, which helps reduce the damage caused to road surfaces.

Tracks are made as wide as possible to reduce the pressure that the tank exerts on the ground and so improve its ability to move across soft ground. The size of tracks does not increase in proportion to the weight of the tank, so the ground pressure of battle tanks ranges from 11 to 13 psi (0.76–0.90 bar) whereas that of light tanks

▼ For much of the late 20th century, Warsaw Pact forces maintained some 26,000 tanks in Eastern Europe. These tanks are on display in a May Day parade in Moscow, then capital of the USSR.

such as the Scorpion is only 5 psi (0.34 bar). This makes it possible for light tanks to move over extremely soft ground, difficult even for infantry to cross on foot.

The weight of a tank is transferred onto the tracks, and hence to the ground, by four to seven road wheels on each side. The wheels have solid rubber tires and in most cases are independently mounted on single arms pivoted in the hull. They are also independently sprung by means of torsion bars mounted transversely within the hull. Exceptions to this are the Chieftain and the earlier Centurion tanks, whose wheels are mounted in pairs and sprung by means of coil springs. The S-tank and several experimental tanks have been equipped with hydropneumatic suspensions, which are more compliant. Hydropneumatic suspensions can also be made adjustable, permitting the raising or lowering of the tank within limits and even tilting it sideways or fore-and-aft. Hydropneumatic and hydrogas suspensions are now fairly common in MBTs.

The characteristics of the suspension have a major influence on the cross-country speed of a tank, which is limited by the amount of pitching and bouncing that the crew can withstand rather than the power of the engine. Even the best suspensions cannot prevent the speed of tanks from

▲ Many of the armor features developed for military vehicles also find applications in civilian vehicles. Security trucks such as this one are heavily armored to protect their occupants and valuable contents from criminal attack.

being much slower over rough ground than it would be on paved roads. To minimize the pitching and bouncing when moving over rough ground, a tank should be as long as possible, but the longer its tracks, the more difficult the steering. A compromise between these requirements resulted in a length-to-width ratio of about 1.5 to 1.

The cross-country operation of tanks sometimes calls for the crossing of rivers and streams. Where bridges are not available, a tank can cross water in one of three ways. If the water is not more than 3 to 6 ft. (1–2 m) deep, most tanks can ford a river merely by having their hulls and turrets sealed for the crossing.

Where the water is deeper than 6 ft. (2 m), light tanks and even some of the lighter MBTs can swim across, either because they are inherently amphibious or because they carry equipment that can convert them into amphibious vehicles. Despite its weight, the Russian PT-76 reconnaissance tank is sufficiently bulky to float. Two water-jet propulsion units can propel it through water at up to 6 mph (10 km/h). The Scorpion and the S-tank, on the other hand, carry collapsible flotation screens, which, when erected, provide them with sufficient buoyancy to float. These tanks paddle by means of their tracks at up to about 4 mph (6.4 km/h).

Heavier MBTs are designed to be able to operate submerged at depths of up to 18 ft. (6 m). They draw air for the engine and crew through a snorkel that protrudes from the turret. Apart from the snorkel, such battle tanks remain completely sealed as they cross a river by crawling along its bed using their tracks.

FACT FILE

- *Early forerunners of the tank were the battlewagons of Jan Žižka, a Czech Hussite religious zealot of the early 15th century. These modified farm carts revolutionized warfare tactics. They had reinforced built-up sides, were armed with cannon, and could quickly be arranged into mobile fortresses from which the enemy could be engaged.*

- *In the 19th century a British inventor, James Cowan, designed a steam-powered, helmet-shaped wheeled battle vehicle armed with protruding, rotating scythes. British prime minister Lord Palmerston rejected it as being too uncivilized for military use.*

- *The earliest British tank in World War I, introduced in January 1916, was the Centipede, later known as Big Willie or Mother. It required four of its eight crew members just to drive it: one was coordinator-commander, one changed the main gears, and two controlled the tracks.*

SEE ALSO: AMMUNITION • BOMB AND MINE DISPOSAL • TRACKED VEHICLE

Artificial Intelligence

Marvin Minsky, a U.S. pioneer of artificial intelligence, defined artificial intelligence as the science of making machines perform tasks that would require intelligence if done by humans. A weakness of this definition is that there is no fixed definition for natural intelligence. As it stands, Minsky's definition of artificial intelligence would include almost everything that computers do. Some of the earliest computers performed complicated financial calculations for banks, for example; although these tasks would certainly require a degree of intelligence if done by a human, few would accept the ability of a computer to perform mathematical calculations as proof of intelligence.

Many of the elements of artificial intelligence, or AI, are already within the capability of some of today's computers. Given the appropriate hardware and programming, a computer can solve problems, make decisions, learn how to perform tasks, recognize faces and handwriting, prove theorems in geometry and logic, write its own programs, and play games such as chess, checkers, and backgammon with great skill. With voice synthesis and voice recognition, a computer can communicate in natural languages, such as English, French, or Japanese, and it can provide instruction signals to operate mechanical arms and other robotic devices. Some types of activities, such as learning or problem solving, can be applied to a variety of tasks. Problem solving, for example, is just as important for a robot trying to find its way out of a maze as it is for a computer to win an endgame in chess.

The hardware

The hardware of human intelligence consists of the 10 trillion or so synaptic connections that form the human brain. If a machine is to have a degree of humanoid intelligence, it might be reasonable to expect it to require the same scale of hardware to support its "thought" processes. The pace of computer development since the mid-20th century has now put that goal within reach.

The first generation of electronic computers, dating from the mid-1940s, used vacuum tubes in their circuitry. The tubes were so unreliable that it was often only possible to run such computers for seconds before one or more tubes had to be

▲ IBM's Deep Blue was the computer that took on the Russian chess grand master Garry Kasparov in 1997 and won. The machine has the ability to examine over 200 million board positions a second.

replaced. First-generation computers were also cumbersome, weighing as much as 30 tons (27 tonnes).

The second generation of computers was made possible by the invention of the transistor in the late 1940s by three U.S. physicists, Walter Brittain, John Bardeen, and William Shockley, at the U.S. Bell Telephone Laboratories. Transistors can perform all the tasks done by vacuum tubes, but they are much smaller and more reliable and require much less electrical energy to make them work.

Third-generation computers employed integrated circuits—thin wafers of silicon—with circuit elements such as transistors, diodes, and resistors etched into their surfaces. The minuteness of such circuit components allowed large-scale integration, or LSI, of several thousands of circuit elements on a single chip not much larger than a fingernail. The introduction of LSI chips vastly increased the processing power that could be packed into a computer's housing, just as transistors had done when they replaced tubes. Very-large-scale integration, or VLSI, packs millions of circuit elements onto a single chip and has made possible the use of parallel processing to perform a number of tasks simultaneously.

Since the mid-1960s, the density of circuit elements that can be packed on a chip has doubled every 18 to 24 months, as has the speed at which a chip can perform mathematical operations. This rate of development made possible such devices as personal computers and can be witnessed in the constantly increasing processing power of home computers and the progressive shrinkage of

◄ Prospecting for minerals is one of the applications that can now be undertaken using intelligent systems.

microprocessor-driven devices such as mobile telephones. More important for the AI researcher, the trend for increasing processing power has made it possible for even a home computer to perform tasks such as voice and character recognition, which are elements of artificial intelligence.

The scope for further development of silicon-based processors is not endless, however: it is limited by the minimum size of components that can be etched on a chip and the speed at which electrons can move through a circuit of such components. Ultraviolet light has already replaced visible light for the etching of integrated circuits, since its shorter wavelengths can etch finer details. Researchers are evaluating alternative semiconductors, such as gallium arsenide and indium phosphide. Other possibilities for future developments could come from research into using light or magnetic pulses to replace electrons as the signal carriers in processors. Researchers are also looking into the possibility of using single chemical bonds, or single electrons, trapped on so-called quantum dots to do computations.

In fact, the current generation of super-computers already have the capacity to perform at least as many logic operations as the human brain, and certainly more quickly. The challenge now lies in developing structures of logical operations that mimic human thinking.

▼ Fifth-generation computers use three basic systems—user interaction and input, software modeling, and processing and support hardware. Machines can now recognize voice patterns, and some can read handwriting. Robot arms linked to the computer can identify an object by comparing its image with one stored in its memory.

Expert systems

One derivative of AI research that has already had widespread success is the expert system. A typical expert system combines enormous databases of knowledge from a specific field, such as medicine, with software that can identify relevant entries in the database to perform a problem-solving task such as the diagnosis of a disease.

An interrogation of an expert system might start with a display screen that instructs the user to enter one or more keywords—words that have particular relevance to the user's query. A person suffering from concussion might enter "dizziness" at this point. The software would then eliminate all entries from the database that contain no reference to dizziness. It might also note that several groups of entries in the database share alternative keywords to those that the user entered. It can then prompt the user to accept or reject alternative keywords as a way to home in on relevant information.

Once the number of qualifying entries has been reduced by keyword analysis, the software might ask a series of questions to eliminate further options. If the search identifies a single entry in the database that conforms to all the information entered by the user, it will display the appropriate course of action. If it finds several entries that are indistinguishable on the basis of the user's information, the system might display all the available options or suggest that the user seek a human expert to resolve the remaining confusion. Since the 1960s, expert systems have played an important role in fields such as geological prospecting, medicine, and financial consultation, and they are related to the search engines that help users of the World Wide Web

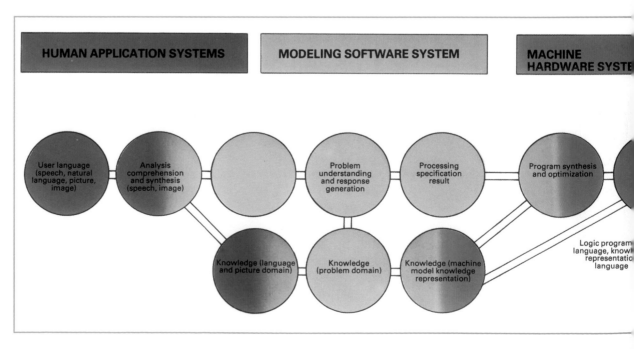

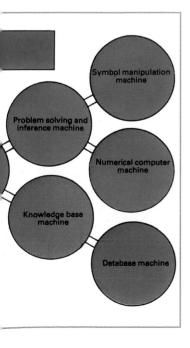

to locate websites that contain information that is of relevance to their interests.

Fuzzy logic

A characteristic of human thought is the ability to consider possibilities and probabilities in the absence of a definite answer. In terms of computing, this corresponds to values between 1, which represents "true," and 0, which represents "false." A value close to 0.8 might represent "probably true," while 0.2 might represent "unlikely to be true." Systems that accommodate values between "true" and "false" are said to use fuzzy logic.

Forward chaining

The challenge for an AI developer is to devise a set of rules whereby a computer can establish and quantify the likelihood of a result in fuzzy logic. This can be understood by considering the mechanism used by a chess-playing computer when there are only a few pieces left on the board. Before each turn, the computer knows two things with certainty: the positions of the pieces on the board and the moves that it can make according to the rules of chess. It cannot know with certainty what its opponent's next move will be. What it can do, however, is calculate all the possible sequences of moves that could follow from each of the moves that it could make next. This is an example of forward chaining. If one move could be the outset for a total of 100 possible sequences of following moves, and only 15 result

in the opponent being put in checkmate, the computer can assign a value of 0.15 ($^{15}/_{100}$) for the likelihood of that move leading to a win. If another possible move could be followed by 25 possible sequences, of which 10 lead to a win, that move has a 0.40 ($^{10}/_{25}$) likelihood of leading to success. Once the computer has calculated a value for each possible move, it chooses to make the move that has the greatest likelihood of winning.

Evaluation

The fact that a forward-chaining chess computer would have to calculate all the possible consequences of its actions before it made a move explains why artificial-intelligence systems can demand great resources of processing power. If there are so many pieces on the board that each player can choose from 20 potential moves, it would take $20^5 = 3,200,000$ calculations to predict all the possible outcomes of the next five moves and $20^{10} = 1.024 \times 10^{13}$ calculations for ten moves.

In fact, the number of calculations can be reduced enormously by evaluating the winning potential of all the configurations of pieces that could result from the next three or four moves. Each configuration can be given a score that reflects factors that could indicate a future win. These factors might include the number of pawns in the center of the board or the ratio of the numbers of each player's pieces on the board. The move of choice is the one that potentially leads to the greatest number of high-scoring configurations after the three or four moves that could follow. Such a scoring system is an example of a heuristic, or rule of thumb; it can be revised by the programmer according to its success rate.

Establishing rules of thumb

Programs that reduce the requirement for calculations by using the rule of thumb method are useful only when they improve the chances of a computer achieving the desired outcome in a task. If the heuristic is wrong, the program will direct the computer to incorrect outcomes more often than necessary. The most direct way to develop a rule of thumb is by backward chaining. This procedure concentrates on the goals of a task and establishes the actions that could lead to that goal.

In the case of chess, backward chaining would start with all the possible checkmates—the goal of the game—and calculate all the possible moves that could lead to those checkmates. By doing this, the configurations of chess pieces that could lead to a successful outcome are revealed. These potentially successful configurations are then used as the basis for formulating a heuristic.

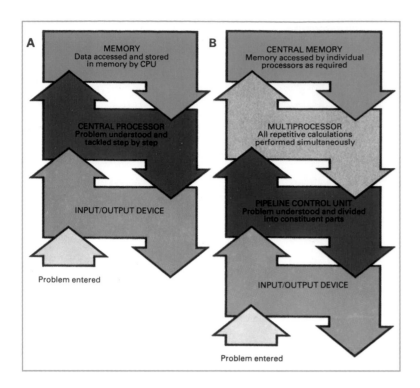

A
MEMORY
Data accessed and stored
in memory by CPU

CENTRAL PROCESSOR
Problem understood and
tackled step by step

INPUT/OUTPUT DEVICE

Problem entered

B
CENTRAL MEMORY
Memory accessed by individual
processors as required

MULTIPROCESSOR
All repetitive calculations
performed simultaneously

PIPELINE CONTROL UNIT
Problem understood and divided
into constituent parts

INPUT/OUTPUT DEVICE

Problem entered

Monte Carlo modeling

Many tasks that an artificial intelligence system might be required to perform have a continuous range of acceptable outcomes. A financial system might simply be required to make a profit, for example, without specifying the exact amount of profit. In such a case, it would require an infinite number of calculations to apply backward or forward chaining. Instead, heuristics can be established by trial and error. The heuristics for a problem-solving program are first defined using numerical parameters. The program is then run maybe thousands of times using random starting points to reveal how frequently the goal of the program was achieved. Each of the parameters can then be adjusted in turn and the program run thousands of times for each change. The success of a change is indicated by an increase in the frequency of successful outcomes. The changes are continued until the runs show no further improvements or until an acceptable rate of success is attained. This type of parameter testing is sometimes called Monte Carlo modeling, since it uses randomness to achieve results, as do the roulette wheels in the casinos of that city.

Natural-language processing

The capability of a machine to communicate in natural language remains one of the most fascinating goals of AI research. To communicate in natural language, a machine would have to recognize spoken words, interpret their meaning, formulate an appropriate response, and express that response as sound. The first and last stages of this process have already been achieved to some

▲ Conventional computers tackle problems by serial processing (A) whereas supercomputers use parallel processing (B).

▼ Dyson's robotic vacuum cleaner uses AI to guide itself away from obstacles.

extent. Voice-recognition software takes the input signal from a microphone and splits it into sound fragments called phonemes. It then checks for combinations of phonemes that form words and constructs sentences from those words. Most voice-recognition software has the ability to adjust the phoneme-detection process to suit its user's accent. Voice synthesis reconstructs phonemes from written sentences. It also adds the inflexions of pitch that indicate questions and commands.

Interpretation and response formulation require context-based judgments and are more difficult to program. The phrase "I saw a man on a bus" could be interpreted in three logically correct ways: it could mean that the speaker saw a man riding in a bus, that the speaker saw a man standing on the roof of a bus, or that the speaker was riding a bus when he or she saw a man. Humans use information from phrases around such an ambiguous statement to identify which meaning is more likely to be correct. Similarly, a question such as "Where am I?" would require different responses depending on whether the speaker was regaining consciousness or in a gas station on a highway. In both cases, there are numerous accurate responses, but the speaker is likely to be interested in only one. Successful natural-language processing will require programming that extracts contextual information and uses it to interpret speech and formulate responses.

SEE ALSO: BINARY SYSTEM • COMPUTER • INTEGRATED CIRCUIT

Astronomy

Astronomy, the science devoted to discovering the shape and structure of the Universe, has fascinated mankind for thousands of years. With the unaided eye, early astronomers recorded movements of objects in the sky with amazing accuracy, enabling man to tell the time, establish seasons, and predict eclipses and comets. The advent of the telescope allowed a closer look at our nearest neighbors, the Sun, Moon, and planets. The biggest revolution in astronomy, however, has taken place in only the last 70 years, with the accidental discovery of radio waves emanating from outer space.

Most of the information that reaches Earth from astronomical objects in space is in the form of electromagnetic radiation, ranging from the shortest wavelengths of gamma rays through X rays, ultraviolet, visible light, infrared, microwaves, and finally, to the longest wavelengths, radio waves. Much of this radiation, however, is blocked by our atmosphere before it reaches ground level. It is therefore hardly surprising that astronomers have tried to observe from above the atmosphere, usually from satellites. This field, which has become important only within the past three decades, is known as space astronomy.

Gamma ray sources

Only the very highest energies of gamma rays can penetrate Earth's atmosphere. They originate from the most energetic and chaotic objects and events in the Universe, such as supernova explosions, quasars, (which are believed to be the nuclei of very distant active galaxies), and neutron stars and pulsars (the spinning superdense remnants of stars that have exploded).

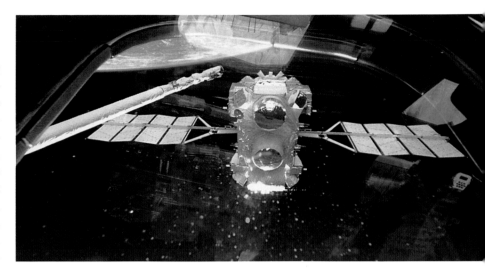

In 1988, the Earth-orbiting Solar Maximum Mission satellite was used to observe gamma rays coming from SN1987A, the brightest supernova to be seen since 1604. The astronomers found gamma ray spectral lines resulting from the decay of the short-lived radioactive element cobalt-56. These observations confirmed the theory that heavy chemical elements are both made and dispersed by such massive stellar explosions.

The Compton Observatory, launched in 1991, was the first spacecraft not only to study gamma rays with a broad range of energies but also to reveal exactly from which direction they came. It has looked at gamma rays from point sources, such as neutron stars and distant galaxies, together with the diffuse emission originating in our own galaxy and beyond.

Many distinctly separate gamma ray sources have been identified, including two supernova remnants: the Crab nebula and the Vela pulsar. Another source, Geminga, in the constellation of Gemini, is one of the strongest gamma ray emitters known, but for many years there was no other trace of its existence. It shows up at the

▲ NASA's Compton Observatory rising from the cargo bay of the space shuttle *Atlantis* at its deployment in 1991. Expected to be in service for 20 years, Compton had to be brought back down to Earth in 2000 when one of its gyroscopes failed.

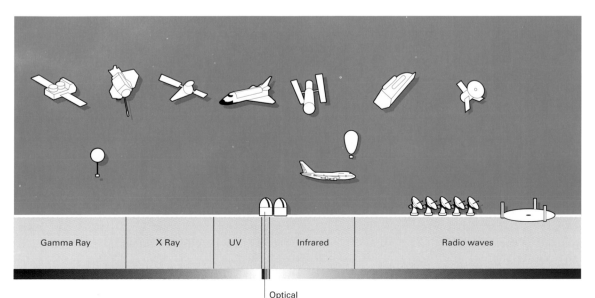

| Gamma Ray | X Ray | UV | Infrared | Radio waves |

Optical

◄ Astronomers can now observe stars across the electromagnetic spectrum using a variety of instruments. Satellites include (top left–right) Compton, ROSAT, Chandra, Astro, Hubble, the ISO, and the Cosmic Background Observer. These are complemented by the aircraft-mounted SOFIA, the Arecibo and Very Large Array of radio telescopes, and various balloon projects.

◀ An artist's impression of the European satellite ROSAT in orbit. ROSAT was capable of observing both X-ray and extreme ultraviolet wavelengths but has now been replaced by the Chandra X-ray Observatory and FUSE, the Far Ultraviolet Spectroscopic Explorer.

highest energy gamma rays but is invisible at lower energies. However, it has now been identified as a neutron star several hundreds of light years distant.

Compton has also recorded a gamma ray glow inexplicably concentrated toward the center of our galaxy. Further investigations of the source of this glow with a radio telescope have revealed an object very close to the center of the galaxy emitting two jets of radiation, in a manner characteristic of a black hole. Then there are the mysterious energetic random gamma ray bursts that appear to be spread almost uniformly across the sky. By chance, an X-ray satellite managed to locate one burst right after it happened. Follow-up with an optical telescope pinpointed a dim galaxy and seemed to confirm the theory that active galaxies right at the edge of the Universe could be the source of these gamma rays.

X rays from the stars

Significant advances in understanding some of the more violent processes in the Universe have been made studying X rays from space. ROSAT, a satellite launched in 1990 by the European Space Agency, made the first ever complete survey of the sky in the little-explored extreme ultraviolet (EUV) region lying between ultraviolet and X-ray wavelengths. Of particular interest have been observations of active galactic nuclei, or AGNs, including the special varieties of active galaxies known as quasars and Seyfert galaxies. They have confirmed that some quasars have spectral features that resemble those of the less luminous Seyfert galaxies, suggesting that the two are more similar than they appear. Many of the spectral features observed in these objects are thought to originate from X rays generated in cold material close to massive black holes at the centers of these galaxies. When this cold material is sucked into the black hole, it provides the "fuel" for the huge energy output observed.

Analysis also showed that a large part of the low-energy X-ray background radiation comes from distant quasars. However, ROSAT was unable to determine the origin of the higher-energy X rays that contribute most energy to the cosmic X-ray background radiation. Early results from the Chandra X-ray Observatory, launched in July 1999, showed that most of this background radiation comes from discrete sources rather than from radiation from hot intergalactic gas. One-third of the background comes from galaxies whose cores are very bright in X rays, yet optically almost invisible. These "veiled galactic nuclei" are thought to harbor massive black holes, producing X rays as gas is pulled into their center.

A second class of new objects is believed to be the source of the other third of the background radiation. "Ultra faint galaxies" also emit little or no optical light because the light is either blocked by dust around the galaxy or relatively cool gas is absorbing the light as it travels through space. If the latter proves to be true, these galaxies would have a redshift of 6, making them, at 14 billion light years away, the most distant objects ever identified.

Ultraviolet

Ultraviolet astronomy is also of great importance. Most ultraviolet sources are unusually hot but otherwise normal stars that have strong gas flows. These celestial searchlights also illuminate nearby gas, yielding information on the chemical elements in the gas. Even in the case of other galaxies, where the stars themselves cannot be distinguished individually, ultraviolet observations reveal the presence of these hot stars. Variations in the ultraviolet spectrum of the active galaxy NGC 4151, for example, led to an estimate of one billion solar masses for the massive black hole believed to lie in the nucleus of the galaxy.

The most successful ultraviolet satellite has been IUE, the International Ultraviolet Explorer. It was launched in 1978 with an expected lifetime of two to three years, but it continued to work until 1996, providing material for more research papers than any other spacecraft in the history of space research. Ultraviolet studies were also carried out by astronomers using the Astro 1 and 2 payloads carried into orbit by the space shuttle in 1990 and 1995. Before Astro 1, no detailed ultraviolet photographs of any object apart from the Sun had been obtained.

The Astro-1 payload carried two telescopes for studying the spectra of quasars and active galactic nuclei and for imaging stars and galaxies, with a photometer sensitive to polarized radiation. The highest-energy objects such as active galaxies were also studied by a fourth instrument, an X-ray telescope. The sensitive ultraviolet telescope obtained images of very hot stars and gas, including the hottest stars in the globular cluster Omega Centauri and shock waves in the Cygnus Loop, a ring of hot gas and debris expanding from the site of a supernova explosion.

Astro 2's priority was to detect the presence of the primordial intergalactic medium (IGM), a hypothetical gas thought to stretch between galaxies and believed to have been created in the Big Bang. It was first detected by the Hubble Space Telescope, but its characteristics could not be observed. Using a faint quasar as a reference, Astro 2 measured how much of its light was absorbed at ultraviolet wavelengths. Spectrum analysis showed that high redshift quasars are the source of ionization of the IGM and that there is between four and six times more mass of material in the IGM than in all the stars and galaxies put together. Although this is not enough to account for the "missing mass" astronomers have been searching for, it does indicate that

only 20 percent of matter created in the Big Bang formed into the recognizable structures we see today.

Interesting results also came from NASA's Extreme Ultraviolet Explorer (EUVE) satellite, launched in June, 1992. During a six-month survey of the entire sky, it recorded the radiation emitted by the multimillion degree outer atmosphere of a star much like our Sun and the hot surfaces of white dwarf stars. An explosive outburst of EUV radiation was also observed from a close pair of stars, as very hot stellar material, pulled from the outer layers of a normal star, fell on to the surface of its white dwarf companion. The EUVE also caught flares, similar to those that occur on our own Sun, on two very dim red dwarf stars, and the first EUV-emitting object outside our own galaxy.

The latest ultraviolet telescope is FUSE, the Far Ultraviolet Spectroscopic Explorer, launched in June 1999. It differs from other projects in that it has been sent up to find answers to specific questions, such as the conditions that existed

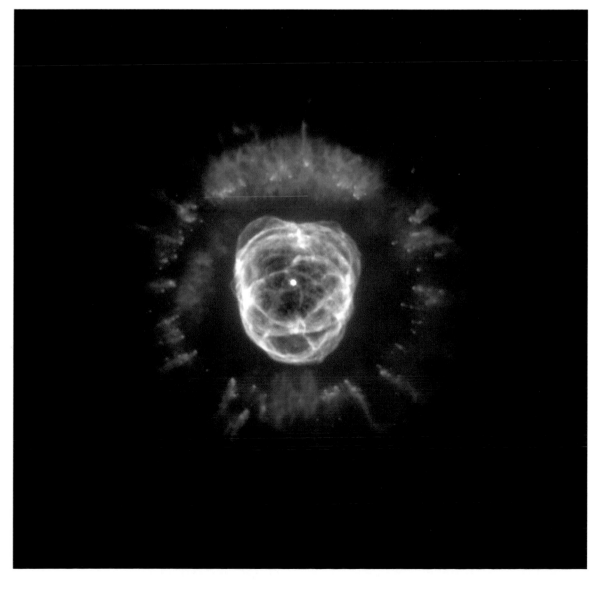

◄ The first picture of the new millennium taken by the Hubble Space Telescope was of an unusual object called the Eskimo nebula. From the ground, the object looked like a face inside a furry parka hood, which gave rise to its name. With the sharp focus provided by Hubble, the "parka" has been revealed as a disk of material with cometlike structures pointing away from the center of a dying star. How they formed and what they are made of is a puzzle to astronomers. The "face" is composed of two elliptical bubbles of gas, one lying in front of the other, being blown into space by the wind from the star's explosion. The bubbles are not smooth but contain filaments of denser material. Each bubble is one light year long and half a light year wide.

▼ These incredible structures photographed by HST in the Eagle nebula are thought to be incubators for new stars. Composed of molecular hydrogen gas and dust, these dense pillars have so far survived photoevaporation by the intense UV light given off by nearby extremely hot newborn stars, but are slowly being eroded to reveal smaller globules of even denser gas dubbed "EGGs" (Evaporating Gaseous Globules). Inside the EGGs are embryonic stars, which will be revealed when the EGGs become separated from the pillar and are themselves eroded by photoevaporation.

immediately after the Big Bang, how chemical elements are dispersed throughout the galaxies, and the properties of interstellar gas clouds. An early finding is that the hot halo of gas that surrounds the Milky Way contains a large amount of oxygen VI (oxygen atoms with five electrons stripped away). Scientists previously thought that the halo was due to ultraviolet radiation from hot stars, but the quantity of oxygen VI found by FUSE can have been formed only by collision with blast waves from supernovas. With this knowledge, study of supernova halos within other galaxies may provide more clues on how galaxies evolve and form new stars and planets.

The Hubble Telescope

Following several overhauls of the much-maligned Hubble Space Telescope (HST), it is now providing some of the most spectacular views of the Universe. With a resolution ten times better than ground-based telescopes, it has revealed the structure of planetary nebulae such as the Helix and Eskimo nebulas, discovered a nursery of stars in towering gas clouds in the Eagle nebula, and shown that some galaxies are engaged in multiple collisions with as many as five galaxies crashing together. Another HST find is the existence of a class of stars called brown dwarfs, a class of objects too large to be planets but too small to be stars.

HST carries a number of different instruments, covering a spectral range from the ultraviolet to

the near infrared. It provides unmatched capability for observations in the ultraviolet because its main mirror is very clean, and ultraviolet reflectivity is good. The telescope can also make excellent spectroscopic observations in both visible and ultraviolet light. The Wide-Field/Planetary Camera has been used to study bright, high-contrast objects, such as the planets and nearby star clusters and galaxies. It has revealed new detail in the compact cores of galaxies. Bright clouds of gas in the active galaxy NGC 1068 provide evidence that a black hole with a mass of 100 million suns lies at its center. An even larger black hole with a mass of 3 billion suns may lie at the heart of the giant galaxy M87.

The HST's Faint Object Camera has imaged high-energy jets in distant galaxies, resolved close, rich star clusters into separate stars, and probed the core of a nearby exploding star. Hubble's two spectrographs have achieved excellent results on brighter sources, particularly in the ultraviolet part of the spectrum. Finally, the fine guidance sensors, although designed primarily for precise pointing of the HST, may also be used for astrometry, complementing those of the European satellite Hipparcos.

Hubble has not just been looking at far away objects. It was ideally placed to see the 21 cometary fragments that made up comet Shoemaker-Levy 9 crash into the planet Jupiter in 1994. HST has also taken the first direct look at the surface of Pluto, showing that it has a varied surface mottled with light and dark regions. Beyond Pluto, the Kuiper Belt of icy debris has been revealed as a huge reservoir of potential comets, with a population estimated at well over 100 million objects.

Infrared

At wavelengths longer than visible red light is the infrared region. The most successful infrared satellite to date has been the Infrared Astronomical Satellite (IRAS). Although its mission lasted only ten months in 1983, it mapped the whole sky and catalogued 245,000 infrared sources, more than 100 times the number known before the launch. Analysis of the vast quantity of information sent back by IRAS still continues to yield some surprises.

IRAS has found that some nearby stars, such as the brilliant

FACT FILE

- *Operating from an orbit 380 miles (610 km) above ground level, the HST has perfect skies all the time. When launched, it was expected to outperform any Earth-based telescope, even though its 94 in. (2.4 m) diameter mirror is much smaller than those of many ground-based telescopes.*

- *During construction of the HST's main mirror, a mistake was made in testing that misled those making it into believing that it was correctly shaped, when in fact it is too shallow by an amount equal to $\frac{1}{50}$ the thickness of a human hair. This fact was not discovered until after Hubble was in orbit. A tiny fleck of paint that had chipped off a part of the test equipment during installation was later found to be responsible for the error.*

- *Hubble orbits the Earth every 97 minutes. As it passes from shadow into sunlight, the temperature rockets from 250 degrees below zero to over boiling point within minutes. It is protected from these extremes by a protective thermal blanket that keeps it at an even temperature.*

- *The telescope's pointing systems can lock onto an object with a precision equivalent to pointing and holding a laser on a small coin 400 miles (675 km) away. Once it is locked on, sensors check for movement 40 times a second. Gyroscopes ensure that if movement occurs, Hubble will smoothly move back into position.*

Vega and Fomalhaut, are associated with cool material that may indicate the presence of planets or a forming planetary system. With one such star, Beta Pictoris, the material was subsequently photographed at optical wavelengths and showed a disk of dust circling the star. Hubble has since found a twist in the disk, suggesting that a giant planet lying at an angle to the disk may be responsible. IRAS also sent back new data about objects such as the hidden stars inside the famous Orion nebula; these stars are young and extremely luminous, but it is not possible to see them optically because of the intervening nebular material. Perhaps IRAS' greatest discovery was a new type of galaxy, which has been termed a "starburst" galaxy. In these starburst galaxies, as much as half the gas is being turned into new stars at once, releasing an enormous amount of infrared radiation.

Two new infrared telescopes are expected to be operational by the end of 2001. The Stratospheric Observatory for Far Infrared Astronomy (SOFIA) will be the largest airborne telescope in the world, carried above the clouds by a specially modified Boeing 747. The Space Infrared Telescope Facility (SIRTF) is planned to complete NASA's line-up of space observatories (Hubble, Compton, and Chandra), providing a complete range of observations across the electromagnetic spectrum.

Future observatories

Even this array of telescopes in space will still be unable to provide answers to a number of questions. Astronomers have a good idea of how the Universe was formed and what it is like today, but they are lacking information on what was happening when it was between one million and several billion years old. This is the crucial period when stars and galaxies began to form. Finding out will be the goal of the planned replacement for Hubble, the Next Generation Space Telescope (NGST).

The NGST will carry a number of instruments covering the ultraviolet, infrared and optical spectrum ranges. Scientists are looking into the use of "distributed optics" for the project, which uses a system of small connected mirrors that can be individually controlled, rather than the rigid, fixed mirrors of the HST. Such an array can be folded up during launch and yet will be larger and more powerful than Hubble.

Another possibility is to leave gaps between the mirrors to create an instrument called an interferometer. Although this initially creates a pattern with gaps in it, these can be filled in by computer to form a perfect image. The farther apart the mirrors are, the sharper the image that results. Plans are already underway to launch a 10-meter interferometer, the Space Interferometer Mission, which will have four times the clarity of a picture from Hubble.

These results show the vital importance of conducting astronomical observations from space. A host of new spacecraft are planned for launch by 2010; they will range over the entire electromagnetic spectrum and will add immeasurably to our knowledge of space.

SEE ALSO: ASTROPHYSICS • BLACK HOLE • COSMOLOGY • RADIO ASTRONOMY • SUPERNOVA • TELESCOPE, OPTICAL • TELESCOPE, SPACE

Astrophysics

Of all the sciences, astronomy, which covers the study of the Universe as a whole, can claim to be the most comprehensive. Astrophysics is the physics underlying the phenomena studied by astronomy—it attempts to explain the objects seen in the sky in terms of the laws of physics that apply on Earth.

Almost all the information about the stars, planets, and cosmic bodies comes in the form of radiation—usually thought of as light, but including radio waves, X rays, and the rest of the spectrum of electromagnetic radiation. The only exceptions to this rule are Moon samples, meteorites, and cosmic rays (high-energy charged particles from space).

Physical observing methods

The astronomical telescope collects light from objects that may well be so faint that they are invisible to the naked eye. Photography makes even fainter objects visible by collecting their light over periods of an hour or longer. A photographic plate registers only about one light particle, or photon, in every hundred. Nowadays much of astronomy is carried out using electronic detectors called CCDs (charge-coupled devices), which can normally detect over 50 percent of incident light. These are super-sensitive versions of the image detectors found in modern home video cameras. Their performance is improved by operating them at temperatures around –95°F (–70°C), provided by liquid nitrogen. One great advantage of CCDs over photography is that the data can be handled digitally and processed by computer software, thus enabling the images to be enhanced to bring out the greatest information. The addition of the spectroscope to these CCDs has made it possible to analyze the light from stars.

The spectroscope splits light into its individual wavelengths, or spectrum. Each chemical element has its own characteristic spectrum. Starlight has a continuous spectrum, with all the colors of the rainbow, crossed by dark lines where particular wavelengths have been absorbed by gases in the outer layers of the star. By comparing the wavelengths of these lines with those produced by gases on Earth, it is possible to discover what elements are present in the star, and their quantities and temperatures and whether the star has a strong magnetic field.

Each star has a predominant color, which depends on its surface temperature. Red stars are cool, as low as 5400°F (3000°C), while the hottest stars are blue, about 45,000°F (25,000°C). The Sun's surface temperature is about 10,472°F (5800°C).

By studying the precise wavelength of the lines in a spectrum, an effect called the Doppler shift shows whether a star is moving toward or away from Earth and at what speed. In the case of a double star, where two stars can be seen orbiting each other, this shift indicates their speed in orbit and can be used to discover the masses of the stars by Kepler and Newton's laws. Since the speed of the stars in their orbits and the time taken to go around are both known, it is possible to calculate the actual diameters of their orbits. These diameters can also sometimes be measured as small angles in the sky, from which the distance of the stars from Earth can be calculated.

The distance of the nearby stars can be found by observing the small shift in their positions as the Earth circles the Sun—in effect, giving a stereo view of the sky. This shift is known as the star's parallax. When a star's distance is known, it is possible to decide how bright it is compared with, say, the Sun. The Sun is found to be about midway between the brightest and faintest stars.

The Doppler effect can also be used to estimate how far galaxies are from Earth. As galaxies move away from us, their radiation is stretched toward the red end of the spectrum a phenomenon termed the *redshift*. Some of the most distant objects of all, quasars, have been estimated to have a redshift of six, putting them right at the edge of the known Universe.

How stars shine

From the stars' spectra, it has been found that the main elements in stars are the gases hydrogen and helium; furthermore, the stars are producing vast

◄ The Carlberg Automatic Transit Circle is a fully automated system that can measure and record the positions of hundreds of stars each night.

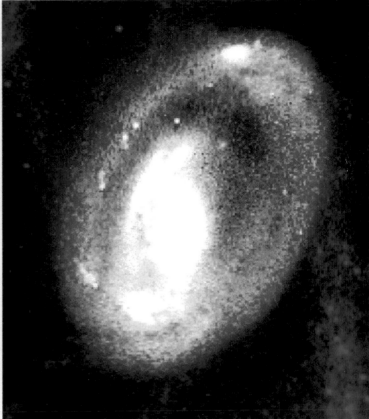

amounts of energy. The source of this energy was a mystery until the U.S. physicist Albert Einstein suggested in his Relativity Theory that matter itself could be transformed into energy. It is thought that the Sun and stars are powered by nuclear-fusion reactions, in which energy is produced by the conversion of hydrogen into helium deep in their interiors.

Because the brightest stars are using their hydrogen supply very rapidly, they cannot continue to shine brightly for more than a few million years. The blue stars are therefore the youngest that can be observed. The younger, more recent stars are found to contain more of the elements heavier than helium than the old stars. This is because the heavier elements can be produced only at very high temperatures inside very massive stars. These stars become unstable because eventually they cannot produce enough energy to support their outer layers and they explode. These events are known as supernovas. The explosion distributes the elements throughout space, and when a new star forms, it will have a certain proportion of heavier elements in it.

This phenomenon was observed in January 2000 by the Chandra X-ray Observatory, which has found a ring of oxygen and neon expanding away from a supernova in the Small Magellanic Cloud, a neighboring galaxy. By measuring how fast the ring is expanding, astronomers can estimate the amount of energy liberated in the explosion. Shock waves are heating the gas to temperatures of nearly 10 million degrees and stripping electrons from atoms as they pass. Small wavelength changes caused by the Doppler effect can be used to measure the velocity at which each element is traveling. Results like these can help explain how newly made elements become part of other stars and planets.

Cosmic questions

Research in astrophysics usually consists of making large numbers of observations of stars, galaxies, and the many other objects that fill the Universe. In general, advances are made slowly as information is pieced together, building up a picture of the way the Universe works. Quite often, what may seem to be academic investigations into the structure or movement of distant objects can alter our understanding of more immediate concerns, such as energy production or particle physics. But occasionally an event occurs that provides a wealth of new data and transforms our knowledge. Such an event was the explosion of supernova 1987A.

On February 23, 1987, a bright star suddenly flared into the southern sky. It was a supernova; not a new star but the death of an old one. Its appearance provided astrophysicists with a long-awaited glimpse of star death, and the observations made of the event provided a crucial test for many modern theories.

▲ The Cartwheel galaxy is an unusual feature, formed by the crashing of a small galaxy into a larger one 200 million years ago. Scientists are puzzled as to why the center of the galaxy contains very few new stars and what has caused the spoke pattern that gives the galaxy its name. Close-ups of the center (see right) have now revealed intriguing cometlike structures several thousand light years in length. It is thought they might have formed from gas clouds oscillating as a result of the shock wave of the collision and the gravitational pull of the material at the center of the galaxy.

Although astronomers had seen many supernovas in distant galaxies, 1987A was the closest and most spectacular since the Italian astronomer Galileo first turned a telescope on the stars almost four centuries ago. The supernova occurred in the Large Magellanic Cloud, a small companion to our own galaxy. The proximity allowed astronomers to make observations that had never before been possible.

The instant of collapse was signaled by a burst of neutrinos—tiny subatomic particles—that swept through Earth on February 23 and were picked up by detectors in Ohio, Japan, and the former Soviet Union. Such a burst is predicted by current theories of supernovas but this was the first time one had been observed.

Pictures from the Hubble Space Telescope have revealed three rings of gas surrounding the supernova. It seems that the central ring consists of gas blown off from the star many thousands of years before the explosion but only now being illuminated. Astronomers noted that 250 days after the explosion the ring became energized with ultraviolet radiation. From this measurement, they could calculate that the supernova, and hence the Large Magellanic Cloud, lay at a distance of 169,000 light years from Earth.

What astronomers are waiting for most of all is to see whether supernova 1987A will become a pulsar. These rapidly spinning neutron stars, emitting regular pulses of radio waves, are believed to be created in supernova explosions. Although there have been some false alarms, the pulsar has yet to show itself, probably because it is still shielded by enveloping gas. If it finally appears, many theories will be vindicated.

The search for gravitational waves

The waves of the electromagnetic spectrum are not the only carriers of information about the distant Universe—in fact only 10 percent of matter can be observed this way. Einstein, in his theory of relativity, predicted another class of waves—gravitational waves—that should be generated whenever a massive object is accelerated.

So far, no one has definitely detected gravitational waves, though their influence on a binary pulsar has been measured accurately, and the measurement is in agreement with predictions. They must be so weak that only catastrophic events on a cosmic scale, such as supernova explosions or colliding black holes, would be powerful enough to produce observable quantities.

The problem is to design a detector to sense them. The effect of a gravitational wave is to stretch and compress any objects through which it passes. But even the most violent cosmic events will produce only fantastically small distortions of one part in 10,000 million million million.

In an attempt to measure gravitational waves, a team of scientists from the California Institute of Technology and the Massachusetts Institute of Technology have built two gravitational wave observatories, one in Hanford, Washington, and the other in Livingston, Louisiana. They look nothing like conventional astronomical observatories. Each consists of two metal vacuum tubes, 2.48 miles (4 km) in length, joined to form an L-shape. A weight hangs at the end of each arm and at the vertex of the L. When the experiment starts, a laser beam will be sent down each tube, reflected from mirrors on the weights, and the two beams will be brought back together to form an interference pattern. Any small changes in the length of the laser beam's path, such as those caused by a passing gravitational wave, will disturb the pattern and generate a signal.

Even with arms 2.48 miles long, the detectors will need to sense movements thousands of times smaller than the size of an atomic nucleus. Scientists are confident that improved techniques of laser interferometry will do just that.

Similar projects are being planned in Europe, with German-British and Italian-French proposals at advanced stages, and an Australian-Japanese observatory is also being discussed. At least four widely spaced observatories will be needed, both to pinpoint the source of the waves and to convince astrophysicists that the detections are real and not caused by local interference.

The neutrino problem

Since the 1930s, astrophysicists have known that the Sun is powered by nuclear fusion. Every second, over 600 million tons of hydrogen are converted into helium in searing heat and crushing pressure at the heart of the Sun. The fusion theory has been extremely successful in explaining how the Sun and other stars work and how they pass through their life cycles. But there is a problem.

▼ Left: This doughnut-shaped object at the center of a nearby galaxy is believed to be evidence of a black hole. At the disk's center, a bright spot shows where gravity is compressing and heating the material.
Right: Formerly the world's most sensitive gravity-wave detector, this instrument at Glasgow University (U.K.), which is 30 ft. long (10 m), has now been superseded by detectors in the U.S. with arms 2.48 miles (4 km) long.

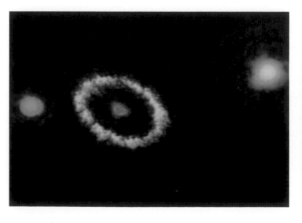

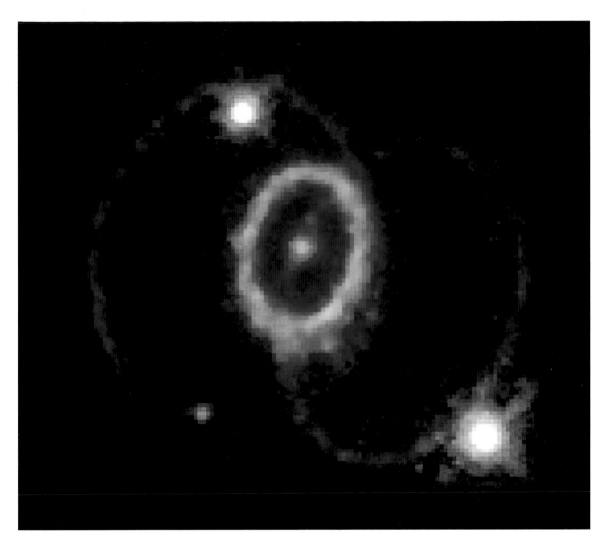

◀ Supernova 1987A is providing astrophysicists with a rare opportunity to witness directly the effects of shock waves on the debris of a stellar explosion. Eleven years after the supernova appeared, the central ring, which formed 20,000 years before the star exploded, began to light up as the force of the wave heated gas atoms to over 1 million °F. Observations should reveal the nature of the original star, whether it was single or a binary system, and how the two larger rings are connected to the system.

The only way to see what is happening in the center of the Sun is to observe the neutrinos that are created in the reactions. The heat energy and light may take tens of thousands of years to reach the solar surface, as it is absorbed and released repeatedly by atoms along the way. Neutrinos are tiny, neutral elementary particles thought to have no mass, or almost no mass. They interact with matter via the weak nuclear force, which makes matter largely transparent to them. If our eyes were sensitive to neutrinos, we would be able to see the nuclear reactions as an intensely bright spot in the middle of the Sun's disk.

Astrophysicists can accurately predict how many neutrinos should be produced, but they are so elusive that it is very difficult to detect them. Nonetheless, four neutrino detectors are now running, in the United States, Japan, Russia, and Italy. All four show that there are not enough neutrinos coming from the Sun. This worries astrophysicists as it suggests that theories of the processes in the Sun, and hence nuclear fusion, may be wrong.

A possible answer is that something happens to the neutrinos on their way to Earth. Scientists know that there are three different types of neu-trinos—electron, muon, and tau—and it is well known that other elementary particles can change versions, or "flavors." In theory, the Sun should produce only electron-neutrinos and current detectors can only identify electron-neutrinos. If the neutrino has only a very small mass, however, then it is likely that the three types continuously convert into each other as they travel through space, so that by the time they reach Earth only a third are electron-neutrinos. A new Canadian detector will be sensitive to all three types of neu-trinos. Scientists shall have to wait another few years before they know for sure whether there is something wrong with their understanding of the Sun or with their understanding of neutrinos. Finding out is important—if the neutrinos are found to have mass, it will mean that the prevail-ing theory of elementary particles will have to change. As neutrinos are the most common parti-cles in existence, by implication, the Universe would be more massive than was first thought.

SEE ALSO: Astronomy • Charge-coupled device • Doppler effect • Electromagnetic radiation • Elementary particle • Gravity • Spectroscopy • Telescope, optical

Atomic Structure

An atom is the smallest possible particle of a chemical element. Smaller particles exist, but they do not have the chemical characteristics that identify an element.

The nature of matter was one of the key concerns of the early Greek philosophers. Empedocles proposed that all matter was composed of just four elements: earth, air, fire, and water. The Greek philosopher Leucippus and his disciple Democritus were the first to suggest that matter was composed of tiny particles that could not be divided. In fact, the word *atom* derives from the Greek word *atomos*, meaning "indivisible." Only a few years after Democritus put forward his theory, the Greek philosopher Aristotle put forward an alternative theory of matter that added a fifth element, "quintessence," of which the stars and planets were made, to Empedocles' list. Aristotle also believed that matter could be divided indefinitely and that an object was the result of an abstract "form" being imposed on matter. Because Aristotle's theory was more consistent with the teachings of the Christian religion, his theories were endorsed, while those of Democritus were dismissed for nearly two thousand years.

Dalton's atomic theory

In the late 18th century, chemists discovered a number of substances that could not be broken down into other substances by the chemical methods of the time. They realized that there were more elements than the four of Empedocles' theory. A French chemist, Joseph Proust, made a great breakthrough when he observed that elements always combine in fixed proportions by weight when they form compounds, so a gram of hydrogen will always react with eight grams of oxygen to form water.

In 1803, the British scientist John Dalton proposed that the fixed proportions of combination

▶ Atoms are made of one or more electrons that whirl about the tiny central nucleus. The nucleus consists of protons (red) and neutrons (blue). The number of electrically positive protons balance the negative electrons to make the atom neutral overall. Protons and neutrons are themselves made up of three quarks bound together by the strong nuclear force. The proton is made of two "up" quarks (dark blue) and one "down" quark (green). Neutrons are made of two "down" quarks and one "up" quark. The atom shown is beryllium, which has four electrons, four protons, and five neutrons.

▼ An atom of helium (left) has two protons and two neutrons in its nucleus and two electrons. Lithium-7 (right), an isotope of lithium, has three protons, four neutrons, and three electrons. The proton carries a single positive charge and holds the atom's negatively charged electron in orbit.

observed by Proust could be explained if the elements consisted of atoms—just as Democritus had suggested—and if atoms of different elements formed compounds by joining together in simple, fixed ratios. Dalton also drew up the first table of atomic weights, but it contained some errors: thinking that the formula of water was HO, Dalton gave oxygen an atomic weight of 8 units relative to hydrogen, which he gave an atomic weight of 1 unit. In fact, the formula of water is H_2O and the atomic weight of oxygen is 16.

Although Dalton had proposed the existence of atoms, he was unable to describe their composition. The first clue to the structure of atoms came in 1897, when the British physicist Joseph Thomson discovered the electron while studying cathode rays—a form of radiation emitted by a hot metal when it is connected to a negative voltage. By studying how these rays were deflected by electric fields, Thomson calculated that they consisted of negatively charged particles with a mass nearly $\frac{1}{2000}$ the mass of a hydrogen atom.

Realizing that he had managed to split negatively charged fragments from atoms, Thomson proposed the "plum pudding" model of atomic structure, which envisaged tiny, negatively charged electrons embedded in a mass of positive charges. The number of positive charges in a neutral atom had to be equal to the number of electrons, and Thomson gave the name *atomic number* to the number of electrons and positive charges in an atom of a given element.

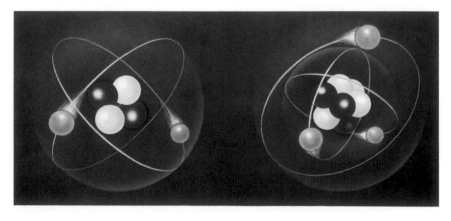

The nucleus

Thomson's model failed to explain why the atomic weights of the elements increase out of step with their atomic numbers. Helium, for example, has an atomic weight four times greater than hydrogen, even though its atomic number is two compared with one for hydrogen. The explanation for these apparent discrepancies would come with the discovery of the nucleus.

In 1911, the British physicist Ernest Rutherford was studying the properties of beams of fast-moving alpha particles, a form of radiation that he had been studying for ten years. Alpha particles consist of two protons and two neutrons, and so have a double positive charge. When Rutherford fired a stream of alpha particles at a thin gold foil, he found that a fraction of 1 percent of them bounced back from the foil. Given the momentum of the alpha particles, they should have penetrated the foil with ease, according to the plum pudding model of the atom. Indeed, Rutherford compared the rebounding alpha particles to cannon shells bouncing off tissue paper.

Rutherford calculated that the electric field necessary to reflect alpha particles could only exist if all the positive charge of each gold atom were concentrated into a central core with a radius around one ten-thousandth the radius of an entire atom. He called this core the nucleus and proposed that nuclei consist of two types of dense particles, each some 2,000 times heavier than the electron. One type—the proton—has a positive charge equal in magnitude to the charge of an electron; the other type—the neutron—has no electrical charge but contributes to the mass of heavier atoms.

Atomic spectra and the Bohr atom

Although Rutherford's description of the nuclear atom was a great contribution to modern understanding of atomic structure, it did little to explain the properties of electrons in atoms. Electrons were thought to orbit the nucleus somehow, but the precise nature of those orbits was unknown. A clue to electronic structure came from atomic spectroscopy, the study of the frequencies of light absorbed and emitted by atoms.

In 1885, a Swiss physicist, Johann Balmer, discovered that the lines in the visible spectrum of hydrogen occur at frequencies that obey the formula *frequency = constant* x $(\frac{1}{4} - \frac{1}{n^2})$, where $n = 3, 4, 5$, and so on. In 1914, a U.S. physicist, Theodore Lyman, discovered lines in the ultraviolet spectrum of hydrogen frequencies proportional to $1 - \frac{1}{n^2}$, and other physicists found a series of lines in the infrared region. All these lines correspond to frequencies that obey a general formula *frequency = constant* x $(\frac{1}{n_1^2} - \frac{1}{n_2^2})$, where n_1 and n_2 are whole numbers.

In 1900, the German physicist Max Planck introduced the idea that light consisted of individual packets of energy, which he called photons. The energy of a photon is directly proportional to its frequency, so the fact that atoms emit and absorb energy at certain specific frequencies implies that there is a limited number of possible energy states that an atom can have, and these vary between atoms of different elements. The emission or absorption of light happens when an atom changes from one energy state to another.

The Danish physicist Niels Bohr was the first person to propose that atoms absorb or emit photons as their electrons jump from one state to another. Between 1913 and 1915, Bohr published a number of research papers in which he suggested that electrons in atoms could exist only in orbits with certain fixed values of angular momentum. Bohr calculated the possible energies of an electron in a hydrogen atom for the allowed orbits and found they were consistent with the formula for the frequencies of spectral lines. Bohr's model of the atom introduced the idea of electron shells: collections of electron orbits that accommodate distinct numbers of electrons with the same energy.

Wave functions

In 1923, the French physicist Louis de Broglie interpreted Bohr's condition as meaning that electrons behave like waves as they orbit the nucleus and that the only "permitted" wavelengths are those that complete a whole number of cycles in one circuit of the nucleus. The shorter the wavelength, the greater the energy of the electron. In the late 1920s, the Austrian physicist Erwin Schrödinger refined the wave description of electrons and produced an equation that gave a fuller description of the behavior of electrons in atoms. The Schrödinger equation is based on the kinetic and potential energies of a negatively charged electron that is moving around a positively charged nucleus to which it is attracted. There are

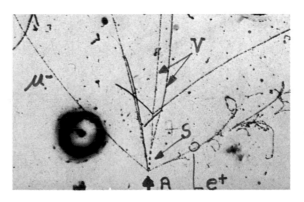

◀ Particle tracks in a bubble chamber show that when a neutrino (A) hits a nucleon, a muon (μ⁻), a positron (e⁺), and an uncharged particle (S) are produced. Tracks like these indicate that atoms are made up of even smaller particles than electrons, protons, and neutrons.

ATOMIC ORBITALS

In 1926, Erwin Schrödinger developed an equation to describe the wave motion of an electron in a hydrogen atom. He discovered that only certain combinations of energy and angular momentum were allowed by the mechanics of wave motion, and these were characterized by the principal quantum number, n, and the angular momentum quantum numbers, l and m. These three quantum numbers can have only whole-number values. The angular momentum quantum number l can have values from 0 to $n-1$, and m can have values from $-l$ to $+l$.

Each combination of quantum numbers describes a distinct type of motion of the electron around the hydrogen atom, and each can be represented by mapping the probability of an electron being at a particular point in space at any given time. These maps of probability density are called orbital diagrams, and they help to visualize how the electrons of neighboring atoms can overlap to form bonds.

The shapes of the different orbitals depend on the values of l, m, and n. The principal quantum number, n, determines the mean distance of the electron from the nucleus. The greater the value of n,

the greater the mean distance. Since there is an electrostatic attraction between the electron and the nucleus, those orbitals that have lower n also have lower energy and they are more stable. The quantum numbers l and m determine the angular form of the electron orbital. An electron with $l = 0$ occupies a spherically symmetrical orbital; as l increases, the number of lobes in an orbital also increases. Angular momentum is a vector quantity: it has size and direction. While l indicates the size of the angular momentum vector, m indicates the direction of the vector relative to the z-axis in a three-dimensional orbital diagram. This has a bearing on which way the orbital "points."

Spectroscopers observed light given out by electrons moving between orbitals of different energies long before Schrödinger's equation was formulated.

They marked the different sets of lines in their spectra s, p, d, and f—sharp, principal, diffuse, and fundamental. These letters are now given to the atomic orbitals that are responsible for such spectral lines.

The fourth quantum number that defines an electron state is s, the spin quantum number. Electrons spin as they orbit, and their spin has an angular momentum of $\frac{1}{2}$. The quantum number s can be $+\frac{1}{2}$ or $-\frac{1}{2}$, depending on the direction of the angular momentum vector along the z-axis used to draw the orbital diagrams. Quantum mechanics dictates that no two electrons can have the same set of quantum numbers. Electrons that share an orbital already have the same values of l, m, and n, so each orbital can contain two electrons with different values of s and no more.

Orbital	Minimum n	l	m	Number of orbitals	Number of electrons
s	1	0	0	1	2
p	2	1	−1, 0, +1	3	6
d	3	2	−2, −1, 0, +1, +2	5	10
f	4	3	−3, −2, −1, 0, +1, +2, +3	7	14

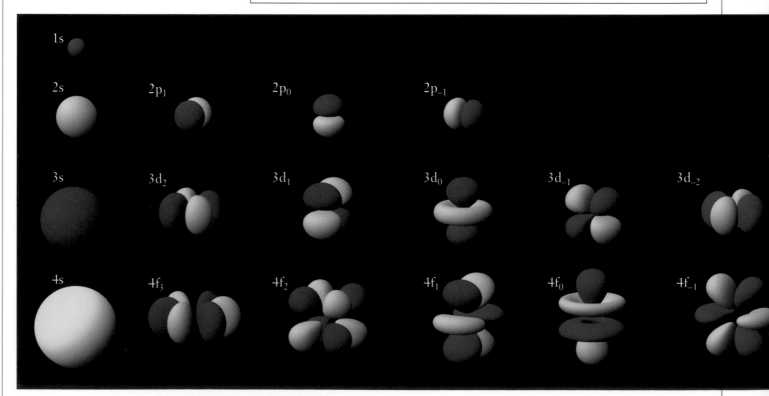

SUBATOMIC PARTICLES

Particle	Symbol	Mass (kg)	Relative atomic mass	Charge (C)	Relative charge
Electron	e	9.11×10^{-31}	0.0055	-1.60×10^{-19}	−1
Proton	p	1.67×10^{-27}	1	1.60×10^{-19}	0
Neutron	n	1.67×10^{-27}	1	0	+1

▼ The electrons in atoms occupy three-dimensional envelopes of space called orbitals. The shapes of these orbitals are dictated by equations called wave functions. The diagram shows areas where the wave function has positive values (blue) and negative values (yellow). The orbital angular momentum of an electron in an orbital increases in the order s, p, d, f, as is reflected in the increasing number of lobes of those orbitals.

similarities with a marble moving inside a shallow soup bowl: the total energy is constant, so the farther the electron is from the nucleus, the greater its potential energy, and the smaller its kinetic energy, the slower it moves. The Schrödinger equation predicts the likelihood of an electron being at a particular point in space; this likelihood is called a probability density.

Self-consistent fields

The Schrödinger equation can only be solved exactly for atoms and ions that contain only one electron, but it still provides a basis for computing the behavior of electrons in more complicated atoms. Imagine an atom of helium, which has two electrons. Whereas the electron in a hydrogen atom moves in a simple electrical field caused by a positively charged point—the nucleus—a helium electron moves in a field in which it is attracted to the nucleus and repelled by the other electron, which is smeared around the atom. An approximate electric field is calculated from the probability density of that other electron in a hydrogen-type orbital, and a whole new set of atomic orbitals is calculated to correspond to that field. These orbitals are more accurate than the hydrogen orbitals but still not exact, since the orbital of the electron that modifies the field has now changed. A whole new set of orbitals is calculated using the electric field for the improved orbital set. This process is repeated until the change

in orbitals from one calculation to the next becomes insignificant. At this point, the modified orbitals are said to be self consistent, since the electric field that they produce is the same as the field that is used to calculate them. Such orbitals are as close as possible to the real behavior of electrons in complex atoms.

Orbital occupation

The arrangements of electrons in atoms are indicated using notations such as $1s^2 2s^2 2p^2$, which indicates two electrons in an s orbital with $n = 1$, two in an s orbital with $n = 2$, and two in a p orbital with $n = 2$. In the lowest energy state of an atom, its electrons occupy the lowest energy combination of orbitals available.

The Schrödinger equation for hydrogen predicts that the energy of an electron depends only on its principal quantum number, n. In fact, this energy is proportional to $\frac{1}{n^2}$, which is consistent with the formula produced by Johann Balmer. When orbital energies are calculated for more complex atoms, the energy of each orbital depends also on the angular momentum quantum number of the electron, l. This is because the different shapes of orbitals with different values of l interact with the electric field in different ways. Electrons with more angular momentum spend more time farther out from the nucleus, so they experience more repulsion from electrons that lie between them and the nucleus. This is why the orbital energies for a given value of n increase in the order s, p, d, f.

For lighter atoms, the orbitals for any particular value of n are always lower in energy than those with a greater value of n. This changes at potassium (K), which has the electron configuration $1s^2 2s^2 2p^6 3s^2 3p^6 4s^1$. Although the $3d$ orbital exists, its energy is higher than that of the $4s$ orbital, which is occupied instead. The $3d$ orbital starts to accept electrons only at scandium (Sc), which has a full $3s$ orbital.

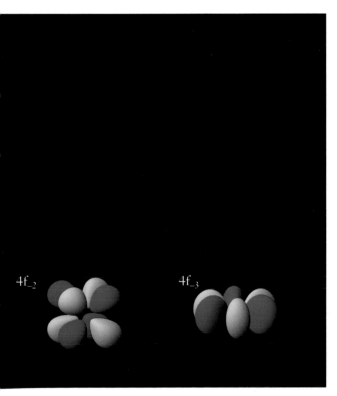

4f_2   4f_3

SEE ALSO:	CHEMICAL BONDING AND VALENCY • ELEMENT, CHEMICAL • ELEMENTARY PARTICLE • QUANTUM THEORY

Audio and Video Recording

Finding convenient ways to store sounds and pictures for repeated use has been the aim of scientists since the U.S. inventor Thomas Edison first discovered the link between the physical impact a sound could make and the reproduction of the sound. His early use of fragile wax cylinders was soon replaced by flat vinyl discs, which allowed prerecorded material to be played at home. Among broadcasting organizations, however, was a growing need for an easy method of storing material they might want to use again or broadcast at a later date.

Recording onto magnetic tape was first perfected in Germany during World War II. Reel-to-reel systems could be made in a relatively small format and became a popular domestic hobby during the 1950s and 1960s. Tape recording also proved useful in the making of records by providing multiple tracks for recording different instruments and by allowing for correction of errors. The first video recorders appeared at about the same time, again making use of magnetic tape. The upsurge in the use of audio and video recording tapes in the home began when the practicalities of recording were simplified by enclosing the tape in a sealed cassette.

Cassettes

Cassettes were introduced by Philips in Holland in 1963, and consist of a flat plastic box containing magnetic tape running between two flangeless reels called hubs, the ends of the tape being attached to the hubs by means of a plastic leader tape. Rollers and guides support the tape along the front edge of the cassette, where apertures allow the recording and playback heads and tape-driving rollers of the recorder to come into contact with the tape. Two thin foils of low-friction material such as PTFE- (polytetrafluoroethylene) or graphite-coated plastic prevent the tape from jamming against the top or bottom of the box. A pressure pad in the cassette ensures good contact of tape and head. The magnetic tape is shielded from stray magnetic fields from the motors by including in the cassette a piece of metal called a screen. This is made from an alloy, usually of nickel and iron, designed to trap magnetic fields.

A cassette has a number of advantages over the use of reels on an open tape recorder: the tape does not require threading into the recorder, a cassette can be stopped and removed at any time without rewinding, and contamination by dust and damage to the tape through handling are minimized.

The major advantages, however, are in size and in playing time. Elimination of handling allows the manufacturer to make tapes very thin, thus getting much longer lengths of tape into a small space. Total tape thickness ranges from 0.00037 to 0.00075 in. (0.0095–0.019 mm). In addition, thin tapes give better recording quality at slower tape speeds, so that a standard speed of 1⅞ in. per sec. (4.76 cm/s) is used on cassette recorders with results as good as at 3¾ in. per sec. (9.53 cm/s) on reel-to-reel recorders.

Playing times are expressed in minutes (designated C60, C90, C120), taking into account that the cassette can be turned over to the other side for further recording on the other half of the tape.

Cassettes can be purchased blank, that is, ready for home recording, or containing prerecorded material. In the latter case, the plastic tabs at the back of the cassette are removed, so that when the cassette is put into the recorder, a safety catch engages in the tabhole and prevents accidental erasure or rerecording. Cassettes are used mostly for music or other entertainment, but they are also used for computer tapes.

Magnetic tape

Tape manufacture for cassettes has become a very specialized business. Advanced techniques are needed for mass production of blemish-free plastic films less than a thousandth of an inch (0.025 mm) thick in strong materials such as polyester. The coating of a magnetic powder set into plastic resins has to be carried out with accuracies of a few millionths of an inch in thickness and with very smooth surfaces. The methods used are normally proprietary secrets, but it is known that the coating is generally applied by a gravure

▼ In the standard audio cassette, the tape is attached at either end by leader tape to the two hubs, runs freely between them, and makes contact with the recording heads through a gap in the front.

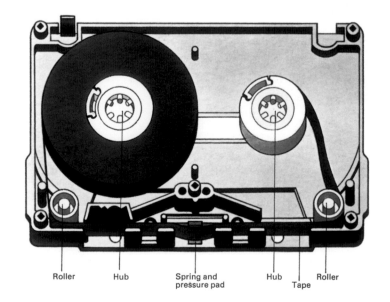

Roller   Hub   Spring and   Hub   Roller
                 pressure pad   Tape

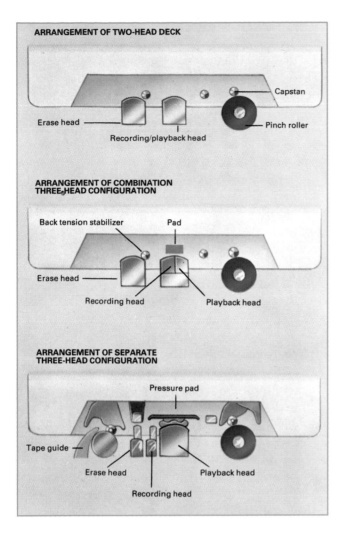

ARRANGEMENT OF TWO-HEAD DECK

Capstan

Erase head

Pinch roller

Recording/playback head

ARRANGEMENT OF COMBINATION THREE-HEAD CONFIGURATION

Back tension stabilizer

Pad

Erase head

Recording head

Playback head

ARRANGEMENT OF SEPARATE THREE-HEAD CONFIGURATION

Pressure pad

Tape guide

Erase head

Playback head

Recording head

◄ The basic tape recorder configuration (top); for higher quality, separate record and playback heads are incorporated (center); high-quality systems use discrete heads for each function (bottom).

process similar to that used in printing and that, after drying, it is compressed and smoothed between rollers. This achieves the tolerances and high finish required—the process is known as calendering.

The wide rolls of tape are then slit to the correct width and supplied in reels of up to 6,000 ft. (1,800 m) in length to the cassette assembly. Where the tape is to be prerecorded, the reels are first sent to a duplicator, who specializes in running these reels across high-speed recorders at speeds of 60 in. per sec. (1.5 m/s), putting onto them repetitive program lengths from a master tape and recording control signals between each program so that the assembler knows where to cut the section out of the tape for each cassette with instant precision.

Assembly of the plastic parts and the tape can be done fully automatically, but at present, most are made on semiautomatic equipment, which provides the operations of joining and winding in the tape but leaves the insertion of hubs, rollers, and so on to the operator. Another method, especially for prerecorded tapes, is first to make cassettes containing short lengths of plastic leader only. These are fed, together with reels of tape, to an automatic loader, which splices in and loads

▶ The tape heads of a professional recording system. Advanced systems like these use separate heads for recording, erasing, and playback.

the required length of tape, either to a preset footage for blanks or in response to the program interval signals on prerecorded tapes. Finally, the cassettes are sealed by ultrasonic welding or by screws, labeled, and packed in their boxes.

Advances in performance and use of cassettes continued in the 1970s. The familiar iron oxide tapes were replaced for the highest quality work by such materials as cobalt-modified iron oxides, chromium dioxide, and finely divided metal. In most cases, the recorder has to be adapted by means of a switch to give conditions suited to the new material.

Video cassettes

The rapid growth of the home video market has led to increased development and competition in the field of recording tapes as well as in the cassettes themselves. Unfortunately, unlike the situation with the audio cassette, no universal standard has been adopted in home video. Initially there were three major formats in use with no compatibility between the systems: VHS, Betamax, and V2000. VHS eventually gained supremacy in the market, pushing the other two systems into relative obsolescence. A recent development of VHS has been the VHS-C for use in camcorders. These tapes are the size of a pack of cards, allowing camcorders to become smaller and easier to transport, but they need an adapter to be played in ordinary video recorders.

Another system has since been developed by manufacturers, called 8 mm video. It uses a much

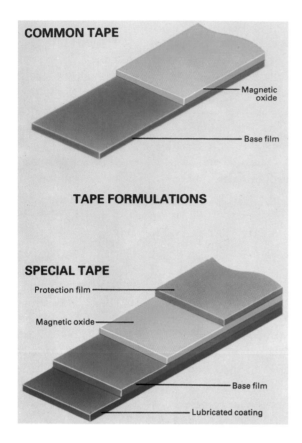

COMMON TAPE

Magnetic oxide

Base film

TAPE FORMULATIONS

SPECIAL TAPE

Protection film

Magnetic oxide

Base film

Lubricated coating

◄ Tapes are typically composed of magnetic iron oxide on a very thin plastic film. Better-quality tapes may contain other metal oxides, such as chromium, barium, and cobalt.

▼ A typical video recorder and its internal mechanism. Although in principle the same as an audio tape, the video counterpart has a more complex formulation and records in a different manner.

smaller cassette than VHS, only slightly bigger in dimensions than an audio cassette, and has led to the development of new forms of magnetic recording tape. Pure-metal formulations are used instead of metal oxides, thereby increasing the available magnetizable material on tape.

Improved versions of these three formats have since become available—Super VHS, Super VHS-C, and Hi8. These offer a better picture resolution (400 lines of horizontal picture resolution as against 240 lines) as they use a better quality tape, but they have the drawback of only being playable in camcorders and video recorders that can handle the super format.

Recording on tape

Recording onto video tape requires a different technique from audio tape recording. Video signals consist of millions of electrical vibrations compared with the thousands typical of audio. In an audio recorder, these signals travel to a small, stationary electromagnet, or "head," which magnetizes a tiny part of the tape as it passes. With audio signals, the vibrations are sufficiently far apart to make each one recognizable, but with video, they would be unintelligible if they were recorded linearly on the tape.

Instead, a spinning head has been devised that creates a diagonal line of magnetism on the tape. Inside a VHS or SVHS camcorder or video recorder is a drum-shaped object with a tiny electromagnetic head at either end. The drum rotates as the tape moves past it, but because it is slightly tilted relative to the tape, one head slides across the tape diagonally. The other begins its own swipe when the first has reached the opposite side of the tape. By doing this, the magnetism is spread over a wider area and the vibrations are separated.

Sound to accompany the pictures must also be recorded. This can be done in the ordinary manner with a linear audio track along one edge of the tape. Being separate from the video, the audio tracks can be dubbed or erased, and vice versa, but sound quality is only moderately good. Stereo sound can be achieved by mixing the audio signal with the video signal and recording it alongside the pictures, but it cannot then be edited.

Both 8mm and Hi8 equipment record stereo sound in the same way, but an editable format that uses pulse-code modulation has been developed. As the head passes across the tape, it records a mixed signal for most of its swipe. As it nears the edge, it stops recording both signals and lays down sound only as a magnetic pulse. The sound can then be edited without affecting the picture.

Digital technology

By far, the biggest advances in audio and video recording have come with the rise in digital technology. Ordinary, or analog, audio tape recorders degrade the sound they are trying to capture, both in recording and playing back. Tapes can accumulate hiss, vary in speed, and distort frequencies. Digital audio tape (DAT) overcomes these problems by converting the signal to binary numbers.

Digital audio tapes are only half the size of an ordinary cassette and ⅛ in. (3.81 mm) wide. They come in various lengths, playing for between 15 and 180 minutes. Blank tapes are coated in metal oxide, though prerecorded tapes more frequently use a barium-ferrite oxide. When the cassette is inserted into the recorder, two spindles penetrate the hubs and lock it in place. A door in the casing flips open, and as the cassette is drawn into the machine, the tape becomes wrapped around a rotating drum, the same way as in a video recorder.

Sound is recorded onto DAT like a video cassette—in diagonal stripes. The difference between it and analog tape lies in how it records sound. First, the signal goes through a low-pass filter, which removes any frequencies higher than 20 kHz. The filtered signal then runs through an analog-to-digital converter, which measures the voltage of the wave form several thousand times each second. As it does so, it converts each measurement into a binary number that is then stored on the tape. The longer each binary number, the more accurate the measurement or quantization. DAT and compact discs are currently standardized on a 16 bit code.

In playing back the tape, the process is reversed. Because the head reads only two binary numbers, 1 and 0, it does not pick up any hiss or distortion on the tape. The numbers are fed into a buffer memory and read out at a constant rate, eliminating any variations in the speed of the tape.

DAT has now become the standard archiving technology used in the production of professional master recordings. Although the tapes cannot be spliced physically without loss of detail, they can be fed into a computer for precise editing using audio software. This allows recording engineers to alter features of the performance such as pitch and tempo and repeat or move sections. Copies made from digital tapes are true to the original, regardless of how many are made. The information can also be stored in different file formats for recording CDs or downloading from a computer as MP3 files.

▲ A digital recording console being used in the production of a pop video. Computerization enables engineers to manipulate the sound and pictures to get exactly the effect they want.

SEE ALSO: ANALOG AND DIGITAL SYSTEMS • COMPACT DISC, AUDIO • ELECTROMAGNETISM • MAGNETIC TAPE AND FILM • SOUND • VIDEO CAMERA • VIDEO RECORDER

Autoclave

The autoclave is a pressure vessel used in hospitals for sterilizing surgical instruments, dressings, bedding, rubber gloves, or any other materials required to be free from bacterial or similar contamination. They are widely used in medical and dental clinics, surgeries and operating rooms, veterinary clinics, and intensive care units.

Microorganisms can be killed by prolonged dry heat, but sterilization is achieved much more rapidly in the autoclave by treating its contents with moist steam under pressure at a high temperature. The increased pressure has no direct effect on microorganisms, but it allows steam to be used at a temperature well above that of boiling water. On contacting the material to be sterilized, the steam condenses, giving up some of its heat and raising the temperature of the materials. Once the material reaches steam temperature, no further condensation will take place, and temperature equilibrium is reached. If the temperature is too high, superheated or dry steam will be produced, and moisture will be evaporated from the material in the autoclave, resulting in much less efficient sterilization. Consequently, temperature and pressure are carefully controlled to maintain optimum conditions.

A typical autoclave consists of a large cylindrical pressure vessel, up to 20 ft. (6 m) long, and 6 ft. (2 m) in diameter. This is closed with a pressure-tight door through which articles to be sterilized are loaded, packed in containers that allow free circulation of steam. Air is pumped out to produce a near vacuum, then steam is fed in from an external boiler supply. This process ensures almost instant penetration of steam into porous materials, which might otherwise not reach a high enough internal temperature. When nonporous materials are to be sterilized, air may be flushed out with steam, rather than by using the vacuum technique. To reduce sterilization time when large loads are being processed, the material is sometimes preheated with a flow of steam before the final vacuum and steam sterilization cycle takes place.

Pressure builds up until the required working temperature is reached; for example, a pressure of 15 psi (one atmosphere) results in a temperature of 250°F (121°C), which would be maintained for 15 minutes or more to effect sterilization. A timing device locks the autoclave door, preventing removal of material before completion of the sterilization cycle. When sterilization is complete, steam is pumped out, and the autoclave allowed to cool. Cooling results in a pressure drop within

◄ A portable autoclave, capable of working at 608°F (320°C) and 4,000 psi (278 bar), being tested by completely dissolving a sample, contained in a silica tube, in a suitable liquid medium.

the autoclave, and filtered air must be admitted before it can be opened. Additional safety features mean that the elements cannot be energized with the door open. A boil-dry cut-out prevents overheating, and a safety valve operates if the chamber reaches a pressure above 36 psi (2.45 bar).

In hospitals, jacketed autoclaves are often used. After sterilization, high-temperature steam is fed into the jacket around the pressure vessel, which dries the contents by driving off moisture. In large units, and for industrial use, the entire process can be automated. Goods to be sterilized are prepacked in suitable containers, loaded on a roller track, and fed automatically to the autoclave. An inverted pressure vessel is lowered over the containers and is sealed by a gasket before the sterilizing cycle takes place. The pressure vessel is then raised, and the container moves off on the roller track.

Autoclaves are also used for the heat stabilization of synthetic fabrics, to minimize shrinking. Other types are used for impregnation of timber, the vacuum cycle forcing preservative into the wood. Food processing industries employ high-pressure sterilization techniques during canning. An ordinary domestic pressure cooker is perhaps the most basic example of an autoclave at work. The term autoclave can also be used to describe a high-pressure-reaction vessel. Manufacturers of dyes, zeolites, and composite materials frequently use this type of autoclave. Minerals such as gold can also be extracted by an autoclaving process.

SEE ALSO: PRESSURE • PRESSURE COOKER • TEMPERATURE • VACUUM

Automatic Teller Machine (ATM)

Cash-dispensing systems have been established as a service offered by banks since the late 1960s. The concept of cash dispensing originated in Britain, where systems were developed for British banks as a substitute for opening for business on a Saturday. In fact, they provided an automated system allowing bank customers to withdraw cash from their current accounts at any time of day or night. The idea was quickly taken up by banks in the United States and Japan, and today there are several different systems in widespread use in most countries of the world.

To facilitate access by the customer 24 hours a day, cash dispensers, or automatic teller machines (ATMs), are normally built into the outside wall of a bank, but they may also be free-standing units located in airports, shopping centers, or large office buildings; in the United States, this type of equipment is also used in drive-in banks.

Initially, cash dispensing was looked upon by the banks as a customer convenience item, but as usage grew, new applications were studied, and the existence of other advantages became apparent. The transfer of the personal type of cash withdrawal transaction to the cash dispenser during normal business hours relieved the cashiers of routine operations and gave them the opportunity to provide personal service on nonroutine matters. It was also found that by installing these machines, more efficient use of expensive bank premises could be made.

Modern cash dispensers are linked directly to the bank's computers, so that a customer who withdraws cash from a dispenser will have his or her account automatically debited by the computer, thus avoiding the handling of paper records.

Self-contained machines

A cash dispenser must exercise the same controls as a cashier who cashes a check for a customer. It must therefore be able to recognize a person using the system as a bona fide customer of the bank, accept some form of instruction from the customer, give the right amount of money, and finally, record the transaction, debiting the correct account. So that the customer can be recognized by the machine, he or she is normally given a secret four- or six-digit code number and a magnetically coded card, depending on the type of system being operated. The bank can exercise some form of credit control by giving the card to suitable customers only.

Systems differ, but in most cases customers key in their personal number on a keyboard after inserting their card into the machine. A bona fide customer will be recognized from the sequence of the individual numbers keyed in and from the information contained in the card. In the case of most card-operated systems, the personal number is keyed in after identification has been verified from the card. The machine reads the card electronically using a magnetically coded strip on the back. The information contained in the card is then correlated with the customer's keyed personal number.

If the machine is unable to correlate information, perhaps because the customer has made a mistake keying in the number, the card may or may not be returned, depending on the system, but in every case a displayed instruction appears for the operation to be repeated. If the information cannot be correlated after a total of three attempts, the card is returned by the machine and no money is issued. In some systems the card is retained.

When the machine is satisfied with the authenticity of the information, a signal will be given for the money to be dispensed to the customer. The magnetically coded card will be returned direct to the customer, the machine having printed out and stored details of the transaction either in the machine or centrally for record-keeping purposes. Most systems are flexible and the information concerning the transaction can, if required, be recorded on magnetic tape for direct input to a remote computer or even directly to the bank's main computer.

▲ Autoteller terminals are now a common feature in all sorts of locations. Advances in computer technology have enabled these machines to become more sophisticated, to the extent that giving out cash will soon become just one of a range of services that can be provided.

◀ The computer control room of a typical national bank. Transactions from ATMs across the country can be processed rapidly and customer accounts updated without the intervention of bank staff or the use of paper records.

On-line cash dispensers

Initially, all systems were designed to dispense fixed amounts of money, which were stored in individual bundles of banknotes in a cassette in the machine. Once the acceptance signal had been given, a packet of notes was released from the cassette mechanically and delivered.

More advanced systems now used are linked directly to the bank's central computer system and are capable of dispensing variable amounts of cash and performing other functions such as giving account statements and balances. Customers key in their number code and use their magnetically encoded card for identification purposes as usual, but in addition, they now key in the amount of money required. This information is transmitted to the computer, which then checks the customer's account balance and the validity of the information keyed in.

The amount of money keyed in is converted into electronic pulses that drive a mechanism that peels off the correct number of banknotes for delivery to the customer. This type of system has also been adapted to accept withdrawals from deposit and savings accounts that have been computerized. In this case, the account passbook is placed into the machine by the customer, and details of the transaction, together with a new balance, are printed out in the book.

Advanced systems

Not only can ATMs (automated teller machines) talk to central computers, they can, using information from the card, securely check the card and the PIN (personal identification number) and pay or refuse cash to the appropriate credit limit.

ATMs can also be used for paying money in to the bank, to be used for bills or deposits into savings accounts. There are already ATMs that can give out a number of different foreign currencies. Cooperative links between banks' computer systems enable customers to draw money from an ATM that belongs to a different bank.

Even with the growth of telephone and on-line Internet banking, people still need cash for small transactions, and the ATM is a convenient way to supply customers. But the technology has the potential for uses outside banking and is already being used to dispense postage stamps, movie tickets, and ski-lift passes. Some airports around the world are already using a type of ATM that allows passengers to check themselves in and collect boarding passes. Supermarkets are also using "do-it-yourself" checkouts, where customers scan in their purchases and pay by cash or check. It may soon be possible to combine getting cash with ordering flowers or booking airline tickets in a single visit to an ATM.

Interactive ATMs

The ATM of the future will also be radically different in design—one company has a model looking very much like an upside down pyramid, with a pressure-sensitive mat that recognizes when a customer is in front of it. Instead of a card, the machine will scan the iris of the customer's eye to confirm identity. Speech recognition and synthesis will allow the customer to give verbal instructions to the ATM and the machine to talk back. There will also be no screen. Customers will be able to download information about their account from the ATM directly to a mobile phone or other portable digital device, which can then be transferred to a home computer.

▶ Chase Bank offers its customers the facility of linking up directly with the bank's computer via the telephone system.

SEE ALSO: Cash register • Computer • Counterfeiting and forgery • Internet • Voice recognition and synthesis

Automatic Weapon and Machine Gun

When describing small-arms mechanisms, the term *automatic* refers to a weapon that fires a round, extracts the empty case, ejects the case, compresses a return spring, feeds a round from the magazine, and places it in the chamber ready for firing. The hammer, or firing pin, then strikes the cap of the cartridge and another round is fired.

In a fully automatic weapon, this sequence starts as soon as the trigger is pulled and repeats until the trigger is released. A great number of so-called automatic weapons are, in fact, only semiautomatic, since their trigger mechanisms are so designed that the trigger must be released and pulled again to fire another round. These weapons are better described as self-loading.

Early automatic weapons

The earliest handguns, in use from the early 14th century to the late 19th century, were equipped with matchlock or flintlock firing mechanisms. Once such a gun had been fired, its carrier would be defenseless until the gun had been reloaded.

As early as the 14th century, a number of devices were designed to increase the rate of fire by putting more than one weapon under the control of a single person. These weapons usually took the form of a number of muskets mounted on a frame or on a wagon and so arranged that the application of the sparks from a match or flint to a black powder train set off a number of barrels in quick succession. This type of weapon was known as an organ gun, since the multiple barrels resembled the pipes of a musical organ. Organ guns became more widely used in the 15th century, when a variety of types were produced, some firing in concentration and some producing dispersed fire.

In 1718, a British notary and author, James Puckle, patented a remarkable weapon. Called a Defence, this tripod-mounted weapon had a single 1.2 in. (30 mm) caliber barrel, 32.7 in. (0.83 m) in length, that could be fed with either round or square bullets from a choice of nine chambered cylinders. The cylinder rotated on a ratchet mechanism, positioning the bullets between a flintlock and the barrel. Two interchangeable cylinders increased the rate of fire. The British newspaper *The London Journal* reported on March 31, 1722, that in a demonstration the weapon managed to fire 63 rounds in 7 minutes, with an impressive average interval of 8.6 seconds between rounds.

In 1861, Richard Gatling, a U.S. dentist and inventor, developed the first truly successful rapid-fire gun. It had six barrels mounted in a frame that rotated around a central axis by a hand-operated crank. Each barrel would fire in turn as the frame rotated; the crank powered the loading, firing, and discharging operations. In some versions, a stacking mechanism continuously fed cartridges to the barrels as they emptied. By 1865, the U.S. Army started to purchase Gatling guns; soon after, every major army followed suit. In a British Army demonstration in 1870, a Gatling gun fired 616 shots in two minutes—more than five rounds per second—although only 369 hit the intended target. The Gatling gun remained in service with the U.S. Army until 1911.

Recoil weapons

In 1885, a U.S.-born British inventor, Hiram Maxim, demonstrated a weapon that would revolutionize the format of machine guns. Instead of requiring manual cranking, the Maxim gun used the weapon's own recoil to eject and reload. In effect, the propellant of the rounds provided the energy for the firing operations.

At the instant of firing a recoil gun, exploding propellant in a cartridge pushes the bullet in one direction and exerts a force in the opposite direction on a movable bolt, which is locked to the barrel at that point. This force drives the bolt and barrel back, compressing two springs: the barrel spring and the bolt spring. At a certain point, the bolt lock disengages and the barrel spring drives the barrel forward. The bolt continues to recoil and the bolt gets caught on a latch so that an opening forms between the barrel and the bolt. The spent cartridge ejects at this point, and a new round takes its place. As the barrel reaches its forward position, it triggers a mechanism that unlatches the bolt. The bolt spring then pushes the bolt back into place, and if the trigger

▼ Members of the British Gurkha battalion in the Falklands with 7.62 mm LIAI self-loading rifles.

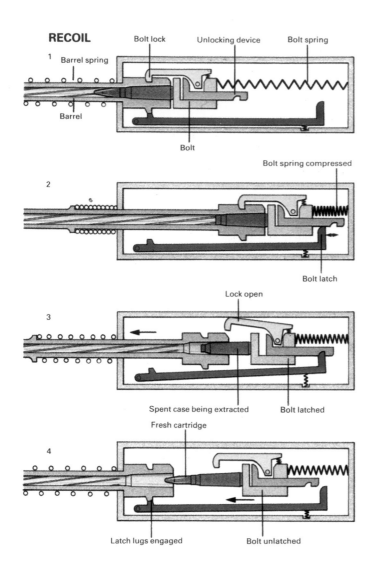

RECOIL

1. Barrel spring / Bolt lock / Unlocking device / Bolt spring / Barrel / Bolt

2. Bolt spring compressed / Bolt latch

3. Lock open / Spent case being extracted / Bolt latched

4. Fresh cartridge / Latch lugs engaged / Bolt unlatched

is still in firing position, the gun fires again. The original Maxims had a water-cooled jacket that encased the barrel and prevented overheating during prolonged bursts of fire.

The Maxim gun could fire 500 rounds per minute from an ammunition belt, only stopping when the belt was empty. Maxim's gun was taken up by most of the major European armies between 1889 and 1890. In 1912, the British Army started to purchase a 0.303 in. (7.7 mm) machine gun manufactured by the Vickers company; in 1917, the U.S. Army adopted as a standard weapon a 0.300 in. (7.6 mm) machine gun presented by a U.S. inventor, John Browning. Both these designs were water-cooled recoil-operated weapons derived from the Maxim gun. The U.S. Army was still using a 0.5 in. (12.7 mm) variant of the Browning gun in the early 1950s.

Gas-operated weapons

Recoil-operated weapons were not the only machine guns developed in the late 19th century. Another type was the gas-operated machine gun, developed by the U.S. inventor Benjamin Hotchkiss in 1872.

▲ The recoil mechanism of a machine gun. (1) The instant of firing. (2) At full recoil. (3) The block is held back while the barrel is allowed to return. (4) As the barrel reaches the forward position, it releases the block, which then runs forward, chambering a fresh cartridge.

Unlike the Maxim gun, the barrel of a Hotchkiss-type gun is fixed. On firing, exploding propellant gases in the barrel pass through a duct to a piston. The piston releases the bolt catch, and the gases then drive the piston and bolt back against a return spring. As this happens, a gap opens between the barrel and the bolt. The discharged cartridge escapes, and a fresh round enters through this gap. The bolt returns to the firing position and the sequence starts again. The original Hotchkiss gun also differed from the Maxim gun in that its barrel was air-cooled by metal fins, and its ammunition was joined in metal strips that could be linked together for continuous firing. The Hotchkiss gun was first adopted by the French Army in 1892. After several modifications, the Hotchkiss gun became a key weapon of the French armed forces in World War I.

Blowback weapons

The Austrian Schwarzlose machine gun, which was widely used in World War I, used a mechanism called retarded blowback to automate the firing sequence. Whereas recoil- and gas-operated guns lock the bolt to the barrel at the start of the firing sequence, blowback guns rely on a strong spring and a retarding mechanism, which hold the cartridge inside the barrel during the initial pressure buildup after firing. This is important, since the exploding gases could rupture the cartridge without the support of the surrounding barrel. The blowback mechanism is only suitable for short-barreled weapons, since the bullet must leave the barrel before the bolt has recoiled too far to secure the spent cartridge.

A toggle-head retarding mechanism consists of a lever device that forces the firing pin back against a spring while the main part of the bolt recoils relatively slowly. The bolt travels back under its own momentum after the bullet has left the barrel and the pres-

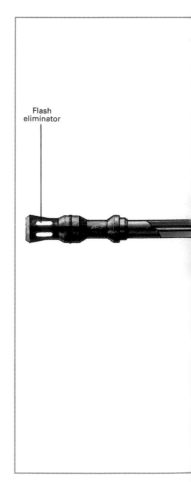

Flash eliminator

sure has dropped. This makes room for the discharging and charging operations. The firing pin drives forward through the bolt, detonating the cartridge propellant, when the spring forces the bolt back to its firing position.

Submachine guns

A submachine gun is a light, handheld automatic weapon that fires pistol rounds from a magazine using a blowback mechanism. Submachine guns are also called machine pistols or machine carbines. They are less accurate than rifles, but provide more rapid and more accurate fire than handguns. Most designs have a shoulder stock and forward hand grip for stability of aim.

The first submachine gun to enter widespread service was the twin-barreled 0.35 in. (9.0 mm) Villar Perosa, a design used by the Italian Army in World War I. The Villar Perosa was intended to be a light machine gun for use in the field or from aircraft. In fact, it was scarcely used in these roles and soon became a single-user weapon for close-range support fire.

A superior design of submachine gun was the Bergmann Maschinenpistole, introduced by the German Army in 1918. This weapon, also called the MP18, had a barrel less than 8 in. (20 cm) long and was designed to use 0.354 in. (9.0 mm) rounds originally designed in 1908 for Luger

pistols. Rounds were fed from a simple box magazine mounted to the left of the barrel to cover the chest of a right-handed user.

John Thompson, a U.S. Army officer, patented his first submachine-gun design in 1920. He would later become famous for the Thompson Model 1928 submachine gun, popularly called the tommy gun. The Model 1928 was favored by gangsters and law enforcers alike and was characterized by its disk-shaped drum magazine, which held 71 0.45 in. (11.5 mm) rimless Colt pistol cartridges under the weapon's body. In World War II, the Thomson submachine gun was redesigned to use box magazines of 20 rounds each. These were lighter and less clumsy than the earlier drum magazines.

The first wartime Soviet submachine gun was the PPSh-41, designed in 1941. This weapon carried 50 0.301 in. (7.65 mm) pistol rounds in a drum magazine similar to the early Thompsons. The 0.301 in. round fires a fairly light bullet at a reasonably high velocity. Later models abandoned the drum magazine in favor of a vertical box. The original submachine guns were made in the traditional gun style with long wooden stocks, bodies machined from the solid, elaborate sights, and, in many cases, long barrels and complicated trigger mechanisms. Modern guns are made from steel pressings and plastic. In most models, the

▼ The British Army's 5.56 mm Individual Weapon is part of the SA-80 small arms family, developed from the Royal Small Arms Factory's experimental 4.85 mm assault rifle.

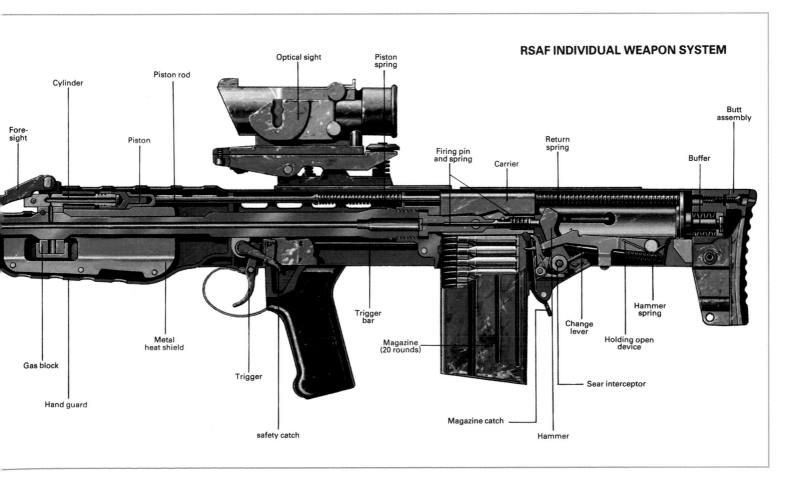

RSAF INDIVIDUAL WEAPON SYSTEM

Foresight · Gas block · Hand guard · Cylinder · Piston rod · Piston · Metal heat shield · Trigger · safety catch · Optical sight · Piston spring · Firing pin and spring · Trigger bar · Magazine (20 rounds) · Magazine catch · Carrier · Return spring · Change lever · Sear interceptor · Hammer · Holding open device · Hammer spring · Buffer · Butt assembly only precision machining is in the bolt and barrel. This type of gun is cheap—less than half the cost of a typical rifle—but has a comparatively short service life. Almost all designs now have folding stocks, and a few are so compact that when folded the weapon is little larger than a big pistol.

Modern submachine guns, such as the Israeli Uzi, are based on the Czech Model 23 of 1948. This design was the first to use a bolt with a sleeve that fits around the end of the barrel when the bolt is in the firing position. This ingenious feature makes it possible to design weapons with shorter barrels. The barrel of the Uzi, for example, is only 10 in. (25 cm) long, making it an extremely portable weapon.

General-purpose machine guns

The general-purpose machine gun was introduced by the German forces, whose Maschinengewehr of 1942—the MG-42—used interchangeable components such as tripods, sights, shoulder stocks, and barrels to modify the performance of the gun according to requirements. A quick-change barrel system allowed the MG-42 to operate almost continuously without the barrel overheating.

The U.S. Army's M60 is a typical general-purpose machine gun, or GPMG. Although it performs all its tasks adequately it is not entirely satisfactory in any of them. As a light machine gun, which is what an infantry section requires, its portability suffers from its unloaded weight of more than 30 lbs. (14 kg). An additional disadvantage is the belt feed, whose trailing edge can become caught in undergrowth and hedges as the gunner moves to a new firing position. If this happens, the entire feed mechanism can become jammed, leaving the weapon inoperable. Despite these disadvantages, GPMGs are valued for their versatility.

Light machine guns and assault rifles

Portable machine guns for infantry use are almost all gas-powered weapons. Light machine guns, sometimes called automatic rifles, are designed to use rifle rounds. Guns that use lighter, lower power rounds are called assault rifles. These rounds are intermediate in power between the pistol rounds used by submachine guns and rifle rounds. Automatic rifles and assault rifles can be used as self-loading or fully automatic weapons by changing the position of a switch.

The most outstandingly successful rifle since World War II has been the Soviet AK-47, one of the Automat Kalashnikov series designed by Soviet military designer Mikhail Kalashnikov. The elegant design of the AK-47 makes it easy to maintain and robust in unfavorable environments, such as jungles and deserts. Although less precisely manufactured than some other designs, the AK-47 fires 7.62 mm ammunition with acceptable accuracy. The AK-47 is fed by a 30-round, detachable magazine and can be used to fire single shots as well as bursts of fire.

The AK-47 has not been without rivals. The most significant of these is the U.S. M16. Designed by the U.S. inventor Eugene Stoner and originally called the Armalite AR-15, the M16 has been the standard automatic rifle of the U.S. Army since 1963. The chief advantages of the M16 are its lightweight construction and light recoil on firing. The weight of the weapon was kept to a minimum by using lightweight alloys and engineering plastics in its construction, while the use of lightweight 0.223 in. (5.6 mm) rounds ensure gentle recoil. Once some early problems caused by inappropriate propellants producing residues that blocked its pipework, the M16 proved itself a highly reliable weapon. New rifles with smaller, lighter rounds are now entering service.

Self-loading pistols

Truly automatic pistols are rare, but amongst the few that are found are the Russian Stechkin and the Czech Vzor 61 (Skorpian); both of these can be set to produce either self-loading or fully automatic fire. The reason for the unpopularity of the fully automatic pistol is its lack of accuracy. The

Foresight

Butt (shown folded)

Magazine spr

◄ An Ingram MII submachine gun has a 20-round magazine and collapsible wire stocks, and is small enough to be hidden under a coat.

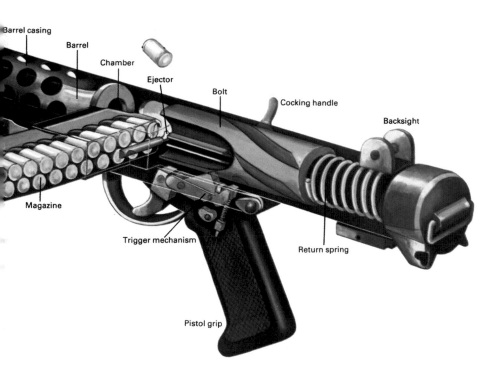

Barrel casing

Barrel

Chamber

Ejector

Bolt

Cocking handle

Backsight

Magazine

Trigger mechanism

Return spring

Pistol grip

lightness of the recoiling parts and the softness of the return spring produce a high rate of fire. On firing, the pistol kicks upwards above the line of the firer's aim, which causes the muzzle to rise to a successively increasing angle as each round is discharged.

After a short burst of firing at 750 rounds per minute, which is typical of the fully automatic pistol, the muzzle could be pointing upwards at 60 degrees. With self-loading pistols, the aim can be corrected between shots and a greater chance of a hit can be expected.

Pistols of small caliber—up to 0.320 in. (8 mm)—are almost invariably of blowback design, operating with an unlocked breechblock. Above this caliber, locked breech designs are used. Nearly all types employ the recoil method of operation, where the breechblock is locked to the barrel. On firing, they move back together until the gas pressure is at a safe level, when the barrel stops and the breechblock continues to the rear.

The gun is prepared for firing by pulling the slide fully back, allowing a round to be placed in the chamber. It then moves forward, and the barrel is locked on to the slide by ribs on the top slotting into recesses in the slide. When the trigger is pulled, the hammer is released and drives the firing pin forward through the breech face. The bullet moves down the bore, and the gas pressure against the cartridge case pushes it back hard against the breech face, which forms part of the

▲ A Sterling submachine gun, which operates on blowback. When a round is fired, the propellant gas pressure accelerates the bullet, and also the case and bolt, in opposite directions. The empty case is carried back until it hits the ejector.

slide. The slide goes back, but is connected to the barrel, which recoils with it.

The underside of the barrel has a link connected to the fixed frame. As the barrel goes back the link rotates and drags the rear end of the barrel down. The ribs on the barrel come out of engagement with the slide and the slide continues to recoil on its own. The slide extracts and ejects the empty case, then feeds in a new round and springs forward to reconnect with the barrel. It carries the barrel forward and the weapon is ready to fire again. The trigger mechanism includes a disconnector, which ensures that to release the hammer the trigger must first be released and then pressed again. This type of pistol is simple, reliable, and robust. Because the barrel moves up and down, the front bearing must have a large clearance.

The automatic pistol has frequently been compared with the revolver, and both have advantages and disadvantages. Automatic pistols have the advantages of a larger ammunition capacity than revolvers, quicker reloading provided a loaded magazine is available, higher muzzle velocity, lightness, and compactness. Automatic pistols are less reliable than revolvers in dusty or sandy environments, and they have closed mechanisms that make inspection difficult, detracting from safety. The complicated mechanism of an automatic pistol also requires more frequent maintenance than a typical revolver.

Motor-driven machine guns

While most modern machine guns are developments of the Maxim gun, in that they are driven by the energy of the exploding propellant, a few are descendants of the hand-cranked Gatling gun. The U.S. Vulcan aircraft cannon, for example, is a multiple-barrel Gatling-type gun that is driven by two electric motors. One electric motor rotates its barrels while another feeds ammunition. The added weight of the motors is not a great problem for ship- or aircraft-mounted guns, and the motorized mechanism fires 0.8 in. (20 mm) rounds at up to 6,000 rounds per minute, or 100 rounds per second.

The idea of using a motor to produce automatic firing is not confined to multiple-barrel weapons. Hughes Chain Guns have a single barrel and a rotating bolt mechanism that is powered by a reliable chain drive. The gun is manufactured with a range of calibers from 0.180 to 1.2 in. (7.62–30 mm).

SEE ALSO: AMMUNITION • BALLISTICS • RIFLE AND SHOTGUN

Automobile

◀ Motor shows like this give consumers the chance to see latest developments in automobile technology. The wide variety of body types, engines, and choice of fuels means that consumers can pick the exact specification that suits their purpose and their pocket.

An automobile is a self-propelled carriage designed to transport small groups of people and their baggage. The first vehicle to conform to this description was a steam carriage built in 1769 by a French military engineer, Nicolas-Joseph Cugnot. Cugnot built two steam tractors—the second in 1770—that could carry four people each but were intended mainly to haul artillery. These vehicles could travel at 2 mph (3.2 km/h)—slightly slower than walking pace—and had to stop every 20 minutes to recover steam pressure.

For almost a century, steam engines powered these horseless carriages, as early automobiles were sometimes called. This situation changed in 1862, when the French inventor Étienne Lenoir fitted his recently invented internal combustion engine to an automobile. This engine had a single cylinder and burned kerosene. In the same year, a German engineer, Nikolaus Otto, built a four-stroke gasoline engine that was the forerunner of modern automobile engines. Otto did not himself apply the four-stroke engine to automobiles—that was done in the mid-1880s by two German engineers: Karl Benz and Gottlieb Daimler. The first Benz was a lightweight three-wheel car that owed much to the bicycle designs of the time; the Daimler was a heavier four-wheeler that resembled a horse-drawn carriage.

If Germany was the country where the first automobiles were built, France was where many early automobile developments took place. During the 1890s, French engineers such as Armand Peugeot and Louis Renault began to transform the primitive automobiles into more logically designed vehicles that were better suited to the needs of both driver and passengers. By

1898, rival French companies Panhard–Levassor and Renault had both arrived at a layout that would remain largely unchanged for the next 60 years: their cars were front-engined, rear-wheel-driven vehicles with a jointed shaft to connect the engine to a differential between the rear wheels.

20th-century developments

Although the main design elements of the modern car were in place by the turn of the century, cars were produced in small quantities and sold at high prices. This changed in the first decade of the 20th century, when the American engineer Henry Ford pioneered the use of assembly lines to produce large numbers of automobiles that could be sold at prices that thousands of people could afford. The first Model T came off the line in Detroit in October 1908—barely 20 years after the first trickle of Benz and Daimler cars had emerged from German workshops.

Automobile development proceeded along different paths on the two sides of the Atlantic. In the United States, automobile engineers developed devices that made the automobile easy to use. The electric starter motor was developed as early as 1912—earlier models had been hand cranked to start. Later developments included coil-and-distributor ignition, synchromesh transmission, low-pressure tires, automatic transmission, and power-assisted steering. Until fuel prices rose spectacularly in the 1970s, the trend was to build ever larger and more luxurious cars that were not constrained by a need for fuel efficiency.

While American engineers worked on comfort and convenience, their European counterparts were seeking ways to make more economical designs for markets that were much more depressed than those in the United States. Imaginative European engineers such as Lancia in Italy and Citroën in France designed lighter cars that consumed less fuel. Lancia was the first to point out the benefits of unitary body construction, while Citroën pioneered front-wheel drive. Also, the intense competition of European motor sport—fed by fierce international rivalry—led to notable technical advances such as independent suspension, four-wheel brakes, and highly efficient engines. By the 1940s, typical U.S.-built automobiles were already larger and better equipped than European cars. At the same time, however the better European models had a fuel economy no U.S.-built car could match.

The three main areas of concern in modern automobile developments are safety, fuel efficiency, and emissions control. These are achieved by the application of new materials and technologies, such as lightweight alloys and electronic-control and engine-management systems.

Safety is provided by designing the front and rear of the body to crumple in the event of an accident, while a rigid passenger cabin protects the occupants of the vehicle.

High-strength steel and other alloys—notably of aluminum and magnesium—are used to make components that are lighter than traditional components but just as strong. Plastics and synthetic rubber compounds are used to make lightweight components where less strength is required.

Aerodynamic designs are tested and improved by using results from wind-tunnel testing and computer modeling to minimize air resistance. This approach has led numerous car designs to converge on a similar shape.

Corrosion resistance is achieved by avoiding curves that can trap water and by treating the underside of the body with wax, silicone-rubber sealants, and other water-repellent coatings.

Many car manufacturers now have a policy of using materials that are suitable for recycling and labeling them as such for ease of recognition.

▼ Using alternatives to sheet metal in order to reduce weight is not a new concept. This 1953 model Chevrolet Corvette had an excellent power-to-weight ratio as a result of its lightweight but strong glass-reinforced plastic bodywork.

The body

In 1900, automobile designs were based on a chassis that consisted of two lengthwise members joined by crossbeams. A superstructure mounted on this chassis served to keep out wind and rain, as well as to make the vehicle look better.

By the mid-1920s, engineers were starting to develop stronger body shells that were self-supporting, and so dispensed with the need for a substantial chassis for support. Lancia in Italy and Budd in the United States pioneered this type of design, and the Budd system of welding pressed-steel panels together to form a torsion box was eventually widely adopted, especially in Europe. In the United States, the bodies of larger automobiles sometimes had a hybrid construction with a welded steel shell partly supported by a perimeter frame. More modern auto designs have the main mechanical components mounted on subframes that are then bolted to the body. Subframe designs benefit from ease of assembly and better sound insulation.

Modern car bodies are designed with four principal requirements in mind: safety, lightness, aerodynamics, and resistance to corrosion.

The engine

Automobile engine designers seek a good compromise between power output, fuel efficiency, and smooth running. Key factors are how fuel is mixed with air and delivered to the engine, how the fuel mixture gets into the engine's cylinders and is ignited, and how the engine is lubricated and cooled. The earliest engines had only one cylinder—they relied on the momentum of a flywheel to exhaust and fill the cylinder. It was quickly realized that multiple cylinders made for smoother running, since one cylinder powered the other cylinders through nonfiring strokes.

Four cylinders became the norm for smaller cars; six or eight cylinders were used for larger models. Six cylinders may be arranged in a line or in a more compact V-shaped layout—two banks of three cylinders, usually with a 60-degree angle between them. Eight-cylinder engines nearly always have a V-8 configuration, with two banks of four cylinders at right angles to one another.

Early gasoline engines took their fuel-air mixture from a carburetor—a device that uses suction from the cylinders to evaporate fuel. Early carburetors were limited in the amount of fuel they could deliver. Later designs featured multiple barrels that delivered more fuel.

In most modern cars, the carburetor has been replaced by fuel injectors—devices originally developed for diesel engines. A fuel injector sprays fuel from a high-pressure gallery either into the main engine intake or directly into the inlet passage to each cylinder.

Ignition and combustion

Most injection systems depend on electronic control systems to work out the correct amount of fuel to inject for a given engine-operating condition. These electronic systems often also control the generation and timing of the ignition spark. Electronic ignition systems are becoming the norm even for carburetor engines—especially where exhaust-emission regulations are severe.

A number of modern engines use turbocharging to increase the air supply and thus the maximum power available; some automobiles are powered by diesel engines, which have no ignition system. Instead, they depend on the heating effect of compression to ignite fuel.

The way fuel and air mix together before they burn has a profound effect on the burning characteristics of the mixture and on the exhaust gases produced by the engine. A recent innovation, called stratified charging, uses a fuel mixture that is richer in the part of the cylinder near the ignition spark. Once this mixture ignites, the flame passes to the part of the mixture that contains more air. This ensures a cleaner burn and produces less pollution than a uniform fuel mixture.

The inlet and exhaust valves of an engine are operated by one or more camshafts driven at half crankshaft speed. At one time, almost all camshafts were chain driven, but most engines now use toothed rubber belts that run smoothly without requiring lubrication.

Alternative power sources

A number of alternative power sources have been tested as a means of reducing pollution. Electric engines are capable of providing acceptable acceleration and mileage for urban use, and hybrid engines that combine an electric motor with an internal combustion are used to provide a wider range of performance. Although carbon dioxide is still produced if the electricity is generated in a fossil-fuel power plant, a smaller volume is produced for the same amount of energy from a gasoline engine, and pollutants such as carbon monoxide are not released into the air.

Liquefied petroleum gas burns more cleanly than gasoline, and alcohol from cane sugar produces no more carbon dioxide than is consumed by the growing cane. Hydrogen forms only water when it burns, but the difficulty of transporting enough fuel for a long journey has limited its use.

Transmission

An automobile transmission performs three tasks: it enables the engine to run when the vehicle is not moving, it multiplies the engine torque and enables the engine to run at an efficient speed at all times, and it carries the drive to the wheels.

Manual transmissions have a pedal-operated clutch and multispeed gears that are selected by operating a hand lever. This type of transmission continues to be popular in Europe, where some drivers prefer the extra degree of control offered by manual gearshifts. Most U.S. automobiles have automatic transmission, in which a hydraulic torque converter and an epicyclic gear train take the place of the manual clutch and layshaft gears.

Traditional car designs have the torque from the engine delivered to a differential between the wheels of the rear axle. The differential allows the two wheels to turn at slightly different rates when cornering. A number of cars now have front-wheel drive, in which power is delivered to a differential between the front wheels. This configuration has the advantages that the power points in the direction of steering, improving control, and the transmission shaft is shorter and does not need to pass through a hump through the center of the passenger cabin.

Another type of transmission drives all four wheels instead of just two—a configuration that was once confined to off-road vehicles. Each axle has its own differential, and a secondary gear system switches between two-wheel and four-wheel drive according to road conditions.

◀ Modern vehicles are designed to give better aerodynamic profiles that reduce drag and aid fuel consumption. This energy-efficient electric-powered automobile produces no polluting emissions.

Suspension

Early automobiles used leaf springs to soften the ride. Such suspensions offered poor comfort if they were stiff enough to locate the axles properly and suffered from tramp (driven-wheel bounce) and poor stability if the springs were soft enough to give a comfortable ride.

Almost all automobiles now have independent suspension, in which the wheels are not joined by a rigid axle but can move independently. Typical independent-suspension systems use coil-type springs together with telescopic hydraulic dampers whose purpose is to stop the springs from oscillating out of control. In an active suspension system, a microprocessor responds to road conditions by changing the size of a hole in the damper piston according to road conditions. The larger the hole, the less damping.

Some automobiles—notably those of the Citroën company—are fitted with high-pressure hydropneumatic suspension systems. This type of suspension benefits from automatic body leveling and adjustable riding height.

Steering

Older steering systems used a rack and pinion to transfer the motion of the steering wheel to the front wheels. As vehicles became heavier, particularly in the United States, manual steering gradually lost favor to power steering, which requires a fraction of the driver effort required for manual steering. In power steering, the movement of the steering wheel lets high-pressure hydraulic fluid into cylinders that turn the wheels. Alternatively, the steering wheel can operate servomotors that turn the wheels directly.

▲ Electric vehicles like this are becoming popular for driving in urban environments as they are quiet and also economical for short journeys.

Brakes and tires

Disk-type front brakes are now standard, since they have a superior resistance to brake fade. More traditional drum-type brakes are often used on the rear wheels, not least because they make for simpler designs of parking brakes.

Another near-universal feature is the brake-assistance servo, which uses suction from the engine inlet manifold to activate cylinders that apply a force to the brakes.

A more recent development in braking systems is antilock braking. This type of system causes a momentary release of the brake if an electronic sensor detects wheel lock.

Improved braking performance goes hand in hand with the improved stability and grip of radial-ply tires, which have almost completely replaced the traditional cross-ply type. There is an increasing tendency for modern tires to become shallower in relation to their width, with an aspect ratio of 70 percent now commonplace.

Electrical systems

The electrical systems of automobiles have seen enormous developments in the last few decades. Originally, the electrical system operated only the ignition and the headlamps of a car using the power from a DC generator and a six-volt battery.

Modern cars use a rectified alternator and a 12-volt battery to power a wide range of accessories, including internal lights, turn signals, heating and ventilation or an air-conditioning unit, radio and sound systems, as well as the numerous microprocessor-controlled circuits for braking, steering, and engine management.

FACT FILE

■ Although they would remain less popular than gasoline-fueled automobiles for the whole of the 20th century, electric cars had already been built in the 19th century. In 1899, the Belgian inventor Camille Jenatzy designed and drove an electric car that set a speed record of 65.8 mph (105.9 km/h).

■ In 1998, American Honda announced the launch of its prototype ZLEV, or zero-level emission vehicle. The ZLEV is so called because its gasoline engine produces no more pollution than a fossil-fuel power plant would produce in generating power for an electric car of comparable performance.

SEE ALSO: AUTOMOBILE ELECTRONICS SYSTEM • AUTOMOBILE EXHAUST SYSTEM • AUTOMOBILE SAFETY • BRAKING SYSTEM • INTERNAL COMBUSTION ENGINE • STEERING SYSTEM • TIRE

Automobile Electronics System

Until the late 20th century, automobiles relied on basic electrical and electromechanical systems to perform tasks such as igniting the gasoline in the engine cylinders and operating headlamps and turn signals. The growing availability of micro-electronics in the 1960s led to the introduction of garage-based diagnostic systems that were used to assess the performance of car engines. Some car models included centralized multipin sockets that accepted a plug from a diagnostic machine. As the engine was running, the machine would measure and display the conditions in each cylinder. Signals from the ignition system reported the timing and strength of the spark in each cylinder. Checks on the fuel system indicated the amount of fuel delivered to each cylinder and the efficiency with which it burned. Further tests checked for leaks in the piston rings, through the valve guides, and around the cylinder head gasket by monitoring the pressure in the cylinders and the vacuum in the intake manifold, which supplies fuel and air to the cylinders. Some machines would interpret the incoming information and print a report that detailed the adjustments needed for better running. Efficiency improvements of up to 10 percent were regularly achieved by correcting problems that would not have been obvious without such monitoring equipment.

As the miniaturization of electronic circuit components progressed, it became possible to include circuitry in onboard microprocessors. These systems monitor changes in engine status and load conditions through a journey and make suitable adjustments. The introduction of such devices made important contributions to fuel economy and emissions control.

Ignition systems

The traditional form of ignition system, now largely obsolete, used a distributor to divert pulses of current to the spark plugs at the correct point in the firing sequence. A distributor has one

▼ A diagnostic system relates engine performance to exhaust-gas content. The two dials indicate the parts-per-million content of hydrocarbons and the percentage of carbon monoxide in the exhaust.

contact point for each cylinder. These contact points are arranged in a circle around a pivoting arm that has a contact point that supplies current from one terminal of the car battery. When the engine is running, the arm rotates so as to make and break contact with each point in turn. When this happens, a pulse of current flows through the low-voltage circuit of a transformer, called a coil, to the other terminal of the battery. The high-voltage circuit of the coil produces the spark that ignites the fuel in the cylinder. The voltage across the spark plug at this point can reach 20,000 volts. This type of system can include a tachometer—an electronic device that detects electrical pulses in the ignition leads from the coil and calculates the engine speed from their frequency.

Electronic ignition

Since the mid-1980s, a growing number of automobiles have been fitted with electronic ignition systems. These monitor the position of the engine's crankshaft, which determines the position of each of the cylinders. The circuitry then initiates a 40,000-volt spark to each cylinder in turn. The greater spark voltage helps improve performance by ensuring a cleaner, more thorough burn. An electronic ignition system has the further advantage of allowing constant fine tuning of the ignition timing according to instructions from the engine-management microprocessor.

Fuel injection

Fuel-injection systems supply gasoline or diesel to the cylinders of an internal-combustion engine by spraying a fine mist of fuel into the intake manifold—a duct that connects the intake ports of the cylinders to the air inlet—or into each individual cylinder. Until the mid-1980s, most auto engines took their fuel-air blend from a carburetor, a device that used suction from the downstroke of the engine's pistons to evaporate fuel. On startup, a manual or automatic choke would increase the proportion of fuel in the blend to keep the engine running until it reached normal operating temperature.

The weaknesses of a carburetor-fed engine are the inflexibility of the fuel-air blend and the inability to control the flow of fuel into the cylinders—the fuel mixture was simply drawn in as the intake ports of the cylinders opened. Fuel injectors offer the ability to control the timing and volume of the fuel spray, and those that feed into individual cylinders offer more control than those that supply the intake manifold do. Signals from the engine-management microprocessor operate a pump for each injector nozzle according to varying factors such as engine speed and load.

Exhaust-gas analysis

One type of exhaust-gas analysis checks for the concentrations of pollutants in exhaust gases. These pollutants include carbon monoxide and hydrocarbons formed by incomplete combustion, and oxides of nitrogen (NO_x), which form by the reaction of oxygen and nitrogen in the air when the combustion temperature is higher than ideal. The equipment used for such testing is expensive and tends to be used only in centers for emissions-testing and commercial maintenance workshops. In such installations, a hose leads gases from the tailpipe for analysis.

A simpler test device is a lambda sensor, which measures the oxygen content of the exhaust stream. Lambda is related to the ratio of fuel to air in the cylinders. A lambda value of 1 represents the ideal mixture for combustion, while a smaller lambda value indicate a mixture that is too lean, and a lambda value greater than 1 indicate a mixture that is too rich to burn completely.

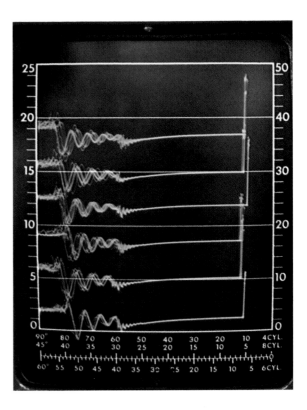

▲ This screen displays the electrical activity in the six cylinders of an engine. For optimal performance, the six traces should coincide from left to right.

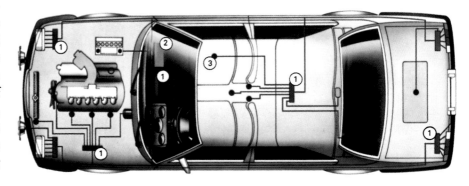

Sensors

A pressure sensor is a type of transducer that produces an electrical signal in response to the pressure that acts on it. A pressure sensor in the intake manifold measures the partial vacuum as each piston descends in its cylinder, which can indicate when a cylinder is suffering from leakage and even the cause of the leakage. Pressure gauges are also used to check the fuel-pump suction and oil-pump-delivery pressure, providing signals for the appropriate driver-warning systems. Pressure

▲ The electronics system of a modern automobile features substations (1) that govern various subsystems, such as engine control, air conditioning, and fuel, oil, and coolant levels. The substations are linked to a central controller (2) and to numerous sensors (3).

sensors can also detect engine knock, which is caused by the fuel–air mixture starting to burn before the ignition spark has been triggered.

Temperature sensors are transducers whose electrical output depends on their temperature. Such sensors are used to monitor the performance of the lubricant and coolant systems—warning the driver in the event of failure—and to monitor ambient air temperature and the combustion temperature in the cylinders.

The third type of sensor used in automobile-control systems is the position sensor, whose electrical output varies with the position of a component. Position sensors are used to monitor the rotation of the crankshaft, for example.

Engine-control module

The engine-control module, or ECM, is the nerve center of any engine-management system. It has a microprocessor that receives signals from sensors around the automobile and that is programmed to calculate the appropriate instructions for various subsystems, including the fuel-injection and fuel-ignition subsytems. This helps ensure the smoothest, most efficient engine performance and the lowest level of emissions for a given power demand and engine condition.

The primary demand for power is determined by the position of the accelerator pedal, but power-assisted braking and steering systems also place a demand for engine power, as does an air-conditioning system and coolant pumps.

The ECM adjusts the rate and timing of fuel delivery and ignition for a given load and engine speed several times per second. It also monitors the signal from the lambda sensor to ensure the best possible conditions for the catalytic converter to function efficiently. Some ECMs also have the capability to lock the torque converter of an automatic transmission when a vehicle reaches cruising speed. This eliminates slip in the transmission and improves fuel economy.

The performance of an engine and its management system can be tested by running the vehicle through a series of load and speed conditions on braked rollers. This type of test rig is called a rolling road. A cable from an output port on the ECM connects to a diagnostic computer, which analyzes signals from sensors and the ECM's actions through the test run. This information can be used to remedy engine malfunctions and calibration problems in the ECM.

Other systems

Microprocessors are increasingly used to provide instructions for the servomotors that operate braking and active suspension systems. In both cases, the microprocessor repeatedly monitors the status of the system and issues corrective instructions.

An antilock braking system, or ABS, applies brake pressure in response to the driver depressing the brake pedal. If the motion sensors of an ABS detect a sudden drop in the rotational speed of the wheels, which would indicate a skid, it releases the brake pressure. When the sensors detect that the wheels have recovered from the skid, it applies more pressure. This process is repeated as long as the brakes are applied firmly enough to cause a skid and is felt as a jerky deceleration.

An active suspension responds to changes in road surfaces by constantly adjusting the response of shock absorbers so as to ensure smooth but firm handling. A microprocessor adjusts the size of a hole in the piston, which damps the suspension, increasing the aperture of the hole for uneven surfaces. This allows easier vertical motion in the shock absorbers and ensures a smooth ride. Reducing the size of the hole helps reduce forward dive when the car brakes and sideways roll when it turns a corner.

Cellular radio and satellite communications systems open the possibility for an automobile to "know" where it is from signals from a global positioning system and to receive traffic information accordingly. These systems already allow fleet vehicles to report their position and status to a central base, and electronic radio tags permit automatic toll charging without the driver having to stop at a tollbooth.

▲ This rolling road permits static engine testing under a variety of simulated driving conditions. The cables carry signals from sensors in the automobile to a diagnostic computer.

SEE ALSO: AUTOMOBILE • BRAKING SYSTEM • CLUTCH • GEAR • IGNITION SYSTEM, AUTOMOBILE • INTERNAL COMBUSTION ENGINE • SPEEDOMETER AND TACHOMETER • STEERING SYSTEM • TRANSMISSION, AUTOMOBILE

Automobile Exhaust System

The exhaust system of an automobile or similar vehicle is what leads the gases produced by an internal combustion engine from the exhaust ports of its cylinders to the tailpipe, where these gases join the atmosphere. The purpose of an exhaust system is to reduce the noise level and the pollutant content of the exhaust so as to lessen the environmental impact of a vehicle.

Back pressure

The catalytic converter and muffler of a standard exhaust system resist the outflow of gases and cause a back pressure at the exhaust ports. Each piston has to push against this pressure on the exhaust stroke, reducing the engine's power output. For this reason, it is important to keep the back pressure to a minimum by avoiding tight bends in the pipework.

In a standard engine, all cylinders pump their exhaust gases into a chamber called a manifold. In a poorly designed manifold, the output from one cylinder can create a back pressure for the cylinder that exhausts next. Engine performance can be improved by using a header-and-collector system instead of a manifold. The header has pipes that lead from each of the ports to a collector, where the individual pipes are smoothly led into a single pipe. The pipes are cut and formed to have such lengths that the pulses of gas from the cylinders are spaced to avoid uneven peaks of pressure.

Pollution control

Gasoline and diesel fuel are hydrocarbon mixtures. When they burn completely, the products are carbon dioxide and water. Unless conditions are ideal, however, a mixture of fuel and air will not burn completely. As well as carbon dioxide and water, the exhaust gases from an engine may contain carbon monoxide (CO) and hydrocarbons (HC—an abbreviation, not a formula). The high temperatures in the cylinders can also cause oxygen and nitrogen from air to combine and form a mixture of oxides of nitrogen, called NO_x. Carbon monoxide is a suffocating poison; hydrocarbons and related compounds can be irritants or even carcinogens (cancer-promoting chemicals); and nitrogen oxides are irritants that contribute to acid rain and photochemical smog.

The most common type of pollution control is called a three-way catalytic converter, since it acts to reduce concentrations of the three main pollutants: CO, HC, and NO_x. The converter occupies a chamber connected to the outlet of the exhaust manifold. Inside this chamber, a ceramic honeycomb structure coated with platinum and palladium metals catalyzes the oxidation of carbon monoxide and hydrocarbons to form carbon dioxide. At the same time, it strips oxygen from NO_x to produce harmless nitrogen (N_2). In some cases, a sensor monitors the oxygen content of the exhaust and increases the air content of the fuel–air mixture if necessary.

Converters function only when they are hot, and they might not even reach their operating temperature during a short journey.

▲ In a variation of the three-chamber muffler, (left), a perforated pipe carries gases to the far end of the muffler casing. The gases then flow back through the casing and exit through a second perforated pipe. In the muffler on the right, the gases flow straight through a perforated pipe surrounded by a fibrous stuffing.

Noise reduction

Exhaust noise results from pulses of pressure in the gases from an internal combustion engine. Mufflers reduce this noise by smoothing the pulses of pressure. A simple muffler consists of a perforated tube that passes through the center of a sealed cylindrical jacket. Fibrous stuffing between the tube and the jacket absorbs some of the pulses of pressure, smoothing the flow of the exhaust gases and reducing the noise.

Some muffler designs use baffles inside a cylinder. Baffles are walls that divert the flow of gases by blocking alternating sides of the cylinder along its length. As the gases switch from side to side, pressure waves reflect off the baffles and cancel one another to some extent, reducing noise.

Some muffler cylinders have three chambers. A pipe leads the exhaust gases through the first and second chambers into a third chamber. A second pipe leads the gases back from the third chamber to the first, and a third pipe leads them from there to the tailpipe. The pipes are perforated where they pass through the second chamber, which allows gas to flow between the pipes. In this way, peaks of pressure in one pipe fill troughs of pressure in another, reducing noise.

SEE ALSO: AUTOMOBILE • CATALYST • INTERNAL COMBUSTION ENGINE

Automobile Safety

Automobile designs include two types of safety measures: active and passive. Active safety measures are those that help drivers avoid accidents; passive safety measures are those that help car occupants to survive in the event of an accident.

Brakes

The ability to slow or stop a car by braking is the most important active safety feature. Modern cars have dual braking systems that make it possible to brake two of the wheels if one system fails. The tendency of brakes to fade, or become less efficient owing to heating, is greatly reduced by new asbestos-free brake-lining materials and by the use of disk brakes in place of drum brakes.

Powerful brakes have the potential to prevent wheels from turning, causing a skid. This effect, called locking, removes the ability to steer and reduces braking, since when locked, the wheels lose their grip on the road. An antilock braking system, or ABS, prevents locking by automatically pulsing the braking force if the brakes are applied hard. Even if the wheels lock, they can regain their grip between pulses, so a skid is avoided and the driver keeps control of the automobile.

Tires

Since the 1950s, low-profile radial tires have largely replaced cross-ply tires. Radial tires offer much more stability and roadholding than cross-ply tires do, and their wide treads allow a large contact area with the road. Improvements in the rubber compounds used to make tire treads have contributed to better roadholding, and water-shedding tread patterns ensure that adhesion is not too much reduced in wet weather.

For a driver to have effective control over a car, the tire on each wheel must grip the road effectively. If one tire suddenly deflates as the result of a puncture, the change in grip characteristics can throw the vehicle out of control. Modern tires resist puncturing much better than earlier high-pressure tires did, but there is still the problem of steering if a puncture does occur. Run-flat tires have reinforced sidewalls. Combined with wheel-rim designs that hold a punctured tire in place, they are usually sufficient to minimize swerving while the car is brought to a halt.

The self-repairing tire has been available since 1998. It features a polymeric repair gel and canisters that contain a reinflating liquid. In the event of a puncture, the increased friction causes the tire to get hotter. The increased temperature then causes the gel to set, sealing punctures up to $\frac{1}{5}$ in. (5 mm) in diameter. The impact on deflation fractures one or more canisters, releasing a liquid that vaporizes to inflate the tire.

Steering and suspension

Steering and suspension systems work together to ensure that an automobile responds to its driver's actions, regardless of terrain. Active suspension systems use a computer to monitor the input from downforce sensors on each wheel and adjust the

◀ This photograph shows a head-on impact in progress. The checkered strips on the side of the car allow engineers to analyze the deceleration of the vehicle by measuring its forward progress between frames of high-speed film. The red arrow on the stand in the foreground is a distance marker, and the dial is a timing device.

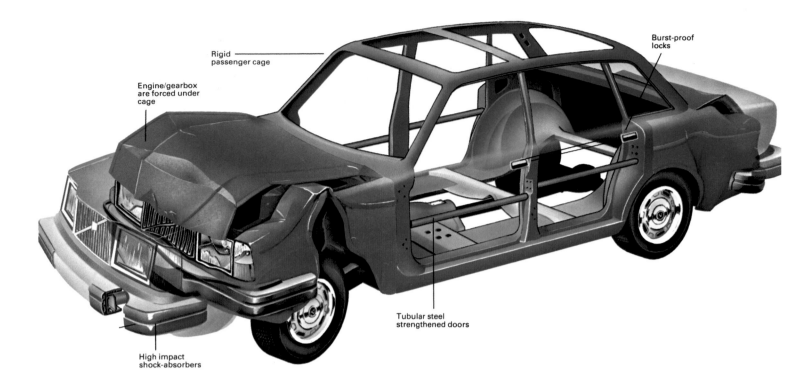

Rigid passenger cage

Engine/gearbox are forced under cage

Burst-proof locks

Tubular steel strengthened doors

High impact shock-absorbers

firmness of the suspension by altering the size of an orifice in the shock absorber restrictor piston in each wheel's suspension.

Variable-ratio steering mechanisms respond more lightly near the straight-ahead position of the steering wheel, more strongly as the wheel turns farther to the right or left. This prevents oversteering at high speed yet maintains maneuverability when turning tight curves at low speed.

Automobile body design

The body of an automobile combines a reinforced safety cell with front and rear crumple zones. The safety cell is a rigid framework that protects the car's occupants, while the crumple zones are designed to deform smoothly during a front or rear impact, absorbing the energy of the impact and avoiding peaks of deceleration that are known to be a major cause of injury. Side impacts are less easy to guard against, since the crush-length of nose or tail is not available, only the thickness of the door. Modern designs use stiff beams inside the door panels. These beams link with the rest of the car's side structure to limit the intrusion of another vehicle's nose as far as possible, while the roof and cabin pillars are made strong enough to resist crushing during a rollover. The steering column of a car is designed to snap during a front-end impact, which prevents it from being driven into the driver's chest as the front end crumples. The fuel tank, which is usually behind the passenger compartment, is placed far enough into the crumple zone to avoid its rupture in all but the most extreme impacts.

Internal safety features

The seats and other fixtures inside a car are fixed rigidly to the safety cell, so they are not hurled violently during impact. The safety belts are anchored to the frame of the safety cell, which supports the restraining force necessary to hold the occupants in place during an impact.

Safety belts are most effective when tight, but would be uncomfortable to wear if they were tight all the time. Some belts reduce the problem of

▲ The design of a Volvo automobile body is typical for modern automobiles. It combines a rigid safety cell (blue) with front and rear crumple zones (red), which are designed to deform in a controlled manner as they absorb the energy of an impact. Large, shock-absorbing fenders can withstand minor impacts, while tubular reinforcing bars in the doors protect the occupants in the event of a side impact.

◀ Renault's hydraulic restraint system delivers a powerful stream of water to a turbine on impact. This tightens the belt against the wearer's chest.

CRASH-TEST DUMMIES

Legislators worldwide demand that cars protect their occupants during a collision; the only way to prove that they do is to strap a dummy into a car and then crash it, and the test most often used is the frontal impact test in which a car is hurled at a concrete block at about 27 mph (50 km/h). Even at this sedate speed it takes only a tenth of a second for an unrestrained passenger to hit the dashboard and fly through the windshield with a fatal force equal to the impact of a fall from a three-story building.

A whole family of mannequins, reflecting all physical types and sizes, used to be subjected to this test. Made of metal and plastic with simple skeletons, they each reproduced with accuracy the injuries a human would sustain in a frontal impact. They were incapable, however, of demonstrating with an adequate degree of accuracy what happens to a human body in other types of impact.

Despite the fact that the major proportion of accidents are not head-on collisions, but oblique collisions at around 30 degrees from head on, lawmakers continued to insist on front-impact tests, for which the older type of dummy was quite an adequate research tool.

The French car manufacturer Renault's safety researchers were the first to realize the need for a more realistic mannequin when they studied slow-motion film of side-impact tests. Some of these were performed using the then-standard range of dummies, others used fresh unembalmed corpses. The dummies seemed hardly affected by the impacts. The corpses, however, were violently disfigured: the scientists discovered that it takes just $^{35}/_{1000}$ of a second for the shoulder to be pushed sideways and up by an impact against the arm, the collarbone to snap, and the ribcage to be crushed sufficiently to cause multiple fractures.

To find out just how much the human body can take, scientists used further human corpses. With accelerometers attached to their spines, they were dropped sideways onto a variety of hard

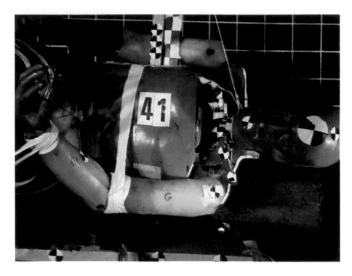

◀ Crash-test dummies were developed by dropping them on their sides and comparing their responses to the injuries sustained by human corpses under the same conditions.

and soft surfaces from different heights. Autopsies after each test revealed rib fractures to be the most common injuries. High-speed photography showed how these fractures occurred, and rib samples taken from each corpse helped establish average bone strength in terms of its bending and shearing capacity.

The scientists then began work on a new mannequin: one that would give the crash-test engineers exactly the information they wanted. A new shoulder was designed to conform more closely to that of a human, one that allowed a similar amount of movement. A new arm was designed with fleshlike padding to absorb some of a side impact in the same way as a human arm. A new linkage was built between the collarbone and sternum to help the shoulder's movement.

Most important, a new rib cage was designed using sprung steel to simulate the ribs, but instead of having them fitted directly to the mannequin's spine, they are mounted on pistons. The pistons slide inside cylinders fixed rigidly to the spine, which allows the rib cage to be crushed laterally by up to 2 in. (55 mm).

Magnetic pick-ups in the piston assemblies—as well as in the head, spine, and pelvis—measure the injuries suffered by the new mannequin in both side-impact and head-on collisions, recording for the auto engineers exactly how their products failed to protect the occupants.

Accelerometers in the mannequin tell them how effective their design was at dissipating the energy of the impact and how hard the mannequin hit, or was hit by, parts of the car's interior.

These new mannequins that ride out the final short journeys of these sacrificial cars look unnervingly real. Impassive, silent, they "tell" the engineers what went wrong and where it hurts. Then, unflinchingly, they go back for more.

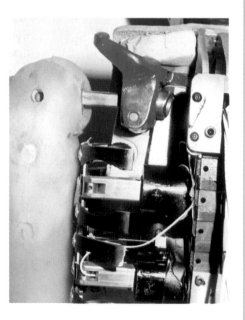

▲ This photograph shows the right-shoulder area of a crash-test dummy viewed from the front. The red assembly is the artificial shoulder joint; below it are the crushable ribs; and the padded arm is at left.

wearer discomfort with an inertia-reel device near one anchor point. The inertia reel allows the belt to slip freely when pulled gently, as when its wearer moves around normally, but locks the belt securely when tugged violently, as in the case of an impact. A safety belt is only effective if it is worn. To ensure that belts are used, some car designs include integral seat belts that fold around the occupants as they close the doors; others have audible warnings or ignition systems that do not function if an occupant is unbelted.

In many countries, the law requires that air bags be fitted in addition to safety belts. Sensors in the air bags trigger inflation if they detect the rapid deceleration of an impact. A triggered air bag blows the cover of the compartment that contains it and expands to cushion the occupant it protects. Some controversy has arisen because of injuries that result when an air bag designed for a larger person inflates in the face of a child or a slightly-built adult. This problem could be resolved by including a weight-sensing mechanism that modifies the explosive force according to the weight of the occupant.

Padded surfaces without sharp corners help to avoid injury in impacts that are too gentle to trigger an air bag, and the use of laminated safety glass prevents the formation of flying shards of glass during impact. Laminated glass consists of layers of sheet glass bonded together by an adhesive layer of plastic. The plastic holds the fragments together if the glass shatters.

A significant potential cause of injury in rear-end impacts is whiplash—the violent backward motion of the head as the body is accelerated forward by the seat back. This motion can cause anything from a painful strain to a lethal or paralyzing neck fracture. The risk of whiplash injuries can be much reduced by the use of an effective head restraint that cradles the back of the head and pushes it forward with the body in the case of a rear impact.

Pedestrian injury

Car occupants are not the only people at risk of injury or death in a car accident: pedestrians also are. While the only truly effective way to prevent pedestrian injuries is to keep pedestrians and moving cars as far from each other as practicable, some automobile design features can help reduce the magnitude of injuries and the risk of death for pedestrians in automobile accidents.

In most developed countries, legislation bans external features that could injure pedestrians. The hood ornaments of car manufacturers such as Rolls Royce and DaimlerChrysler, for example, are designed to collapse telescopically or fold freely backward in the event of impact.

The smooth lines of aerodynamic automobile body designs have the added benefit of presenting a cornerless surface in the event of pedestrian impact. In addition, many states and countries have legislation that requires soft front panels that deform on impact, absorbing much of the blow. These panels and fenders are manufactured using semirigid polyurethane foam or synthetic rubber. Such materials can be painted in the same color as the rest of the bodywork.

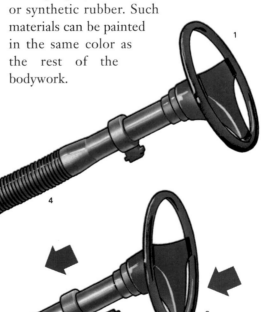

◀ This steering column is designed to reduce chest injuries for the driver in a collision. The rim of the steering wheel is padded to cushion impacts (1). The wheel can also flex to flatten against the driver's chest, spreading the force of impact (2). The column is secured by a breakaway mounting (3) that snaps under the force of impact, so that a telescopic slipsleeve (4) and folding knifejoint (5) can take up any further compression.

SEE ALSO: AUTOMOBILE • BRAKING SYSTEM • STEERING SYSTEM • TIRE

Aviation, History of

Aviation is the design, manufacture, and operation of heavier-than-air flying vehicles. The word derives from the Latin word *avis*, which means "bird." Flying machines fall into two categories: lighter-than-air machines and heavier-than-air machines.

Lighter-than-air craft include balloons and dirigibles; they are so called because they obtain their buoyancy from gases such as helium or hot air, which are less dense than the atmosphere. Heavier-than-air craft are devices that stay aloft by virtue of an upward force, called lift, which results from their motion through air. Gliders and powered airplanes are included in this class. Helicopters are also heavier-than-air craft, but their lift derives from the motion of their rotors through the air and does not require the whole vehicle to move.

Early dreams of flight

Ancient humans were aware of flight from their observations of birds. The notion of human flight became the stuff of myth, such as the Greek myth of Daedalus and Icarus. Florentine artist and inventor Leonardo da Vinci, a man fascinated by birds, took this notion further by designing machines that he believed would make human flight possible. One of them, the ornithopter, was a frame with movable wings that could be flapped by a person inside the frame. Other designs by da Vinci featured crude versions of helicopters, gliders, and parachutes.

By the end of the 18th century, a number of enthusiasts had attempted flight by strapping themselves into devices similar to da Vinci's ornithopter and flapping frantically. None succeeded, however, since the power required to lift the weight of a human in such a device is much greater than the capability of any human.

Gliders

British scientist and mechanic George Cayley is considered by many the pioneer of aviation based on scientific aerodynamics. Just as da Vinci three centuries before him, Cayley was inspired by the flight of birds. He outlined a design for a fixed-wing aircraft with a powered propeller as early as 1799, even though a suitable source of power was not available at that time. Cayley built a number of gliders, including an unpiloted glider with a wing area of 300 sq. ft. (around 28 m²) that he built in 1808. In his paper *On Aerial Navigation*, published 1808–1809, Cayley outlined the roles of thrust, drag, and lift in flight and pointed out

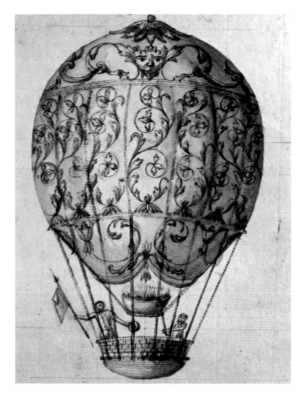

◄ An 18th-century hot-air balloon fueled by the burning of chopped straw. As these early balloons were made of cloth backed with paper, it is not surprising that many of them caught fire, or finished the flight in a damaged condition. Today, ballooning remains a popular leisure method of air travel, albeit for short distances.

the value of the cambered, or arched, wing shape. In 1853, Cayley built a glider in which his coachman flew a few hundred yards across a valley before crash landing. This is believed to have been the first human flight.

German inventor Otto Lilienthal continued the development of gliders, making more than 2,000 successful flights between 1891 and 1896. Lilienthal controlled his gliders by shifting his weight from side to side. At the time of his fatal crash in 1896, Lilienthal was working on a body harness attached to a rear elevator.

Powered flight

Gliders were limited by their dependence on favorable wind conditions and their requirement of an initial drop or tow to put them in flight. Inventors realized that truly sustained flight would require an onboard power source. At first, they looked to steam engines. The most ambitious early design, the aerial steam carriage, drawn up by William Henson in 1842, had a tailpiece to provide control and stability, box-kite wings incorporating spars and ribs, and a three-wheeled undercarriage. It was to have a wingspan of 150 ft. (46 m) and was to be propelled by two six-blade airscrews. It was, however, never built. In 1848, British inventor John Stringfellow, who had worked with Henson until 1847, produced a steam-powered model monoplane (a craft with a single wing) that was capable of sustained flight.

The problem with steam power was the weight of a steam engine compared with the power that it produced. In 1894, for example, British inventor Hiram Maxim staged an elaborate experiment with a device that weighed 3.5 tons (3.2 tonnes) and had two 180 horsepower (134 kW) steam engines. It lifted momentarily from its rails, and there the project ended. With the development of the gasoline engine in the final quarter of the 19th century, however, the mathematics of powered flight became a reality.

In October 1903, U.S. astronomer and engineer Samuel Langley of the Smithsonian Institute, Washington, came close with a gas-powered aircraft launched by catapult from a houseboat on the Potomac River. Two months later, the Wright brothers succeeded in achieving powered flight.

The Wright brothers

Between 1900 and 1902, the Wright brothers, Orville and Wilbur, U.S. aviation pioneers, performed more than 1,000 glider flights at Kitty Hawk, North Carolina. In 1903, they designed and made a propeller and then set about finding an automobile engine that would be light enough to mount on their glider frame and powerful enough to give it lift. No suitable engine could be found, so they hired an engineer to build one for them: a four-cylinder motor that weighed 15 lbs. (7 kg) and produced 12 horsepower (9 kW). It turned two wooden propellers behind a double wing, while the pilot pulled a wire string attached to his waist to twist the wingtips and balance the aircraft in flight. On December 17, 1903, Orville Wright piloted *Flyer I* in a 12-second flight of 120 ft. (37 m). Orville and Wilbur made three more flights on that day, and the last succeeded in covering a magnificent 852 ft. (260 m).

At first, the Wright's achievement caused little stir. It was only their third *Flyer* airplane that generated widespread interest: in 1905, it managed a flight of 24 miles (38 km) at an average speed of 38 mph (61 km/h); its success owed much to the Wright's experiments in control.

In 1908, Wilbur Wright demonstrated the latest model in France, where he made several long flights, including one of 2 hours and 20 minutes on December 31. This flight gave a great impetus to European designers, who had previously concentrated on stability, rather than control.

Meanwhile, in 1907, British engineer Alliot Roe designed and built a tractor biplane—one whose propellers pulled from the front—and British inventor John Dunne built the world's first swept-wing airplane, again a biplane, aimed at inherent stability. Around the same time, British engineer Frederick Lanchester put forward his theory of the circulation of air over wing surfaces in *Aerodynamics* (1907) and *Aerodonetics* (1908), a theory which has since been proved to be true.

At the August 1909 Reims aviation week in France, more than 30 aircraft were on show, six built to the Wright's specification. But their influence on European design was short-lived. French aviator Louis Blériot had already achieved the first crossing of the English Channel on July 25 of the same year—in a monoplane—and European aircraft designers started going their own way. The best performers were still biplanes, but a good deal of work went into monoplane designs and the idea of the cantilever wing, supported by the fuselage instead of wires, was contained in a patent registered by Junkers of Germany in 1910. A year later, another improvement appeared in a German device for raising hinged undercarriage legs to lie flush with the fuselage in flight so as to reduce drag.

By 1913, a host of important achievements and events had been recorded. The air speed

▼ Wilbur Wright, having just let go of the wing, watches brother Orville at the controls of the *Flyer* as it takes off from a wooden rail in December 1903 and flies away from the camera.

record stood at 126.6 mph (204 km/h), a French pilot had looped the loop for the first time, and the Schneider Trophy Race for seaplanes had been inaugurated.

World War I

With the outbreak of World War I, the flimsy, underpowered aircraft of the prewar era would soon be replaced as designers took up the task of building combat aircraft. Aircraft became sturdier and were equipped with more efficient engines. Designs such as Fokker's high-wing monoplane, which had a suspended, stressed-skin fuselage construction, would lead to major advances in later years. The most significant developments, however, were not structural: the most important advances came in the way aircraft were designed for specialized operations. At the start of the war, aircraft were used only for reconnaissance work; by 1918, the British Handley Page V/1500, a biplane powered by four 375-horsepower (280 kW) engines, could carry 7,500 lbs. (3.4 tonnes) of bombs over Berlin, and German Gothas could dump similar loads over

London. Fighters could fly at around 140 to 150 mph (225–240 km/h) and climb to altitudes around 23,000 ft. (7,000 m).

When peace came, there were large numbers of ex-military aircraft available to passenger and mail-transport operators. The large, wire-braced biplanes of the war years scored some significant success immediately after 1918. In May 1919, the NC-4, a flying boat built by the Curtiss Aircraft Company for the U.S. Navy, crossed the Atlantic Ocean. It took two weeks and stopped several times along the way. Two weeks later, British avia-

▲ The autogiro, a basic form of helicopter, derives its forward motion from a small pusher-type propeller motor, and its lift from a free-rotating blade.

◄ The Boeing 747 Jumbo Jet is powered by four Pratt and Whitney JT9D turbofan engines.

tors John Alcock and Arthur Whitten Brown flew nonstop from Newfoundland to Ireland in a Vickers Vimy, a converted wartime bomber, in 16 hours and 27 minutes. During this period, work started on helicopters, pioneered in the United States by Sikorsky and in Germany by Focke and Angelis.

In 1927, U.S. aviator Charles Lindbergh flew the *Spirit of St. Louis*, a monoplane built by Ryan Airlines, 3,600 miles nonstop from New York to Paris in 33 hours and 39 minutes; in 1928, Australian aviator Charles Kingsford Smith crossed the Pacific from the United States to Australia in *Southern Cross*, a three-engined Fokker monoplane. These flights and many others of the time were more than just feats of personal endurance: they underlined the growing reliability of aircraft. Newer designs incorporated navigational and radio equipment to further enhance safety in the air.

Hinged flaps were added to the rear of wings to increase lift and resistance at low speed, allowing planes to land more slowly and use shorter airfields. Then a new range of passenger aircraft emerged, such as the Boeing 247 of 1933 and the Douglas DC range, introduced between 1933 and 1936, that were reasonably large and had soundproofing, offering an unprecedented degree of comfort. For sea crossings, large flying boats were built by Latécoère of France and by Glenn Martin and Boeing in the United States.

During the 1930s, designers began experimenting with jet engines. The first jet-powered flight was made in August 1939, by the German Heinkel He 178. The development of jet propulsion was accelerated by the start of World War II. In May 1941, the first British jet—a Whittle-engined Gloster—made its maiden flight; the U.S. Bell XP-59 followed in 1942. Supersonic flight was achieved in 1947 with the U.S. rocket-powered Bell X-1.

Immediately after the war, U.S. aircraft designers concentrated on developing piston-engine, propeller-driven airliners such as the Douglas DC-7 and the Lockheed Starliner, carrying 100 passengers at over 300 mph (480 km/h); the British concentrated on jet engines, introducing a Rolls Royce turboprop Dart engine to the De Havilland Viscount series in 1948. In 1952, the all-jet Comet appeared, but the original square cabin windows failed in the early models, leading to a series of crashes. By the time the revised Comet 4 appeared in 1958, the Boeing 707—the first U.S. commercial jet airplane—had been tested for four years and was entering commercial service. U.S. plane manufacturers went on to dominate the civil air-transport industry

with ever-larger aircraft, culminating in the "jumbo" aircraft that emerged in the late 1960s. In 1976, British Airways and Air France started operating the Concorde, a supersonic airliner.

New developments

Although the design of commercial aircraft has changed little since the 1960s, a few significant trends emerged. Aircraft operators started to move to small and mid-sized aircraft, which allow more flexibility in their operation. Modifications in engine designs have also made for more powerful, less noisy, more efficient propulsion units that produce less pollution. New lightweight alloys have also reduced the operating costs of aircraft by reducing their weight.

Perhaps the most significant development of recent years has been the introduction of fly-by-wire technology, pioneered by Airbus Industrie of Europe in their Airbus 320. Whereas pilots operate the control surfaces of conventional aircraft through mechanical and hydraulic couplings, the pilot of a fly-by-wire aircraft gives steering instructions to a computer through a control stick, similar to a computer joystick. The computer then signals to electric motors, which adjust the control surfaces. Another important feature of a fly-by-wire is its ability to be flexible in flight, so a slight change in the positions of the control surfaces results in a change in flight behavior, thus making the aircraft more maneuverable. In steady flight, the control computer monitors any slight change in flight behavior and adjusts the control surfaces accordingly.

▲ Ultralight and minimum aircraft are becoming increasingly popular as an alternative to relatively expensive light aviation flying. The *Solar Challenger* took the concept of low-cost aviation a stage further by crossing the English Channel in 1981 driven by a propeller powered by solar energy from wing panels, or photovoltaic cells, in a bid to save fuel.

SEE ALSO: Aerospace industry • Aircraft-control engineering • Aircraft design • Aircraft engine • Airliner • Balloon • Glider • Helicopter • Seaplane and amphibian

Balance

The balance is one of man's oldest measuring instruments and was probably invented by the ancient Egyptians or Babylonians about 5000 B.C.E. It was first used for weighing gold dust for jewelry, commercial goods being exchanged by barter rather than by the payment of money for a weighed amount. These early balances consisted of a simple beam pivoted at its center, with standard weights in a pan at one end and the article to be weighed in a pan at the other.

The Romans made an important improvement to the design of balances when, at the point at which the beam is pivoted, they fixed a triangular section, or "knife edge" fulcrum, to the beam. This made the balance more accurate, especially when measuring very small weights. It was not until the 17th century that Gilles Roberval, a French mathematician, perfected a balance that enabled the goods and weight plates to be placed above the beam and remain accurate wherever the goods were placed on the plate.

Pendulum weighing scales, first developed by Leonardo da Vinci, not only weighed the load but also indicated its weight. By combining the Roberval and pendulum mechanisms at the beginning of the 20th century, a retail scale was devised that did not require the operator to manipulate weights or sliding poises, and indicated the load by a needle moving around a dial. Once common in stores selling loose goods, these scales have since been replaced by electronic weighing machines, which are often connected directly to cash registers.

Just about all modern balances and scales are now electronic. They are more robust, smaller, and much easier to use than mechanical balances.

▶ A digital analytical electronic balance that can weigh with accuracy to 0.0001 g.

All electronic balances use an easily-read digital display so there can be no mistakes when accuracy is needed.

The single-pan electronic balance

Modern balances are classified into different types. Microbalances are used for very fine measurement, say of dust particles in the air, and generally weigh amounts down to one-millionth of a gram. Semimicrobalances are more common and are used in research practices where accuracies to five decimal places are required. Analytical balances weigh to 0.0001 g and are used in research, education, and general laboratory work. Precision balances are those that are generally accurate from 1 g to 0.001 g. Any balance that is not accurate to within 1 g is known as a scale. Scales are widely used in factories, stores, and markets.

For weighing in laboratories where an accuracy of 1 g or better is needed, most electronic balances use a very accurate measuring system. The principle employed is termed "electromagnetic force compensation," which makes use of the very strict linear relationship that exists between the current used and the force generated. To make an electronic balance, a weighing pan is fixed to a wire surrounded by a magnetic field. The location of the wire must be controlled using an indicator. A regulated power source and a current-measuring device are also required. When the pan has no load on it, the system keeps just enough current flowing through the wire to maintain the wire position indicator at its zero point. As weight is added, so the wire in the magnetic field is pushed down. The indicator registers this fact and tells the power regulator to put more

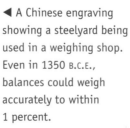

◀ A Chinese engraving showing a steelyard being used in a weighing shop. Even in 1350 B.C.E., balances could weigh accurately to within 1 percent.

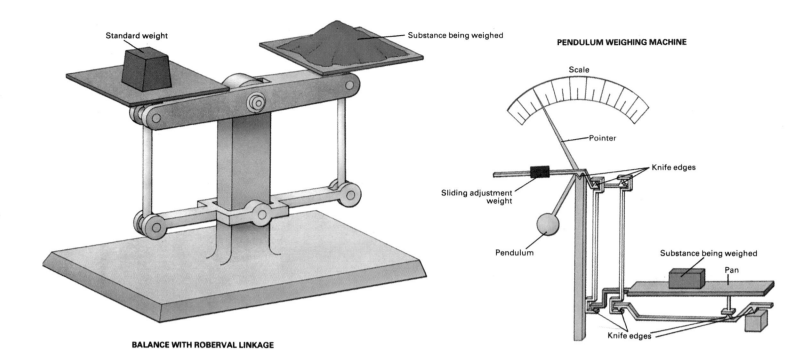

Standard weight

Substance being weighed

PENDULUM WEIGHING MACHINE

Scale

Pointer

Knife edges

Sliding adjustment weight

Pendulum

Substance being weighed

Pan

Knife edges

BALANCE WITH ROBERVAL LINKAGE

current through the wire. Therefore the force generated is also increased. This continues until the position indicator is once again at its zero point. In practice, these processes happen almost instantaneously. The difference in the current indicated by the measuring device between the loaded and unloaded condition is proportional to the weight placed on the pan. Sophisticated microprocessors convert the electric signals produced into digital displays.

Microbalances

A microbalance is a very accurate type of balance that can measure weight differences as small as one-hundredth of a microgram.

Electronic microbalances employ a moving-coil mechanism similar to that used in an ammeter. In one form of this instrument, the beam is attached at one end to a coil, in the same way as the needle of an ammeter, with a small pan at the other end. If an object is placed in the pan, the beam will tilt downward from its horizontal position. The beam is restored to the horizontal by passing an electric current through the coil, and the current required is proportional to the amount of force needed to raise the beam. This analog current is measured, but it is calibrated in units of weight instead of current by microprocessors so that the weight of the sample can be read instantly.

Electronic scales

Electronic scales have been of enormous benefit to the retail food industry through their ability to weigh and price prepacked goods for supermarkets. One type of machine uses a spring combined with a Roberval-type mechanism. The spring

deflection causes a coded disk to rotate, allowing a light source to activate photoelectric detectors according to the pattern on the disk. Each value of weight is uniquely coded. The signals from the encoder exist in the form of a voltage being present or absent on a terminal. With suitable circuits, these signals can operate digital indicators displaying values as numerals. Additionally, the signals can be multiplied by a factor corresponding to the unit weight price of the goods, and the result is fed to a display or ticket printer.

Another form of electric weight transducer makes use of the strain that is produced when load is applied to a material. The strain, which is proportional to the load, is measured by electric resistance strain gauges. Connecting a number of gauges to an electric supply produces an output voltage level proportional to the load. Such a device is known as a load cell, and a number of cells would be used to support a weigh-station platform and provide signals representing loads. These signals are amplified and then converted from analog to a digital read-out device by means of a balancing current. The balancing current is controlled by electronic switches that are turned on or off depending on how much is needed, and the patterns of on and off switches represent the weight signal in digital form. This allows weight changes to be followed as they occur.

▲ Left: A mechanical balance with Roberval linkage. The pans remain horizontal wherever the weight is placed on them. Right: Pendulum weighing machines allow weights to be read directly from the scale.

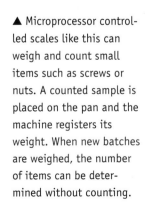

▲ Microprocessor controlled scales like this can weigh and count small items such as screws or nuts. A counted sample is placed on the pan and the machine registers its weight. When new batches are weighed, the number of items can be determined without counting.

SEE ALSO: DIGITAL DISPLAY • ELECTRONICS • WEIGH STATION

Ballistics

Ballistics is the study of projectiles and the extent to which their trajectories are affected by shape, propulsion, gravity, temperature, wind, and so on. Though mainly used for research into ammunition and missiles, ballistics also has applications in such fields as geophysics, meteoritics, and space exploration. There are three branches: interior, dealing with all aspects of propulsion within a gun barrel or at launch; exterior, concerned with the trajectory of the projectile in flight; and terminal, relating to the effects of the missile on the target.

There are a great number of related factors that have an effect on interior ballistics. For a start, there is the propellant and the task of measuring the pressure it exerts upon the projectile. This depends upon the density of the gas given off by the exploding propellant and the rate at which it burns.

Besides the propellant, there is the shape of the projectile and the characteristics of the gun to

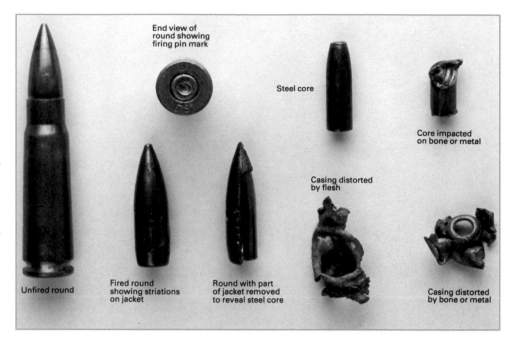

End view of round showing firing pin mark

Steel core

Core impacted on bone or metal

Casing distorted by flesh

Unfired round

Fired round showing striations on jacket

Round with part of jacket removed to reveal steel core

Casing distorted by bone or metal

be taken into account. Whether a gun is rifled or smooth barreled makes a difference to the behavior of shot, as does the efficiency of the weapon's recoil mechanism. It is also evident that, within limits, more muzzle velocity can be imparted to a light, large-diameter projectile than to a heavy, small-diameter one.

The diameter of the projectile and all its aerodynamic properties is also the concern of exterior ballistics—as is its muzzle velocity. An illustration of this is the fact that, although higher muzzle velocity can be imparted to a light, large-diameter projectile, the aerodynamic drag upon it will reduce its velocity much more rapidly during flight than the velocity of a heavy, small-diameter projectile. An example of applying ballistics to get the best of both worlds is the discarding sabot principle, by which a light, large-diameter case is employed to carry a heavy, small-diameter shot out of a gun muzzle to reduce drag during flight.

In the same way, rifling a projectile causes it to spin during flight and is a means of stabilizing it to prevent it from toppling, which would increase the drag on it. Fins are used on bombs and guided missiles to prevent yaw and tumbling. The other main force operating on a missile in the exterior phase is gravity.

Terminal ballistics grows more and more detailed and complex as the task demanded of projectiles becomes more varied. The need to penetrate armor, for instance, has resulted in types of shot with different terminal characteristics. There is shot that uses kinetic energy and is essentially a long, strong, thin round hurled with

▲ A rifle round from a Kalashnikov AK-47 before and after firing, and meeting with different types of target. It has a steel core, a soft lead tip, and a cupro-nickel casing. The identification of a bullet or gun is one of the most basic functions of forensic ballistics.

◄ The aerodynamic properties of a bullet can be seen clearly in this high-speed photograph of the projectile disturbing the waves of heat above a lighted candle.

maximum velocity at an armored target, and there is shot that uses chemical energy or shaped explosive that detonates on the target and blasts through it or causes it to scab. The boundaries of terminal ballistics were only extended in this way because more sophisticated measuring instruments enabled the phenomena taking place to be observed in milliseconds.

Another aspect of terminal ballistics is the study of damage caused to the human body by ammunition, which can be useful in law enforcement, as the direction and range of a shot can be gauged from the wound it makes. Telltale marks left on bullets and cartridges after firing can also be used by forensic ballistics experts to identify not only the type of gun used in a shooting but also the exact weapon that fired the shot.

Gravity-assisted projectiles

Gravity's influence on a projectile has proved advantageous in space exploration. Probes are often targeted at a particular planet or the Sun to make use of the slingshot effect to change the probe's trajectory and speed up its flight. This can be useful in cutting down on the amount of fuel needed for the journey or in cases where the object to be visited is in an awkward position relative to Earth. Voyager 2 took advantage of a unique alignment of the planets to enable it to reach Uranus and Neptune, each time using the gravity of the planet it was passing to speed it on to the next. The Galileo probe had an even more extraordinary journey. After heading for Venus, it looped twice around Earth before being flung toward the asteroid belt. It then made a final swing around Earth before journeying to Jupiter.

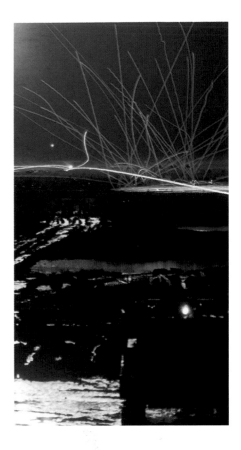

▶ Machine gun tracer and mortar fire at night. The bright paths of the ammunition trajectories can be used to sight in on an enemy position.

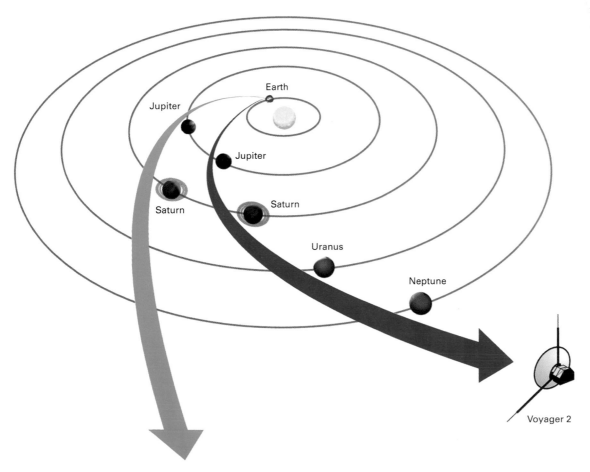

◀ The routes taken by the Voyager probes on their visits to the outer planets. In launching the probes, scientists took advantage of the gravity of the Sun and planets to swing the probes on to their next destination. Voyager 1 was launched after Voyager 2, but its trajectory only took it past Jupiter and Saturn before it traveled out into space. By the time Voyager 2 arrived at Jupiter, the planets Saturn, Uranus, and Neptune were aligned in a unique orbiting position that will not occur again until 2150.

SEE ALSO: AMMUNITION • BOMB-AIMING DEVICE • FORENSIC SCIENCE

Balloon

◄ At 40,000 ft. (12,200 m) the air is –58°F (–50°C); the jet streams at this altitude can average a speed of 100 mph (160 km/h).

Balloons are unique in that they are the only form of aircraft that span the entire history of flight. They were the means by which humans first took to the air, and they are still in use today.

The first manned flight took place by means of a hot-air balloon on November 21, 1783. The balloon, made by the Montgolfier brothers Joseph and Etienne, French paper manufacturers, was 75 ft. (23 m) high by nearly 50 ft. (15 m) in diameter—a frail affair of cloth backed with paper and heated by a furnace burning chopped straw. The pilots were Pilatre de Rozier and the Marquis d'Arlandes.

Only a few weeks later, Jacques Charles, also French, made the first ascent in a hydrogen-filled balloon, and almost at once the gas balloon established itself as superior to the hot-air version. Although it took longer to inflate, it was quiet, easier to handle, lifted more, and above all could be used again. The hot-air balloons had a tendency to catch fire or at the very least to finish their flights in a charred and brittle condition, preventing the balloon's reuse.

The use of hydrogen balloons grew unchecked until the development of airships. They proved useful in both research and war, in the latter particularly as tethered military observation platforms, for which purpose they were used by both sides in the American Civil War and again in World War I. In the latter stages of World War I, the early mono- and biplanes gradually replaced the balloon for aerial observations. The balloon made a comeback, however, in World War II, when barrage balloons were used to protect ships and cities from aerial attack.

Ballooning as a sport reached a peak in the famous Gordon Bennett races, which took place in Europe between 1906 and 1938 and in which the greatest distance covered was 1,368 miles (2,191 km). It was not until 1955 that the modern reusable hot-air balloon was born. Hot-air balloons are now manufactured in varying sizes from 30,000 to 140,000 cu. ft. (850–3,964 m³) to carry from one to six people or an equivalent load.

Principles of balloon flight

A balloon is lighter than an unpowered aircraft. Unlike heavier-than-air machines such as airplanes and gliders, which stay aloft by moving through the air to create dynamic lift, a balloon obtains its lift by displacement, which is a static force and does not require movement through the air to create it. An airship is fitted with one or more engines and also with controls (rudder and elevators), but a balloon has no engine and cannot be steered: it merely drifts with the wind.

A balloon is in equilibrium, that is, balanced in the air and not moving up or down, when its total weight is the same as the weight of the volume of air it is occupying, or displacing. Since the fabric, basket, crew, and equipment are all heavier than air, they must be balanced by filling the envelope with some gas lighter than air.

Gases suitable for filling a balloon include hydrogen, helium, and ordinary air that has been heated. Some gases are lighter than air because the weight of their molecules is less than the average weight of the molecules in the air, that is, they have a lower density than air. Hot air is lighter than cold air because any gas (and air is a gas) expands when heated. The molecules are driven farther apart and therefore a given volume will contain a lower weight of molecules. At sea level, 1,000 cu. ft. (28 m³) of air at 212°F (100°C) will have a lifting capacity of 17.4 lbs. (7.9 kg) when the surrounding air is at 60°F (16°C). A similar amount of helium has a lifting capacity of 65 lbs. (29.5 kg), and for hydrogen the lift available is 70 lbs. (31.75 kg). From the point of view of lift alone, it is obvious that the best thing to fill a balloon with is hydrogen and the worst is hot air.

All lifting media have advantages and disadvantages. Gases are expensive, since they have to be extracted from the air and transported. It costs considerably more to inflate a hydrogen balloon than it does to inflate a hot-air balloon. Hydrogen is highly flammable, but helium, which is safer because it neither burns nor forms explosive mixtures with air, is much more expensive than hydrogen in most countries, except the United States. These factors aside, there are other aspects of gas and hot air that have resulted in the development of two distinct types of balloon, different in design, performance, and to some extent, in the manner in which they are controlled.

Gas balloons

Hydrogen easily penetrates most materials; the fabric of a hydrogen balloon envelope is therefore quite heavy, about half the total weight of the balloon, made from fabric impregnated with rubber or neoprene. The envelope is spherical, the most efficient shape to contain a given volume, and is contained in a string net that distributes the load evenly over the fabric. Below the envelope, the net is drawn together at a load ring from which is suspended a basket to carry crew and equipment.

The envelope is not sealed: at the bottom is a long, narrow open tube called the appendix. As the balloon rises, atmospheric pressure decreases and the gas in the balloon expands. The appendix allows gas to escape, thus preventing the balloon

from bursting as a result of its internal pressure. When the balloon descends, the appendix closes (like a wet drinking straw if it is sucked too hard). This prevents air from getting into the balloon and forming an explosive mixture with the gas.

To ascend in a hydrogen balloon, it is necessary to reduce weight by discharging ballast in the form of sand and thus increase the lift. Similarly, in order to descend, it is necessary to reduce lift. Since additional ballast cannot be obtained while airborne, this is done by opening a small valve in the top of the balloon, which is operated by a cord that leads down to the basket and is held shut by springs or elastic. Ballast and gas escape are the only means of control in a gas balloon. Once the balloon is in equilibrium, these measures will not need to be used unless the balloon is affected by outside factors such as a general cooling or heating of the outside air, which will cause the lifting gas to contract or expand.

Operationally, then, the main advantages of balloons are endurance and lifting power. The disadvantages are the cost and the inconvenience of inflating the balloon, a process that can last as long as two hours.

Hot-air balloons

Modern hot-air balloons are almost the only significant design development to have taken place since balloons were invented. Despite their poor lifting power and endurance, they have been responsible for a tremendous upsurge in the sport because of their low running costs, simplicity, and comparative safety.

Structurally, a hot-air balloon is quite different from a gas balloon. Hot air cannot penetrate material in the way that hydrogen can: the envelope can therefore be made of light fabric, usually rip-proof nylon treated with polyurethane to reduce porosity.

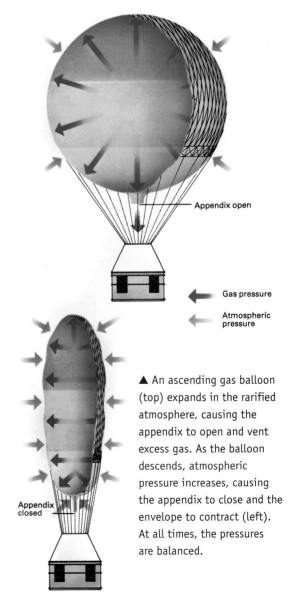

Appendix open

Gas pressure

Atmospheric pressure

Appendix closed

▲ An ascending gas balloon (top) expands in the rarified atmosphere, causing the appendix to open and vent excess gas. As the balloon descends, atmospheric pressure increases, causing the appendix to close and the envelope to contract (left). At all times, the pressures are balanced.

The profile of a hot-air balloon is described as a natural shape: wide at the top, tapering toward the bottom, in the shape naturally created by the internal pressure. Loads are carried on nylon tapes sewn into and integral with the envelope. From these tapes, steel wires lead down to the burner, which is in the same position as the load ring on a gas balloon.

The basket is suspended from the burner by steel wires or a rigid structure, depending on the manufacturer. At the base of the balloon, there is a large opening to allow heat from the burner to enter. A modern hot-air balloon burner uses propane, which is fed under its own bottle pressure to the burner jets. The heat generated may be anything from 8 to 25 million Btu (approximately 3–5 GJ) per hour, much more than many industrial space heaters.

Hot-air balloons are fundamentally different from gas balloons in that it is possible to increase or decrease the lift simply by heating the air or allowing it to cool. When flying a hot-air balloon, the pilot simply turns on the burner if he wants to ascend and leaves it off and allows the air to cool if he wants to descend. The air, in fact, takes some time to cool, and the burner can be left off for quite long periods before the balloon starts to lose height. With the average balloon being between 50,000 and 90,000 cu. ft., inflation can be accomplished in a matter of minutes, which compensates for the relatively poor endurance of hot-air

▲ Balloons can be used for a variety of purposes including recreation (left) and research (right). Almost every country in the world sends up gas-filled radiosonde (remote meteorological) balloons twice daily to gather weather information.

balloons (up to five or six hours, depending on the load), since several flights may be made in a single day.

Scientific balloons

Unmanned gas-filled balloons are used extensively for weather observation and scientific research. Weather balloons carry instruments that collect information on atmospheric conditions such as temperature, pressure, and humidity. Balloons are also used to carry a wide range of scientific instruments into the upper atmosphere, including telescopes and cameras for astronomical research. They are employed in monitoring such things as pollution of the upper atmosphere, cosmic rays, and meteorites.

Weather balloons carrying payloads of 90 lbs. (41 kg) are carried around Earth by circulating winds at a height of over 15 miles (24 km). These balloons are about 65 ft. (20 m) in diameter, made from a double layer of Mylar (a polyester film) 0.02 in. (0.5 mm) thick. Some scientific and meteorological balloons are designed to burst at high altitude, after which their instrument packages return to Earth by parachute. They expand from 5 ft. (1.5 m) in diameter on inflation, to 20 ft. (6 m) in diameter before bursting at a daytime altitude of some 100,000 ft. (30,480 m), which reduces to 80,000 ft. (24,384 m) at night.

Designers and aero-engineers are constantly attempting to advance the frontiers of ballooning, and to reduce size and cost. Hot air is still relatively difficult to fly because balloons are so big. Manufacturers are experimenting with modern materials such as Kevlar, which can resist heat up to temperatures of 750°F (400°C) and would lift four times the weight of a conventional balloon. Experiments are also being made with low-energy balloons, which are much bigger. There is a solar-heated balloon with a transparent top and a black bottom, which absorbs and radiates the heat. The solar energy comes in from the top, hitting the black bottom and reradiating the heat into the center of the balloon. The balloon is inflated with a fan and burner, but once aloft, it is capable of indefinite flight.

Round-the-world flights

Ever since the Montgolfiers' first experiments in ballooning, adventurers have tried to set records for distance and endurance in balloon travel. The ultimate goal—a nonstop round-the-world trip—was finally achieved in 1999 by the crew of *Breitling Orbiter 3*.

For the attempt, the crew used a mixed, or Rozier, balloon, which combines hot air and gas, and is characterized by a helium cell lodged within a hot-air envelope. During ascension, the helium increases in volume owing to the drop in atmospheric pressure and heat of the Sun. The rise can be controlled by venting some gas, which also prevents the balloon from exploding. At night, the helium contracts and the altitude drops. Propane burners are used to heat up the helium and thus stabilize the altitude. A smaller helium balloon is used to create a tent over the main cell, which insulates the peak and diminishes the effect of solar radiation.

For the journey, calculated to take 21 days, 28 titanium canisters of propane gas were strapped to the outside of the pilot capsule. The capsule itself was made of Kevlar and carbon fiber, and measured 17.5 ft. (5.4 m) long, 7 ft. (2.25 m) wide and 9 ft. (2.85 m) high. Flying at high altitudes, the cabin had to be pressurized at a level equivalent to commercial aircraft. Air inside the capsule was filtered to remove CO_2 and regularly topped up with extra oxygen. Power was supplied by five lead batteries, recharged by solar panels. To keep the weight of the capsule down, space was allowed for only a tiny kitchen, a toilet, and a bunk for one crew member to rest at a time.

Nonstop round-the-world flights would be impossible without the existence of natural atmospheric phenomena called jet streams. These are high altitude currents that blow from east to west at heights of 23,000 to 39,000 ft. (7,000 –12,000 m). They resemble a flattened tube several hundred miles wide and about a mile high and are created by differences in air temperature. At the center of the jet stream, wind speeds can reach 190 mph (300 km/h), shortening flight times considerably.

FACT FILE

- Breitling-Orbiter 3 *stands as high as the Tower of Pisa (180 ft. or 55 m) when inflated, and its envelope can hold a volume equivalent of seven Olympic swimming pools. At 18,000 lbs. (8,100 kg) it weighs as much as a fighter plane.*

- *The balloon took off on March 1, 1999, from Chateau d'Oex in Switzerland and landed 19 days, 21 hours, and 47 minutes later in Egypt, having passed over 26 countries.*

- *At its fastest, the balloon traveled at 150 mph (240 km/h). It reached a maximum height of nearly 38,000 ft. (11,750 m).*

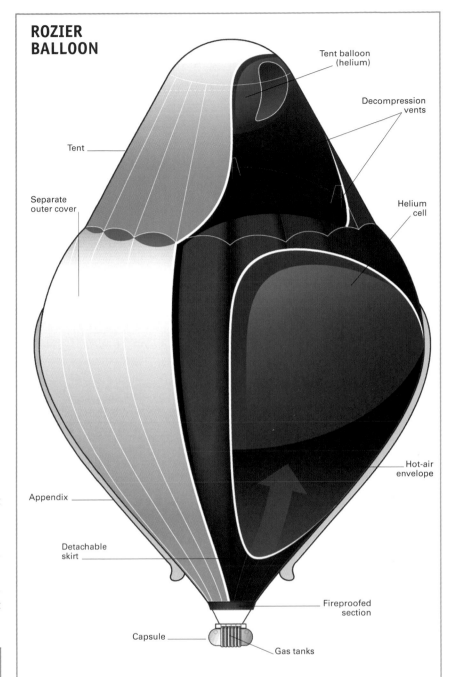

ROZIER BALLOON

Tent balloon (helium)

Decompression vents

Tent

Helium cell

Separate outer cover

Hot-air envelope

Appendix

Detachable skirt

Fireproofed section

Capsule

Gas tanks

A Rozier balloon like *Breitling-Orbiter 3* works by combining the characteristics of hot-air and gas balloons. For the round-the-world attempt, the main helium cell was filled to only 47 percent of its capacity. As the balloon ascends, the drop in atmospheric pressure and the warmth of the Sun makes the gas expand, and the balloon gains altitude. If the expansion is too strong, some helium has to be vented to prevent the balloon from exploding. By the end of a long trip, the amount of gas left is very small.

Safety features on the balloon enable the capsule to separate from the envelope in the case of a sea landing, and stay afloat. The envelope skirt can also be detached, turning the balloon into a giant parachute.

 SEE ALSO: AIRSHIP • GAS LAWS • METEOROLOGY • POLYAMIDE • PRESSURE

Barometer

Barometers are instruments for measuring atmospheric pressure. The atmosphere exerts a pressure because air has weight and is being pulled to Earth by the force of gravity. For this reason, atmospheric pressure depends on the height of air above the point at which it is being measured and is lower on top of a mountain than it is at sea level.

Pressure is the ratio of the force acting on a certain area to the area itself and is commonly expressed in such units as pounds force per square inch (psi), pascals (Pa) equal to newtons per square meter (N/m²), and bars (sometimes millibars, or mb). Another common unit of pressure is the atmosphere, which is defined as the aver- age atmospheric pressure at 32°F (0°C), sea level, and 45 degrees latitude. One atmosphere is approximately 14.7 psi, 101,325 N/m², or 1.01325 bar.

The pressure at the bottom of a container of liquid can be determined in the above units from the height (h) of the liquid column, the density (d) of the liquid, and the acceleration (g) due to gravity, all expressed in compatible units. The pressure is h x d x g. The width of the container does not affect the pressure. For an open container, the pressure calculated this way is the gauge pressure, or pressure above that of the atmosphere acting on the bottom. To find the absolute pressure, one must add one atmosphere to that result.

In atmospheric pressure measurement, a column of a standard liquid (one with known density) in a vertical tube is used, and as gravity is approximately constant at all points on the Earth's surface, it is only necessary to record the column height. The tube is sealed at the top so the only pressure on the top of the column is that of the liquid's vapor—generally much less than one atmosphere. Mercury is the most common liquid used because it is extremely dense and so only needs a short column. One atmosphere is the pressure at the bottom of a column of mercury only 30 in. (760 mm) high. Consequently, one atmosphere pressure is often referred to as 30 in. of Hg (or 760 mm Hg—Hg is the chemical symbol for mercury). Using water, whose density is about ⅓ that of mercury, one atmosphere is about 33 ft. (10 m) of water.

Gases are not used because their densities are very much lower than those of liquids, and the column would have to be extremely tall. For example, normal atmospheric pressure would be the result of approximately 5 miles (8 km) of air, if its density were constant. There is, however, a further complication in that gases are compressible while liquids are not, which means that the density increases with pressure.

Mercury barometers

The fact that the atmosphere has weight and exerts pressure was first demonstrated by the Italian scientist Galileo Galilei in the early 17th century. It was his pupil Evangelista Torricelli, however, who worked out the actual design of the barometer. The mm Hg unit of pressure is sometimes called the Torr in his honor.

In principle, the weight of a column of mercury is balanced against the weight of the air. To do this, a glass tube more than 30 in. (760 mm) long, sealed at one end, is completely filled with

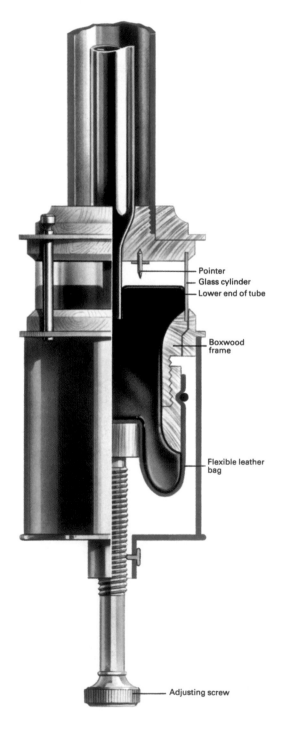

◀ The Fortin barometer, designed by Jean Fortin and first brought into use in the early 19th century. To obtain a reading the adjusting screw is turned, compressing the flexible leather bag until the mercury level in the cistern reaches the tip of the ivory pointer. The difference between the two mercury levels can then be read from the fixed scale and movable Vernier—which increases the accuracy of the reading—by the column.

Pointer
Glass cylinder
Lower end of tube

Boxwood frame

Flexible leather bag

Adjusting screw

mercury. This is then placed upright with its sealed end uppermost and its open end dipped into an open bowl of mercury. The pressure on the open surface of the mercury is the atmospheric pressure, and this must balance the pressure created by the column of mercury. The mercury level in the tube therefore falls until the weight of the column exactly balances the atmospheric pressure; by falling, it creates a vacuum at the top of the glass tube. The fact that the bottom of the tube is submerged prevents air from entering the tube, allowing the mercury to run out.

As the atmospheric pressure changes, so will the height of the mercury column, and by measuring its height above the surface of the open bowl, the atmospheric pressure can be found.

All modern mercury barometers are based on Torricelli's basic design and only differ by a few modifications that enable more accurate and consistent readings to be made. Two important types of mercury barometer are the Fortin and the Kew.

Fortin barometer

In the simple barometer mentioned above, any change in the column height will mean a slight change in the mercury level in the bowl. Yet, as it is from this level that the column height is measured, this would mean using a moving scale to find the height of the top of the column. The Fortin barometer overcomes this problem by employing an adjustable container (called a cistern) so that the open mercury level can be raised or lowered to a fixed point. This point is where the mercury level just touches a fixed ivory pointer. The column height is then measured with a fixed vertical scale. For even more accurate readings, an adjustable Vernier scale is added, which allows readings to be measured to within 0.002 in. (0.05 mm) of mercury.

Kew barometers

The Kew barometer has a fixed cistern, and allowance is made for changes in the open mercury level by altering the spacing of the column scale. If both the column and the cistern are per-

▼ The operating principle of the mercury barometer. Left: Both ends of the tube are open and the atmospheric pressure is equal on both sides. Center: One tube is sealed and evacuated. The pressure now affects one side only. Right: The open end of the tube is replaced by a shallow dish and the closed end by a single inverted glass tube.

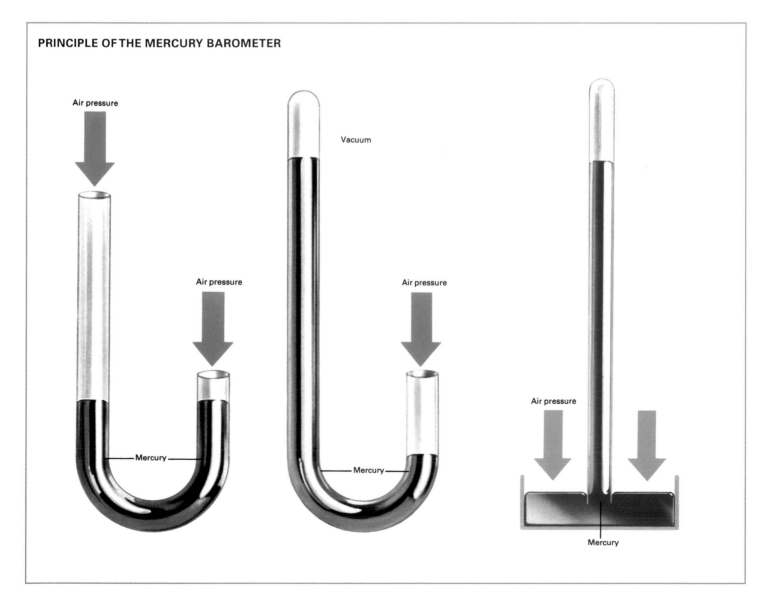

PRINCIPLE OF THE MERCURY BAROMETER

Air pressure

Air pressure

Vacuum

Air pressure

Mercury

Mercury

Air pressure

Mercury

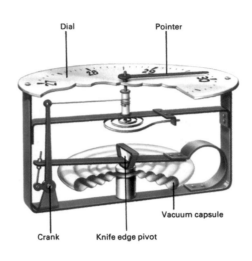

Dial   Pointer

Vacuum capsule

Crank   Knife edge pivot

◄ Far left: An 8-in. (20 cm) Vidie-type aneroid barometer made in Hamburg, Germany, around 1876.
Left: The aneroid barometer consists of two corrugated metal diaphragms enclosing a vacuum. Any change in air pressure on the outside of this chamber is transmitted mechanically to the pointer on the scale.

fectly cylindrical then the change in the column scale compared to the true inch or millimeter will always be in a fixed ratio. This ratio is made very close to equality by making the column very narrow compared with the diameter of the cistern.

Kew barometers are often used in ships, where motion can affect the accuracy of the readings by causing oscillations in the mercury column. This is overcome by introducing a restriction in the column that dampens such oscillations without unduly affecting the sensitivity of the device.

A further modification is an air trap to prevent any air from entering the column from the cistern and reaching the vacuum at the top of the tube, which might happen if the barometer were tilted or shaken. Kew barometers are designed to be portable, usually being carried upside down with the mercury completely filling the glass tube.

Aneroid barometer

In 1843, another Italian scientist, Lucius Vidie, invented the aneroid barometer. The term *aneroid* means "without liquid," and although not offering quite the same degree of sensitivity as the mercury barometer, it has the advantage of being a robust instrument, useful in such applications as altimeters and generally where mobility is required (an aneroid altimeter is exactly the same instrument as a barometer, and is used to measure changes in altitude by comparing air pressures).

The aneroid barometer has a sealed metal chamber, sometimes called the bellows, that expands and contracts with changes in atmospheric pressure. This expansion and contraction can be suitably amplified with a rack-and-pinion arrangement or levers to move a pointer on a suitably graduated scale.

The chamber is usually made of thin-sheet nickel-silver alloy or hardened and tempered steel. High-grade aneroid barometers have a series of steel diaphragms formed into a complete unit and corrugated to provide greater flexibility.

Temperature compensation is necessary with precision aneroid barometers, since the diaphragms expand and contract with temperature changes, and their elasticity alters. Any air within the chamber also leads to unwanted temperature effects from expansion and contraction, and so a high vacuum is generally created in the chamber.

The modern aneroid barometer is a precision instrument, which, when compensation is introduced for temperature and other errors, can easily give pressure readings to within 0.02 in. Hg (0.5 mm Hg) and can be estimated to within 0.001 in. Hg (0.025 mm Hg). When used as an altimeter, this means height readings estimated to within 1 ft. (30 cm) at sea level and 1.5 ft. (45 cm) at 11,000 ft. (3,350 m), where the air is thinner. Altimeters must be adjusted before use to take account of the prevailing air pressure in the area.

Aneroid barograph

A refinement of the aneroid barometer is the aneroid barograph, a self-recording barometer for meteorological and aeronautical applications where a continuous record of pressure variations is required. Instead of a pointer, a pen is attached that traces a graph on chart paper wrapped around a slowly revolving drum.

Because of the friction between the pen and the paper, accuracy is not quite as good as in the aneroid barometer. For better sensitivity, a refined version known as a microbarograph is used. In this device the graph is to a much larger scale, and it is possible to obtain readings to within 0.02 in. Hg (0.5 mm Hg).

SEE ALSO: GRAVITY • METEOROLOGY • PRESSURE • VACUUM • VERNIER SCALE

Battery

An electric battery consists of one or more electrochemical cells that produce power by means of a chemical reaction. A battery can be either primary or secondary: the primary type is normally regarded as unrechargeable whereas a secondary-cell, or storage, battery can be recharged.

There are some indications that batteries may have been used in the third century B.C.E. by the Parthians, a tribe in what is now Iran, for electroplating jewelery. The work that led to modern batteries, however, began with a discovery in the early 19th century. An Italian, Alessandro Volta, found that he could cause an electric current to pass through a wire by immersing two different metals in a salt solution.

All batteries, be they primary or secondary types, produce electricity through chemical reactions in which electrons are deposited on one metal or carbon electrode, the negative terminal, while they are removed from a second, the positive terminal. When the battery is connected to a circuit, the electrons from the negative terminal move to the positive through the circuit, while the chemical reactions restore the original charges.

The outer layer of an atom is composed of electrons, tiny particles each carrying a negative electrical charge. These particles are not all permanently attached to their atoms. In all but a few elements (the rare gases), there are loosely bound electrons that can be exchanged between atoms during chemical reactions.

When an atom gains an electron, it gains an extra negative charge and so becomes negatively charged as a whole. When it loses one, on the other hand, it becomes positively charged. Atoms or groups of atoms in this charged state are known as ions. Positive and negative ions are attracted to each other and, when circumstances allow, will move together and combine to form compounds. Ions with similar charges repel each other.

The chemical reactions that provide electricity in cells involve either atoms leaving one of the metal electrodes to become positive ions and leaving their electrons behind, or ions or atoms accepting electrons from an electrode, or atoms and ions giving up electrons to an electrode. At least two such processes must occur in the cell: one is adding electrons to one electrode and the other is taking electrons away from the other electrode. A solution called an electrolyte is used to provide ions and atoms for such reactions to take place. Electrolytic solutions can be acids

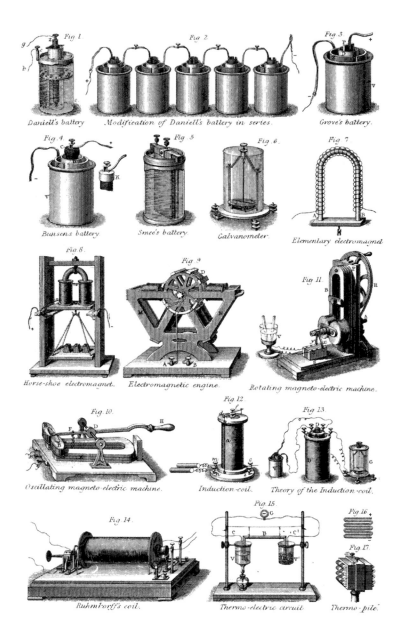

such as sulfuric acid; alkalis, such as caustic soda; or salts formed by the interaction of an acid and a base.

Electricity is generated in cells because when any of these chemical substances is dissolved in water, its molecules break up and become electrically charged ions. A good example is sulfuric acid, H_2SO_4, the molecules of which consist of two atoms of hydrogen, one of sulfur, and four of oxygen. When dissolved in water, the molecules split into three parts; the two atoms of hydrogen separate, and in the process, each loses an electron, becoming a positively charged hydrogen ion (represented by the sign H^+). The sulfur atom and the four atoms of oxygen remain together as a sulfate group (SO_4) and acquire the two electrons lost by the hydrogen atoms, thus becoming negatively charged (written SO_4^{2-}). These groups can combine with others of opposite charge to form other compounds.

▲ Early batteries appeared in a wide variety of different shapes and sizes.

If one plate, or electrode, of zinc and one of either copper or carbon is dipped into a sulfuric acid electrolyte and each is externally connected to a load such as a light bulb, a current will flow through the bulb, lighting it. This is because one of the chemical elements chosen for the electrodes is electrically positive (that is, has a tendency to lose electrons and acquire a positive charge) with respect to the other, and when they are electrically connected, the chemical equilibrium of the cell is upset and reactions start at both plates. Under these circumstances, the atoms of zinc each give up two electrons, which flow through the external circuit and form the current. The positively charged zinc atoms left behind dissolve into the electrolyte, and each one combines with one of the negatively charged sulfate ions. The result is a neutral zinc sulfate molecule. The two electrons originally given up by each zinc atom travel around the external circuit and reach the other plate. There they combine with and neutralize the positive charges on two hydrogen atoms from the electrolyte. These two neutral hydrogen atoms then combine to form a molecule of hydrogen gas, and gas bubbles are produced at that plate or electrode.

In theory, the chemical reaction would go on, and electric current would continue to flow until all the zinc on the zinc plate (known as the nega-

tive electrode, or cathode) has been used up. But in the simple cell, a film of hydrogen bubbles begins to form on the copper or carbon plate (known as the positive electrode, or anode), and as hydrogen has a much higher electrical resistance than the electrolyte proper, the internal resistance of the cell increases, reducing the current that can flow in the external circuit.

If the external circuit is disconnected, the hydrogen bubbles will gradually disappear and the cell can be used again, but the same thing will reoccur. In all modern batteries, this effect, which is known as polarization, is greatly reduced by surrounding the positive electrode with a material known as the depolarizer. This works either by reacting with the hydrogen to form water or by taking over from the hydrogen the task of accepting the electrons as they arrive from the external circuit.

The Leclanché cell

The "dry" batteries used in flashlights and so on, which have a depolarizer, are of a type known as Leclanché with modifications to make the liquid electrolyte a semisolid. In its original form, the Leclanché cell was entirely "wet" with an electrolyte consisting of a strong solution of ammonium chloride. A zinc plate was used for the negative electrode, and a carbon rod packed into a porous pot containing crushed carbon and manganese dioxide (to accept the electrons) formed the positive electrode and its depolarizer. Similar materials are used in a modern dry Leclanché cell. The electrolyte is not, in fact, dry but is made up in the form of a moist paste or jelly.

Additives include mercuric chloride, introduced to inhibit what is known as local action, the name given to the chemical reactions that take place between zinc atoms and carbon and iron atoms, which occur as impurities in the zinc plate. It can be overcome by a process known as amalgamation in which the mercury forms an amalgam, or alloy, with the zinc, preventing it from reacting with its impurities. Other additives include potassium dichromate, which inhibits the corrosion of the zinc—an effect that would otherwise reduce the shelf life of the battery, that is, the length of time a battery can be stored without deterioration.

In the cylindrical Leclanché cell used in flashlights, the zinc forms the outer casing and is also the negative electrode. The positive electrode consists of a mixture of graphite (carbon) and manganese dioxide depolarizer around a graphite rod.

Dry cells are supplied singly or in groups of two, three, or more connected in series to give

◀ When a battery is recharged, a gas is produced by the chemical reaction. Here a silver–zinc unit emits hydrogen bubbles.

higher voltages. In a series connection, the positive electrode of one cell is connected to the negative electrode of the next. High-voltage batteries, in which sixty or more individual cells are connected in series, are available but are very heavy and cumbersome. A lighter and more compact construction, where large numbers of cells are to be connected in series, is the flat, or layer, type. Batteries of this type consist of alternate thin, flat layers of zinc electrolyte and the materials making up the positive electrode and its respective depolarizer.

Other primary batteries

Alkaline batteries are similar to carbon-zinc batteries in that they both use the same materials for the anode and cathode. However, the zinc anode is more porous and oxidizes more readily. Potassium hydroxide, a strong alkali, is used as the electrolyte because it conducts electricity within the cell better than ammonium chloride. As a result, this type of cell can produce a sustained higher current more efficiently than carbon-zinc batteries and is more economical, lasting between five and eight times as long.

A disadvantage of dry cells is that the current quickly falls, principally because hydrogen forms more quickly than it can be removed by the depolarizer. For this reason, they are best suited to intermittent work. A more constant voltage and current is provided by the mercury cell widely used in hearing aids, where almost continuous operation is necessary. In this type of cell, the full name of which is zinc-mercuric oxide, the electrolyte consists of potassium hydroxide. The negative electrode is zinc, as in the Leclanché cell, but the positive electrode and its depolarizer consist of graphite and mercuric oxide. When in use, the zinc changes to zinc oxide and the mercuric oxide becomes mercury, but the potassium hydroxide remains unchanged.

Secondary batteries

A lead-acid battery, as used in a car, does not in practice consist simply of two plates dipped in acid. Lead dioxide is too brittle, and while pure lead is rigid, the lead that is deposited on the negative plate by the charging process builds up as a sort of metal sponge, that is very fragile. Consequently, both plates need some sort of support.

This is usually accomplished by making the plates in the form of grids of an alloy of lead and antimony (which is tougher than pure lead) with the spongy lead or lead dioxide pressed into the grid. There are several grids in each cell of the battery arranged so that positive and negative

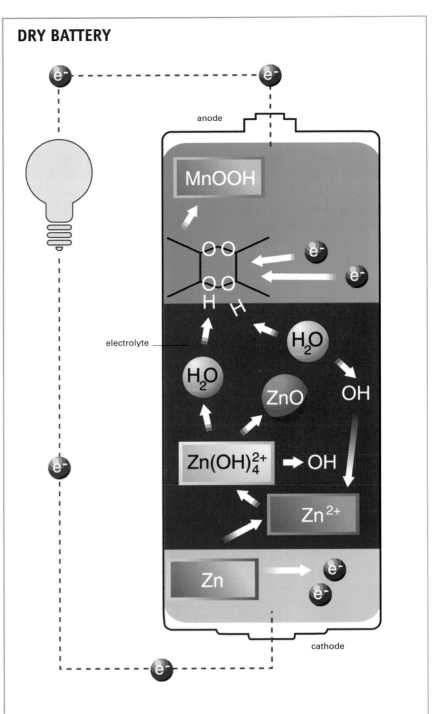

DRY BATTERY

In a typical flashlight battery, the power is provided by electrons released from the zinc anode in a process called oxidation. Each atom of zinc gives up two electrons to leave Zn^{2+} ions behind.

After making the bulb light up, the electrons reenter the battery at the cathode. Here they combine with molecules of manganese dioxide (MnO_2) contained in the electrolytic paste in a reduction reaction, which leaves the manganese dioxide negatively charged ($MnOO^-$). These ions react with water in the electrolyte solution, splitting it into hydrogen ions (H^+) and hydroxide ions (OH^-). The hydrogen ions combine with the $MnOO^-$ to form $MnOOH$, while the hydroxide ions are drawn toward the anode.

When they reach the anode, the hydroxide ions combine with the Zn^{2+} atoms to form a zinc hydroxide compound ($Zn(OH)_4^{2-}$), which splits into zinc oxide (ZnO) and water (H_2O). This completes the circuit, and the reaction is ready to start again and send more electricity to the bulb.

alternate and are spaced a short distance apart by separators to make the construction more rigid.

A single cell, that is, one set of plates immersed in a single container of acid, produces electricity at the comparatively low voltage of 2 V. The electrical system of most modern automobiles runs on 12 V, provided by linking six cells together in series so as to take advantage of their combined voltage. The six cells are completely separate except for linking bars across the top that carry the current from one to another.

A lead–acid battery must not be allowed to remain discharged for a long time because the lead sulfate, which is deposited in microcrystalline form (i.e. small crystals), tends to harden into a solid block. Once it has done this, it will not take part in any chemical reaction and the plate becomes partly or wholly dead, depending on how much of it is affected. This change is known as sulfating. The state of charge of a battery can easily be discovered by measuring the density of the acid. As the battery discharges, the acid turns to water and the battery becomes lighter. Its density is measured with a hydrometer. When the battery is recharged, it becomes warm. Some of the water evaporates, so storage batteries must be topped off occasionally with pure distilled water.

To avoid the inconvenience of topping off, researchers have developed the "maintenance-free" battery. This battery lasts longer because its plates are made of a lead–calcium–tin alloy, which does not discharge when the battery is not in use. It is completely sealed except for a small vent that allows gases produced by the chemical reaction to escape.

Other types of batteries

The lead–acid battery is a simple and durable device, but it is rather heavy. Other, lighter types of batteries have been invented. The most important of these are the NiFe (pronounced knife) cell, invented by Thomas Edison, and the nickel–cadmium cell. The NiFe cell is light and robust, but each cell of a battery only produces 1.2

▼ A battery-powered delivery vehicle and a battery pack (inset) being serviced. The greatest breakthrough in electronic vehicle technology will come in the form of new, lighter batteries with greatly increased power output.

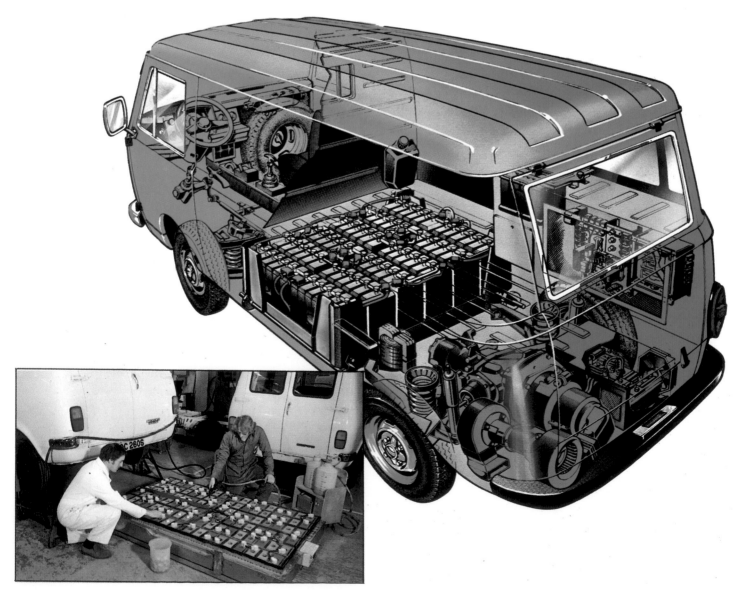

V instead of the 2 V of a lead–acid cell. As a result, more cells are needed to produce a given voltage. This, and greater manufacturing cost, make the NiFe system considerably more expensive. It is used in portable radio transmitters because its light weight makes them easier to carry.

Nickel–cadmium cells are becoming lighter and more powerful, as well as cheaper, and are being developed for use in high-performance electric vehicles. A key advantage with this type of cell is that it can be sealed airtight to prevent its potassium hydroxide electrolyte from leaking out.

Another possibility for use in electric vehicles is the sodium-sulfur battery, which can, in theory, achieve an energy density of 2.5 MJ per kg. The sodium–sulfur battery is unusual because it is made from β-alumina, which is a form of aluminum oxide that allows sodium ions to pass freely through at a high temperature, usually around 570°F (300°C). At this temperature, the sodium and sulfur are both liquid and are held apart by a solid alumina tube, which constitutes the electrolyte. The cells are packed into a thermally insulated stainless steel canister, that controls the heat loss. At the present state of development, it is possible to get an energy density for such batteries better than 0.5 MJ per kg.

At the other extreme are the tiny "button" batteries needed for small portable devices such as watches, cameras, and pacemakers. These use lithium as the anode with a variety of oxidizing substances as the cathode and often a thin plastic film as the electrolyte. Button batteries can produce higher voltages than other cells but are expensive because of the difficulties of working with lithium.

◄ Research into power sources for use in space might lead to more powerful batteries.

▼ Lead-acid batteries, linked in series, have been used to provide power for this truck.

FACT FILE

■ *Acting as a low-voltage battery producing direct current, a photovoltaic (PV) cell produces electricity from light, or solar, radiation. Already functioning in satellites, in private homes, and even in experimental aircraft, PV cells produce electricity when the light reacts with certain semiconductor materials such as silicon, cadmium sulfide, and gallium arsenide.*

■ *New plastic materials called electrically conducting polymers, or synmetals, could be used to make batteries that deliver twice the power of conventional lead–acid automobile batteries while weighing considerably less. Lightweight plastic batteries could be repeatedly charged and discharged without degradation and molded into any convenient shape.*

SEE ALSO: Chemical bonding and valency • Electricity • Fuel cell • Low-emission road vehicle

Bearing and Bushing

A force is always required to slide one object over another in order to overcome the resistance or friction between the two surfaces. Friction is usually a hindrance in machines, absorbing power, producing heat, reducing efficiency, and promoting wear, which limits the life of the machine.

A bearing is a device that will reduce this friction while supporting a load. The moving member can be either rotating, such as the wheel of a bicycle, or it can be a flat surface such as a tool holder sliding along a lathe bed. A bushing is a hollow cylinder or sleeve used as a removable lining for axles and pivots and is generally made of plastic or an antifriction metal.

Bearings can be classified into three groups: the first being rolling-element bearings; the second, fluid-film bearings; and the third, rubbing bearings.

Rolling-element bearings

The ancient Egyptians used a type of rolling bearing when they moved the huge stones needed for the pyramids by rolling them along on logs. They realized that such a system meant less work. Modern rolling-element bearings are precision mechanisms but work on the same principle, using either balls or cylindrical rollers between two surfaces. As with the use of logs in earlier times, the force required to roll one part over the other is very small compared with the force that would otherwise be required to slide one part over the other.

Rolling-element bearings are used today in automobile wheel hubs and transmissions, electric motors, washing machines, ventilation fans, textile machinery, and all types of industrial machines. Such bearings are comparatively friction-free (rolling friction between metals being about one-hundredth that of the sliding friction). Any energy losses that occur are because of the compression of the metals and the motion of the lubricant.

The most common type of rolling bearing for rotating mechanisms consists of four basic parts: the inner ring, or race; the rolling elements (either balls or rollers) of which there are several; a cage to retain and separate the balls or rollers; and an outer race. The inner and outer races and the rolling elements are made in a hard alloy steel to give a long life and to prevent permanent indentation of the races at the contact points when under load. The cage is made of soft steel, brass, or plastic resin.

Types of rolling bearings

Ball bearings are normally used to carry radial loads, that is, loads perpendicular, or at right angles, to the axis of the shaft. Other types are

▲ The outer face of a roller bearing during manufacture. After forming the upper edge, the barrel-shaped cylinder forms the central groove.

available that will accommodate axial or end-thrust loads, while some will carry combined radial and thrust loads. Depending upon the type of bearing, the rolling elements can be cylindrical (log-shaped), convex (barrel-shaped), or tapered. Taper roller bearings are often used in automobile wheel hubs, where the weight of the vehicle has to be supported and the sideways cornering forces resisted.

Fatigue life

When rolling bearings are subjected to load and rotation, the balls, or rollers, and the races undergo repeated application of stress at the contact areas, which may ultimately show signs of fatigue failure. Metal fatigue in rolling bearings gives rise to surface pits, or craters, which cause noisy operation and necessitate replacement. The length of time a bearing will operate until surface pitting begins is known as the fatigue life. The principal external factors that affect the fatigue life are the load, which for a given size and type of bearing, determines the contact stress, and the rotational speed, which determines how frequently the contact stress is applied.

Because of variations in materials and conditions, the fatigue-life prediction is usually based on a rotational life—usually one million revolutions—reached or exceeded by 90 percent of identical bearings operating under the same load and speed test conditions.

Lubrication

Rolling bearings must be lubricated for long life and quiet operation. The majority, including many automobile and household equipment bearings, are partly filled with grease, which in some cases lasts the life of the machine. In most industrial applications where heat is developed in the bearings, circulating oil is used as the lubricant and as a means of removing the heat. In communication satellites, which are required to remain in space for seven to ten years, lubrication of the ball bearings in gyroscope and solar paddle mech-

anisms is critical because grease tends to evaporate and dry up in the vacuum of space. In this and other difficult situations—for example, in high-temperature applications—greases made from synthetic materials are used.

Fluid-film bearings

In fluid-film bearings, the frictional forces are reduced by putting a film of fluid instead of balls or rollers between the two surfaces. The fluid is usually oil, such as in automobile engine bearings, but it can be water (pump bearings) or even air or gas, depending on the application.

The two main types of fluid-film bearing are the hydrodynamic, in which the fluid-film pressure is generated by rotation, and the hydrostatic, in which the fluid is supplied under pressure from an external source, such as a compressor.

The majority of fluid film bearings are hydrodynamic. Here fluid film pressure required to separate the loaded surfaces is generated by the movement or rotation of one part relative to the other. Automobile engine crankshaft bearings operate on this principle, and although there is an oil pump, its only purpose is to supply oil to the bearing, and the pressure is not sufficient to support the load. When the engine is stopped, the oil film is squeezed out and the metals touch. Water skiing uses a similar hydrodynamic principle (aquaplaning), where the movement of the skis relative to the water produces a pressure sufficient to support the weight of the skier. If the speed is too slow, then the skier will sink. Hydrodynamic bearings are used, therefore, in applications where the speed of rotation is high enough to produce a supporting fluid film, such as in automotive engines, steam turbines, alternators for producing electricity, steel rolling mills (though some modern mills use rolling element bearings), and paper-making machinery.

Because there is no film separation when the machine is being started and stopped, bearings of this type have to be made in materials that will permit some rubbing contact with the shaft

▼ Shell bearings in halves, used to separate the crankpin from the crankshaft of automobile engines. At rest (center), the crankpin rests on the bearing (the clearance is exaggerated for clarity) but glides on a film of oil when the engine turns at its normal operating speed (right).

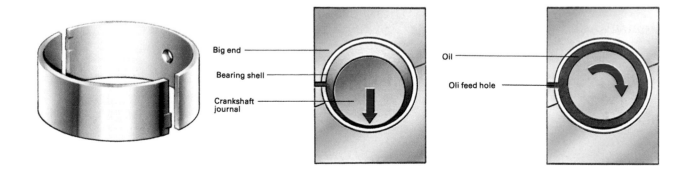

Big end

Bearing shell

Crankshaft journal

Oil

Oli feed hole

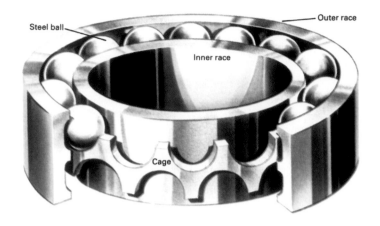

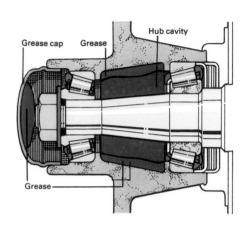

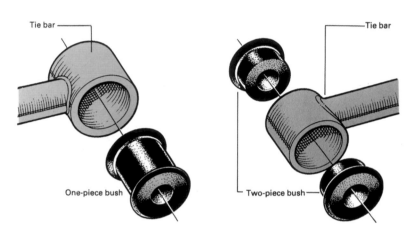

the principle of operation is aerodynamic and not hydrodynamic. Self-acting air bearings have been developed for textile-spinning machinery where the spinning spindles rotate at very high speeds, say 50,000 revolutions per minute, and where oil lubrication is undesirable because of possible staining of the yarn. Other problems associated with spinning machinery—noise, friction, and wear—are all minimized by using air bearings. Air bearings of this type are suitable only for high speeds and light loads and in small sizes, up to 1 in. (25 mm) diameter.

Hydrostatic bearings

Hydrostatic bearings are not widely used as they require a pumped supply of fluid under pressure to separate the two surfaces. The pressure must be high enough to support the load. The bearing itself is not very different from a hydrodynamic bearing except for the addition of pockets, or recesses, in the bearing surface into which the fluid is pumped, and as there is never any metallic contact, steel or similar materials can be used throughout. The system, however, is expensive to make, principally because of the need for a high-pressure pump and motor with a complicated control system.

Hydrostatic bearings are used where heavy loads have to be supported at very slow speeds, or even when stationary, and where under these conditions friction must be kept to a minimum. Some precision machine tools use this type of bearing in the form of flat pads to support the heavy table on which the work piece is carried. A good example of the application of hydrostatic bearings is in large telescopes, such as the famous Hale telescope at Mount Palomar in California. The moving parts weigh 500 tons (450 tonnes) and are supported on three hydrostatic bearing pads. The whole apparatus is driven by a $\frac{1}{12}$ horsepower motor and, in fact, could be moved by hand.

(which is usually of steel) without causing damage. Generally, soft bearing materials are preferred, provided their strength is adequate. Soft materials allow dirt to be embedded that would otherwise score the surfaces. Moreover soft metals generate very little heat when rubbing occurs and do not weld or seize when in contact with a steel shaft. The softest metal bearings for light loads are made from white metals (also known as Babbitt metal). These are alloys, mainly of lead and tin. Next in hardness are the copper–lead alloys, and harder still are the bronzes, which are basically alloys of copper, tin, and lead. Phosphor bronze is the hardest alloy and is used for very highly loaded bearings like diesel-engine-piston pin bushings. Other metals, such as antimony, nickel, and aluminum, are also used in some of these bearing alloys.

There are many applications of slow-speed bearings such as chemical drum driers, plate shears, dock gates, large blanking presses, and so on, where full film generation is not obtained. In such cases, the bearing materials given above are normally used, and the system is lubricated with grease.

In some bearing applications where air is used as the separating medium rather than oil or water,

▲ Above left: A sectioned heavy-duty ball journal bearing, designed to support loads perpendicular to the shaft. This type of bearing is not suitable to support an automobile hub, for example, which needs a tapered roller bearing on each side (above right) to withstand the sideways forces due to turning corners, as well as the weight of the car. Where the motion is not circular, bushings in single or two-piece units (left) can be used to absorb shock.

Bearings of this type but using air as the pressurized support film are properly called aerostatic bearings. Air-cushion vehicles work on this principle: air is blown into the underside of the hull at sufficient pressure to support the weight and to lift the hull. One of the first aerostatic bearings was developed for dental drills, which rotate at about 500,000 revolutions per minute and are driven by a small air turbine that also supplies air to the bearings. Another example where air (or rather gas) bearings have been used is in some gas-cooled nuclear reactors, where, because of radioactivity and the need to prevent contamination of the circuit with lubricating oil, the gas circulators have been completely sealed and their bearings continuously pressurized with circuit gas. In this case, carbon dioxide is used.

Rubbing bearings

In recent years a great variety of plastic materials has been developed that have proved to be very useful in many bearing applications. The materials include phenolic, epoxy, and cresylic resins, which are usually reinforced with cloth, nylon, acetal, and polytetrafluoroethylene (PTFE). PTFE is also used as a coating on nonstick pans.

These materials have the advantage over metal bearings of being able to operate dry—that is, unlubricated. This is a valuable property in some applications, for example, in the food and pharmaceutical chemicals industries where contamination of the product has to be avoided. Other advantages are their cheapness and ease of machining or, in some cases, molding into the required shape.

The life of plastic bearings in dry conditions is limited by wear. Because of this, they are generally suitable only for slow speeds with intermittent operation or light loads. Lubrication of these bearings greatly increases their wear life, and there are today many applications where the performance of lubricated plastic bearings—usually bushings or sleeve bearings—is better than that of

▶ A ball bearing and cage undergoing a seizure test at high temperatures.

lubricated metal bearings. Examples are the steering linkage bearings in automobiles, which are grease lubricated; dock gate bearings, also grease lubricated; central heating pumps and many other water pump bearings, which are water lubricated; and sliding door wheels and furniture casters, which normally operate dry.

Some rubbing bearings are self-lubricating, usually made from sintered metal powders based, mainly, on aluminum, copper, brass, gun-metal, or bronze. They are a result of the technology of powder metallurgy, in which very fine powders of metal are precision compressed to the required shape and dimensions. Their porosity depends upon their degree of compactness.

In essence, they can be thought of as metal sponges, having holes ranging from 1 to 30 thousandths of a millimeter, that can retain an amount of oil up to 30 percent of their volume. Typical applications are as clutch-release bearings and main bearings for automobiles and other light-duty applications. Their main advantage is that they do not depend upon an external oil supply, are cheap to make, and can be installed with relatively little difficulty.

Jewel bearings

Jewel bearings are typically used in mechanical clocks and watches. Such bearings are usually made of natural or synthetic rubies or sapphires. Their hardness of surface and the high polish that can be obtained result in a wearing surface that has a long life and causes little friction. Mainly used as pivot bearings, they can also be applied to the pallets, escape wheel, and impulse pin. In precision clocks, all the holes may be jeweled, and jewels may be set into the acting faces of the pallets.

◀ Ball bearings are examined to make sure they are free from cracks and blemishes.

SEE ALSO: ALLOY • FRICTION • HYDRODYNAMICS • LUBRICATION • POLYTETRAFLUOROETHYLENE (TEFLON)

Beer and Brewing

Beer has been made in various forms for at least six thousand years; it is known to have been made by the Babylonians and ancient Egyptians. In early times, brewing was a cottage craft carried out at the same time as baking, since the initial processes of brewing were then very similar to those of bread-making. Primitive types of beer were produced by steeping partly cooked bread crumbs in water and allowing them to ferment. The bread was made from a mixture of crushed barley, which had begun to germinate (sprout), and yeast.

By the 14th century C.E., brewing had developed into a separate trade with its own specialized skills. To a considerable extent, this was stimulated, over a period of three centuries or so, by the brewing activities of the monasteries. In medieval times, the monks were the main producers of beer, serving not only their own needs but also those of the local people. Brewing was also carried out at home, mostly by women.

As a trade, brewing then expanded steadily for some five hundred years, notably in Europe and, in the 18th century especially, in North America. By the middle of the 19th century, many thousands of breweries were in operation in the Western world. Since then, the production of beer has become a major industry and modern breweries are now large and complex. Over 200 million barrels of beer and lager were produced in the year 2000 by the United States alone.

Types of beer

Beers can be divided into two main groups: lagers, or bottom-fermented beers, and the top-fermented British-type beers. Some varieties of lager are known by the names of the places in which they were first brewed, such as Pilsener (from Pilsen in Czechoslovakia) or Dortmunder (from Dortmund in Germany). Most of them are pale in color, carbonated, and have a less pronounced hop flavor than British beers; both bottom and top fermentation are used to produce darker, more full-bodied beers. Most of the beer brewed throughout the world is of the lager type, generally with an alcohol content of between three and five percent by weight.

Although an increasing amount of lager is being brewed in Britain, the top-fermented ales (beers) and stouts (a type of dark brown beer) are still the most popular. Until the 17th century, the name *ale* referred to a drink brewed from malt, yeast, and water, whereas beer was made by the addition of hops during the brewing. Beer was

▲ Malt being dried prior to crushing.

▼ Concentrated hop granules (top left); the crushed malt and water in the mash tun (bottom left), where enzymes begin to degrade the mash into carbohydrate-rich wort; and the kettle (right) in which the wort is then boiled with the hops.

brought to England from Europe in the 15th century, and by the early 18th century, it had replaced ale as the main English brew. Although ale as such is no longer made, the name is still applied to any beer that is not a stout or a lager, for example, bitter ale, pale ale, brown ale. The alcohol content of ale is usually between 2.5 percent and 6.5 percent by weight. Stout, which is brewed with roasted malt and often a high percentage of hops, has a strong, rich flavor. It is very dark, often black in color, containing up to 5.5 percent of alcohol. Porter was a dark beer of the 18th and 19th centuries, full bodied but milder than stout.

The brewing process

The raw materials used in brewing have a major influence on the type and quality of the beer produced. In theory, beer can be made by fermenting any cereal or other source of starch, such as potatoes in water. In practice, barley is the most widely used cereal. Other cereals are used as additives to the main barley mash to reduce costs, and sometimes to produce a desired flavor. The main additives are rice, corn, tapioca, soyabean meal, unmalted barley, and various sugars.

The initial brewing operation is to make a sugary liquid mixture from barley, water, and hops, which is known as wort. Barley cannot be used, however, until it has been malted, a process not usually carried out at the brewery itself but at plants known as maltings. The malting of barley involves germinating it under controlled conditions to produce natural substances called enzymes, which act as catalysts in various chemical reactions vital to brewing. Commercially produced enzymes from different sources now make it possible to produce wort from unmalted barley, but the use of malted barley is still preferred by brewers.

To soften the barley and promote its germination, it is soaked in water at 55 to 60°F (13–16°C) for between 48 and 72 hours, depending on the type of grain used. After soaking, the barley is put into large drums or boxes, and moist air is blown through it for 7 to 11 days to encourage germination. It is then dried in a kiln until its moisture content is between 1.5 and 2 percent. The rootlets that have grown during germination drop off and are used as animal food. The barley is now known as malt and contains enzymes.

At the brewery, the malt is crushed and made into a mash with water and additives. Mashing sets the enzyme process in operation and brings out the carbohydrates, such as starch and sugar, from the malt. Insoluble material such as protein is made soluble by the action of enzymes, which also convert the malt starch into maltose sugar; the amount of maltose produced determines the alcohol content of the beer. The mashing operation must be very carefully controlled so that all the physical and chemical processes and enzyme reactions are coordinated to produce precisely the type and quality of wort, and therefore beer, that is required. The mashing process for lager beer is different from that for top-fermented beers.

Infusion mashing

Infusion mashing is used to produce top-fermented beers and is carried out in large insulated tanks called tuns, which are generally heated by steam. The consistency of the mash is important, so the tuns are often fitted with mechanical agitators such as rakes. Precise temperature control is vital, since a deviation of only a few degrees can produce a totally different type of wort from that required.

Once the warm mash has reached the point where starch conversion (to maltose sugar) is complete, the temperature is raised to about 167°F (75°C) for a short time. This operation, known as "mashing off," is carried out to deactivate the enzymes, most of which stop working at this temperature. The mash is then allowed to stand for 30 minutes to allow the insoluble grain husks to settle out. The husks form a layer on the false bottom inside the tun and act as a filter. The

▶ A brewery packing hall, where the beers are chilled and pasteurized.

▼ Refrigeration plays an essential part in preserving the flavor of beers that are not pasteurized. The beer is held in huge chillers until it is ready to be bottled.

liquid wort is run through until it becomes clear; the spent or used grains are then washed, or "sparged," with sprays of hot water to ensure that all the soluble matter passes through the false bottom of the mash tun into a receiving vessel.

Decoction mashing

The malted barley used in lagers is not germinated for as long as that used in top-fermented beers, and so it needs to be more finely mashed. The mashing is done in stages: a preliminary mash at 100°F (37°C), followed by subsequent mashes at 122°F (50°C), 149°F (65°C) and 168°F (75°C); or the quick mashing system used in the United States with two mashes at 149°F (65°C) and 172°F (78°C). The temperature is raised to the various temperature stages by removing part of the mash, heating it to boiling, and returning it to the main mash.

Boiling

After mashing, the wort and sparge water are transferred to a large copper or stainless steel vessel, known as a brewing kettle, and boiled vigorously with hops or hop extracts (which are sometimes added progressively) for at least two hours. This operation does several things: it sterilizes the wort and reduces its bulk by evaporation of the water; it draws out the full bitter flavor of the hops and helps precipitate any unwanted protein left in the wort; and it ensures that if any enzymes have survived the mashing-off operation, they are now made completely inactive, preventing spoilage of the beer in cask, bottle, or can by further reactions.

After boiling, the wort is discharged through a filter bed made from spent hops and then cooled, usually by heat exchangers, which can drop the temperature of the wort from boiling to around 55°F (12°C) in a matter of seconds. It can then be aerated to help fermentation later on.

Fermentation

When the wort is at the optimum temperature for starting fermentation, the yeast is added. Yeasts are microscopic organisms related to fungi, and there are thousands of different species. There are many strains of the brewer's yeast (*Saccharomyces cerevisiae*), but they can all be placed into one of two groups: they either rise to the surface or sink to the bottom during fermentation, thus giving top-fermented or bottom-fermented beers. The particular temperature chosen depends on the quality and strength of the beer and is also varied at different times of the year. Weaker beers require higher temperatures than stronger beers. The action of the yeast on the wort is extremely complex, producing alcohol and carbon dioxide as the principal products along with many other substances such as acids, esters, and glycerin, all of which affect the final flavor and aroma of the beer.

For bottom-fermented beers the yeast is added at a temperature of 43 to 50°F (6–10°C), and fermentation takes about eight days, after which the beer is put into storage tanks for up to three months (the name lager comes from the German word for storage). The lager is stored at 32°F (0°C), and a secondary fermentation occurs that clears the beer and improves the flavor.

Top-fermented beers begin fermentation at about 60°F (15°C), and during the process the

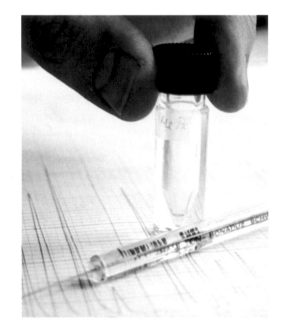

◄ Chemical analysis of beer flavor compounds has identified only 150 of the 400 recognizable constituent components.

▼ The control room of a computerized brewery.

temperature increases to 70°F (21°C). Fermentation takes 5 to 7 days, followed by a low-temperature maturation period, perhaps three weeks.

Whichever process is used, the yeast layers are separated off and may be used in subsequent brews. Fermentation produces more yeast than can be used in this way, and the surplus is used for animal feeds and yeast-extract manufacture. The beer may be given a very fine final filtration in order to polish it—that is, to give it more clarity and lightness before it is put into the barrels, bottles, or cans. Some ales are subjected to a secondary fermentation process in the barrels in which they are sold, but this is now comparatively rare, since most beer in bulk is now supplied under pressure in aluminum or stainless-steel kegs rather than in the traditional wood.

The brewing process yields several useful waste products. Animal feedstuffs are made from the dried rootlets and spent grains of the malted barley and from the yeast residues, which are also used in human foods, pharmaceuticals, and vitamin concentrates (yeast is a rich source of B-group vitamins). Spent hops can be used as fertilizers, but hops as such are gradually being superseded in brewing by hop extract in powder or pellet form, which leaves no major residues. The main constituents of the beer itself are carbohydrates (5 percent); protein (0.6 percent); small amounts of riboflavin, niacin, and thiamine, which are forms of vitamin B; traces of calcium and phosphorus; from 2 percent to 6.5 percent alcohol; and up to 90 percent water. One pint (0.56 liters) contains about 280 calories.

Special beers

Consumer demand has led to developments in the type of beer available to suit people's preferences. "Dry" beers are allowed to ferment longer than normal brews, so that almost all of the residual sugar is converted into alcohol. This type of beer has a crisp flavor and little aftertaste. Low-calorie beers are made by reducing the amount of grain in the brew or by the addition of an enzyme to reduce the starch content, resulting in a beer of only 2.5 percent alcohol. Fruit beers were first brewed by the Germans in the 17th century. A wheat beer or ale is used as a base, and fruit such as raspberries, apricots, or cherries are added during the aging process. Alternatively, the fruit is boiled with the grain and hops, then yeast is added to start fermentation. Most fruits can be used, but seasonality means that this type of beer is brewed in small batches.

Modern trends

Although the trend in the second half of the 20th century had been toward much larger, often international, brewery groups and widespread exporting of beer, there is still considerable interest in home-brewing beer to an individual's own tastes. A recent innovation has been the development of "microbreweries," which allow home brewers to use professional, but small-scale, equipment on-site to produce beer from their own recipe.

SEE ALSO: ALCOHOL • ENZYME • FERMENTATION • WINEMAKING • YEAST

Bell

Bells have been made since prehistoric times. In China, heavy bells are said to have been in use since the third century B.C.E. Eastern bells are basically cylinders closed at the top and with increased wall thickness at the open end: they are struck on the outside near the middle.

In Europe, bells have changed little in general appearance throughout the Christian era, although the early bells were slightly more conical than those of the present day. Some European churches still use bells cast as early as the 13th century, and some bells date even earlier.

When a bell is struck, the metal is set into vibration, and this causes a movement of the air, which the listener hears as the characteristic bell sound. The vibration, and therefore the sound, is very complex, over 60 different frequencies being present just after the impact. Most of these fade rapidly, so that the note soon contains only ten or so components, or partials; of these, five predominate and can easily be distinguished by anyone with a musical ear. The nominal—the note that is heard on the impact of the clapper—and the hum note—which swells up afterward—are the most evident to the unpracticed ear; the others are the minor third, the fifth, and the fundamental, which is an octave above the hum note and an octave below the nominal.

Each partial is produced by a different pattern of vibrations over the bell, normally heard all at

◄ Molten metal at 2102°F (1150°C) is poured into the space between the core and the cope. Casting is carefully controlled to ensure no cracks or stress points develop as the bell is cooling.

▼ Metal is trimmed from the bell on a vertical lathe until the tuning is correct.

once. For each pattern there are certain nodal lines. These occur where the metal does not vibrate at all, and they divide the bell into zones of vibration.

Because a bell is never perfectly symmetrical, each partial usually occurs not as a single frequency but as a close pair of frequencies that combine in the listener's ear to give a surging effect known as beating. For example, a partial may actually consist of two components, 1,000 Hz and 1,004 Hz, but it will be heard as a single note at a frequency of 1,002 Hz, swelling and fading four times every second. Beating can be minimized by careful tuning and selection of the point where the clapper strikes, but it can never be completely eliminated; it is therefore another of the characteristic features of the bell sound, particularly noticeable with small, light types of bell.

Bells are cast in bronze (77 percent copper, 23 percent tin is typical) because this is a very tough alloy—it was used for old-fashioned cannon and Roman swords—and does not rust. The molten bell metal is poured into a mold consisting of an inner core and outer cope, which together fix the shape of the bell. The outer surface usually carries an inscription, cast in raised letters. These are stamped into the loam, the material that lines the cope before casting. The loam is a mixture of clay and traditional additives such as chopped hay and horse droppings. These burn when the molten metal is poured in, providing ventilation holes to help the cooling and to prevent stress points from developing in the finished casting.

Old bells had an arrangement of loops cast on the top by which they were fixed to their supporting wooden beams with chains. These days, bells are usually made with flat tops that are drilled to take mounting bolts and the support for the clapper. This technique was first used in the 19th century, when metal drilling became sufficiently easy.

The general shape of the bell is dictated by experience, but in order to obtain the exact frequencies required, the bell is cast a little thicker than the final value. This gives a slightly higher set of frequencies, which are decreased by turning the inside of the bell on a lathe.

Bells in a church belfry are mounted in a frame and have a freely hanging clapper. They are rung by pulling a rope that swings them through about 390 degrees, each stroke starting in an almost vertical position with the open end facing toward the sky. This system is used only when the British art of change-ringing is being practiced.

Carillons are a set of bells, usually housed in a tower, operated with a keyboard similar to an organ. The mechanism can be mechanical or electrically controlled. When the player depresses a key, a hammer strikes the relevant bell to make it sound. Carillons can have over 70 bells of different tones, allowing melodies to be played.

Electric bell

The electric bell found in many houses is made to ring by a very simple device that makes a clapper vibrate against a bell or gong. The mechanism consists of the bell itself, the clapper that strikes it, which is mounted on a spring, an electromagnet (most bells have one consisting of two coils), and a simple adjustable electrical contact.

When the bell-push is pressed, electricity flows through the contact into the electromagnet. This attracts the iron arm of the clapper, which moves out on its spring and strikes the bell. As it does this, however, it swings away from and breaks the electrical contact, stopping the flow of current through the electromagnet. With the magnetism gone, the arm is pulled back by the spring. When the arm falls back, it touches the contact again, restarting the flow of current to the electromagnet, so that the arm moves out again and hits the bell—the cycle repeating itself. The speed of vibration, and to a certain extent the loudness of the bell, can be increased by reducing the distance that the clapper must travel. This is done by adjusting the contacts. Electric buzzers work on the same principle, but the clapper hits the outer casing of the buzzer instead of a bell, producing a dry sound.

Chimes

The two-tone chimes that some houses have instead of bells are worked in a different way. There is an electromagnet that pulls a clapper over, but no contacts. Instead, the end of the arm has a flexible joint. When the bell-push is pressed, current flows through the electromagnet, causing the flexible end to swing across and hit the first chime. When the bell-push is released and its arm falls back, the flexible end swings back farther than the arm and hits the other chime. It comes to rest roughly halfway between the chimes, ready for next time.

Some sets of chimes have a second bell-push for the back door connected to the electrical circuit through an electrical resistance. Current to the electromagnet is consequently weaker, and the magnetic field produced pulls the arm with less force. If the arm is set off-center between the chimes, it will only hit one of them, thus making it clear whether the caller is at the front door or the back. More complicated chimes with three or more notes are rung by electric motors turning a striker that rings them in order.

Alarms

Some fire and burglar alarm bells on the outside of shops and offices use electric motors rather than electromagnets. Attached to the motor shaft is an arm with a jointed hammer end. The spin causes the hammer to fly outward, striking the bell, but the joint allows the hammer to bend back after striking, so that it can pass the bell. Amplified bells playing through loudspeakers are still found on ambulances and police cars in some countries, although solid-state electronic sirens now prevail.

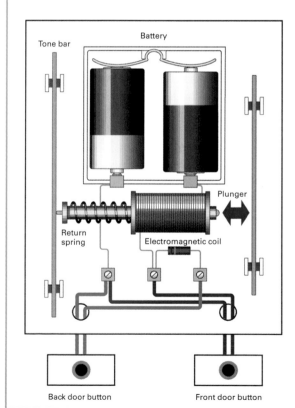

ELECTRIC CHIME

Tone bar
Battery
Plunger
Return spring
Electromagnetic coil
Back door button
Front door button

An electric door chime works when the steel plunger is flung against the first tone bar by the electromagnet, and then against the second tone bar by the reaction of the spring. Chimes with more than two notes are rung by an electric motor turning a striker that hits a series of chimes in sequence.

SEE ALSO: Alloy • Bronze • Electromagnetism • Musical scale • Sound

Bicycle

◄ Structurally, modern racing bicycles are not far removed from early designs such as the Singer Safety Special made in 1896, which was based on a diamond-shaped frame.

A bicycle is a pedal-driven human-powered vehicle with two wheels placed one in front of the other. *Bicycle* derives from the Latin *bi*, meaning two, and the Greek *kyklos*, meaning circle or wheel. Similarly, one- and three-wheeled variations are called unicycles and tricycles, respectively. Bicycles designed for two pedalers are called tandems.

Cyclists can travel three or four times faster than pedestrians, and they consume less energy in traveling a given distance than any other moving animal or machine. This efficiency derives from the fact that the bicycle is propelled by the thigh muscles, the most powerful in the body, operating in a smooth, rotary action at speeds of up to 60 to 80 rpm, thus making extremely efficient use of human power output. The first successful human-powered air flight across the English Channel was achieved by this method, the rider using no more than a quarter of a horsepower (0.18 kW) for almost three hours. Transmission losses in the gears and roller bush chain of a bicycle are low (1.5 and 5 percent, respectively), and narrow pneumatic tires and light, but strong-spoked wheels minimize rolling resistance. For comparison, the energy consumption of a cyclist is equivalent to that of a car traveling 1,250 miles on one gallon of gasoline (530 km/l).

Development

A sketch by the Italian artist and inventor Leonardo da Vinci (c. 1490) is the earliest known depiction of a bicycle, although there is no evidence that the machine was ever constructed. A two-wheeled hobbyhorse, the Draisienne, patented by Karl von Drais in 1817, had a wooden frame, spoked wooden wheels with metal tires, a saddle, and a steerable front wheel.

The first bicycle that could be propelled without the rider's feet touching the ground was a lever-driven model produced by the Scotsman Kirkpatrick Macmillan in or around 1839. The Macmillan machine, which had treadles mounted near the front fork connected to cranks attached to the rear axle, was copied and produced commercially by Thomas McCall, but the idea was not patented, and its influence on the development of later models was quite minimal.

The bicycle was reinvented by Phillipp Fischer of Obendorf in the early 1850s and by another German, Karl Kech, in 1862. The first truly commercial machine was produced by Pierre and Ernest Michaux in 1861. They fitted cranks and pedals directly onto the front wheel of a steerable velocipede (hobbyhorse).

In 1867, the Boneshaker appeared. This had two wheels and pedals on short cranks fitted to the front wheel. In the 1870s, the Ordinary took development a step further. It had a big front wheel measuring 54 in. (137 cm) in diameter for the average man of 5 ft. 8 in., while some had wheels of 60 in. (152 cm) in diameter for very tall riders. By comparison, the back wheel was quite small. These machines became known as penny-farthings, after the British coins.

James Starley of Coventry invented the tricycle in 1882. This was the first chain-driven cycle. In 1885, the Rover Safety set a new trend in design and from it developed the Humber bicycle featuring the diamond frame, a design that has lasted over 100 years. It was popular because its two wheels of equal size and gearing suited any rider. People could mount and dismount in safety.

Until then, tires had been made of solid rubber. In 1888, John Boyd Dunlop's reinvention of the pneumatic tire ended the "bone-shaking" era.

Cycle-frame design remained largely unchanged for many years, except for the Dursley-Pedersen in the 1890s. The frame was made of small-diameter tubes in a triangular design, and instead of a leather saddle, a hammock-type saddle was strung between the handlebars and rear frame tube.

Despite being hailed as the most comfortable bicycle, the Dursley-Pedersen found favor only among enthusiasts; it incorporated the diamond frame, and nothing changed for 60 years, except to modify it and improve accessories.

▶ Professional racing cyclists on the grueling Tour de France on cycles trimmed to the limit for lightness and strength. Despite the weight advantage and a choice of up to 20 gear ratios, the riders are severely tested on the mountainous route.

◀ In parts of southern Asia the Oxtrike, or Oxfam three-wheeler, is an important commercial vehicle.

In the simplest form, fixed-wheel drive, the rear gear sprocket is attached directly to the rear wheel, with no freewheel. Only one gear ratio can be used at a time, and the cranks cannot be turned independently of the rear wheel. The fixed-wheel bicycle can be braked by the rider resisting the motion of the pedals. Although lighter and more efficient than other systems, this method of transmission is used mainly on track-racing bicycles, as the single gear and the necessity to strap the feet firmly to the pedals make it impractical for general use.

Hub gears are available in 2-, 3-, 4-, and 5-speed versions. The gear is built inside an enlarged rear hub and controlled either by a cable or cables passed through the hollow axle or by a back-pedaling action. In a standard Sturmey Archer hub gear, the ratios of direct drive are 4:3, 1:1, and 3:4. Brakes and dynamos can also be incorporated into hubs in various combinations.

Other developments include the Cross frame, first developed in 1886, which reappeared as the small-wheeled Moulton in 1962. This frame has a main tube running straight from the headset to the back wheel axle, crossed by a second tube in the vertical axis carrying the saddle at the top and the bottom bracket axle at the bottom. In the Moulton, this design is reinforced by triangulation around the crossing point.

Transmission systems

The roller bush chain is still used in almost all bicycles, but experiments continue with the belt and shaft transmission. The gear sprockets at the bottom bracket and rear wheel axles are connected by an endless chain, and the cycle is propelled by pedals attached to the front sprocket.

▶ In Beijing, China, rush-hour traffic consists not of automobiles but of bicycles. Bicycles are a popular form of transport in many of the less-developed countries of southern and eastern Asia.

Derailleur gears provide a mechanism for changing gear, in which an assembly fixed to the bicycle frame is used to derail the chain from one gear sprocket to another. Five, six, seven, or eight sprockets are arranged in order of size on the rear axle, and one, two, or three on the crank axle. Both front and rear derailleurs are controlled by cables that pull the arm containing the chain inward against spring tension. The rear derailleur also acts as a pulley to maintain tension in the chain, taking up the slack that is necessary to accommodate sprockets of various sizes.

Even with derailleur gears, the range of available ratios is limited, so various continuous or automatic gears have been developed. Recent examples include the Biocam, a 50-ratio drive system incorporating double cam-shaped chainwheels mounted at 80 degrees out of phase. A nonendless chain is driven by the reciprocating motion of these cams, and the effective gear ratio is varied during the power stroke to parallel the muscle action of the rider.

The Deal Drive has a spring-loaded variable-diameter front chainwheel, which is opened or closed to the effective size by the pressure exerted on the chain. An intermittent locking system allows the gear to change only when the chainwheel teeth are free from the chain.

Freewheeling, which allows the rider to coast without pedaling, is activated by a one-way clutch in the hub. The mechanism uses a ratchet, which is a section of the shaft with projections resembling saw teeth, and a pawl, which in bicycles takes the form of rollers or ball bearings in tapered slot housings, which are jammed by the taper against the outer sleeve when the shaft is turned in the driven direction. The shaft is free to turn in one direction and makes a clicking noise as the pawl slips over the teeth, but when the shaft turns in the other direction, the pawl engages a tooth and prevents the shaft from turning or, alternatively, allows power to be transmitted through it. In the bicycle coaster brake, the construction has additional design features that allow the brakes to be applied by pedaling in reverse.

Brakes

Some heavyweight roadsters still have brakes consisting of a plunger rod mounted on the front forks, which bears directly down on to the tire tread surface. The more efficient rim brakes pinch the metal rim of the wheel from both sides with equal pressure. Controlled by rods or cables, such brakes are used on almost all lightweight models. The force to close the arms of the brakes is applied either from one side (sidepull),

▲ The British Bluebell is a streamlined semi-recumbent. Built exclusively for speed attempts, it has reached speeds of over 50 mph (82 km/h).

from directly above the wheel (centerpull), or from both sides using brake arms mounted directly onto the forks, thus providing extra leverage (cantilever).

The composition of the brake blocks that come in contact with the rim has a marked effect on braking performance, particularly on wet steel rims. Chrome leather blocks work well on steel, and synthetic materials have been developed to improve braking on alloy rims.

Hub brakes, controlled either by back pedaling or by a hand lever, are used on heavy roadsters and tandems. Disk brakes can also be used in some cases, and hydraulic control systems have been produced for bicycle brakes.

Tires and wheels

The development of the pneumatic tire greatly improved the comfort and performance of the bicycle, but it also introduced the problem of punctures. Impenetrable tire casings, tough layers inserted between tire and inner tube, liquid sealants inside the tube, and even solid plastic tires and solid inner tubes have been produced in an attempt to overcome this problem, but none are as good as the pneumatic tire.

The wire-on tire has an inflatable inner tube and a sturdy outer case with patterned tread surface held on by a wire bead that fits inside the rim of the wheel. Lightweight racing bicycles have one-piece tubular tires with a light airproof inner membrane.

As with many parts of the bicycle, steel rims and wheel hubs are cheaper but heavier than aluminum alloy components. All-plastic wheels and plastic rims have been developed, although their main use has been in BMX and childrens' bicycles. The strength and characteristics of the wheel are affected by the spoking pattern, and many variants are used. Most bicycles use ball bearings, but roller bearings are produced for specialist use, and cheaper bicycles have nylon bearings.

Frames

The design and composition of the frame is the major factor affecting the performance of the bicycle. The cheapest frames are made from low-carbon mild steel, which is rolled and welded into seamed tubes. Seamless alloy steel tubing is used to produce lighter and more responsive frames. The best quality frames are made from heat-treated manganese/molybdenum steel, double-butted so that the walls are thicker at the ends than in the center of the tubes to reduce weight without affecting performance. Cheap frames are welded, but lugged and brazed joints are used in most medium- and high-quality frames. The new inexpensive high-manganese-chrome-molybdenum steels can be machine brazed easily because of their higher heat tolerance, but top quality frames are hand brazed, some with silver.

Bicycle frames can also be produced in welded or glued aluminum tubing, and some frames and components have been produced in titanium. The all-plastic bicycle has reappeared every ten years or so, but the major use for plastic materials is likely to be for components such as mudguards.

Frames vary from the long wheelbase and heavily raked forks of the roadster to the tight angles and almost straight forks of the racing model. Roadsters are intended for relatively slow but comfortable traveling, and they have straight handlebars and an upright riding position. Bicycles for faster riding or touring over long distances are stiffer but more responsive, with dropped handlebars to allow the rider to crouch and minimize air resistance.

The only major departure from the diamond frame is the Moulton, a small-wheeled bicycle with a Cross type frame and suspension front and rear. The Moulton combines the riding quality of

◀ The streamlining effect of a plastic windshield more than compensates for its weight.

▼ Powered by five riders, the New Wave human-powered vehicle attempts a speed record.

a full-sized bicycle with compact size and suitability for a wider range of riders. Since the Moulton was introduced in 1962, a sizeable share of the market has been taken up by mass-produced small-wheel bicycles, but most of these lack the riding qualities of the original. Many ingenious designs for lightweight folding bicycles have been produced, notably the Bickerton, which has an aluminum box-section frame and many aluminum components and folds down to a tiny portable package weighing approximately 22 lbs. (10 kg).

Another departure is the BMX bicycle for children, which has 20 in. (50.8 cm) wheels, straight forks, and a rugged frame intended for rough fast riding and various stunts. The adult cruiser bicycle (mountain bike) has wide straight handlebars, broad high-pressure tires, a responsive frame, and high-quality gears and brakes. It is intended for both on- and off-road leisure use.

The recumbent human-powered vehicle, with either two or three wheels, combines greater use of the rider's power with a more efficient aerodynamic profile. The rider lies prone or supine on the vehicle, pedaling with the back braced against the seat. When enclosed in a light plastic shell, human-powered bicycles can travel at over 60 mph (100 km/h) on level ground. With battery motor assist, such vehicles could achieve acceleration rates and cruising speeds comparable to those of automobiles. Although very efficient, they have not become popular, possibly because the low-slung design makes riders feel vulnerable among other vehicles on the road.

Perhaps the most innovative changes in design of recent years have been in racing bicycles, particularly those used for time trials. Tubular frames have been replaced by the all-in-one monocoque, a hollow carbon fiber/epoxy resin structure. Gear and brake cables are carried inside the frame, which has an aerofoil cross section to minimize wind resistance. The wheels, also made of carbon fiber, can be trispoke, solid, or a combination of both. The rider crouches low over the handlebars and, combined with a teardrop-shaped helmet, presents an aerodynamically good profile. The bicycles weigh less than 7 lbs. (3 kg), and cyclists can reach speeds of over 200 mph (335 km/h).

As well as structural developments, there have been technical advances in bicycle design. The Chilcote automatic transmission system uses a computer under the saddle and sensors in the rear wheel hub to monitor the pedal pressure and speed and automatically adjust the gearing.

FACT FILE

- *Before World War I, the British Army instituted bicycle battalions, and a special folding bicycle was developed. Combat techniques from an army manual of the time include instructions on how to deal with cavalry by turning the bicycles upside down and spinning the wheels to frighten the horses.*

- *An experimental four-seater tandem, developed at the University of Queensland, Australia, incorporated a rider-shading canopy that was equipped with 440 photovoltaic cells. The PV cells delivered power to an auxiliary electric motor over the rear wheel. In a 1,150-mile (1,920 km) test run, the solar cells contributed an estimated 25 percent increase in speed.*

▲ Modern racing bicycles have taken advantage of lighter and stronger materials to significantly reduce the weight of the frame and increase the aerodynamic profile of the machine and its rider.

SEE ALSO: Aerodynamics • Bearing and bushing • Chain drive • Gear

Binary System

The binary system of counting is based on the number two. Normally, people count using a decimal, or base-ten, system, which uses the digits 0 to 9. Binary is much simpler—it uses only the digits 0 and 1.

When writing a number in base ten, the far right digit represents units, the next left tens, the next left hundreds (ten times tens), the next left thousands (ten times ten times tens), and so on.

(i) For example: $9533 = 9 \times (10 \times 10 \times 10)$
$+ 5 \times (10 \times 10)$
$+ 3 \times (10)$
$+ 3$

Binary is very similar, except that in writing a binary number the far right digit represents units, the next left twos, the next left fours (two times twos), the next left eights (two times two times twos), and so on.

(ii) For example: $1011 = 1 \times (2 \times 2 \times 2)$
$+ 0 \times (2 \times 2)$
$+ 1 \times (2)$
$+ 1$

or putting it another way, $(1 \times 8) + (0 \times 4) + (1 \times 2) + (1 \times 1) = 11$. So 1011 in base two is 11 in base ten. Fractions can also be represented in binary. To see how, recall what happens when writing a decimal fraction. The first digit to the right of the decimal point represents tenths, the next right hundredths (tenths of tenths), the next right thousandths (tenths of tenths of tenths), then ten thousandths, and so on.

(iii) For example: $0.5333 = 5 \times (\frac{1}{10})$
$+ 3 \times (\frac{1}{10} \times \frac{1}{10})$
$+ 3 \times (\frac{1}{10} \times \frac{1}{10} \times \frac{1}{10})$
$+ 3 \times (\frac{1}{10} \times \frac{1}{10} \times \frac{1}{10} \times \frac{1}{10})$

The pattern is similar in binary, but using multipliers of halves instead of tenths. In a binary fraction, the first digit to the right of the decimal point represents halves, the next right quarters (halves of halves), the next right eighths (halves of halves of halves), and so on.

(iv) For example: $0.1111 = 1 \times (\frac{1}{2})$
$+ 1 \times (\frac{1}{2} \times \frac{1}{2})$
$+ 1 \times (\frac{1}{2} \times \frac{1}{2} \times \frac{1}{2})$
$+ 1 \times (\frac{1}{2} \times \frac{1}{2} \times \frac{1}{2} \times \frac{1}{2})$

So, 0.1111 in base two represents $\frac{15}{16}$ when multiplied out, or 0.9375 in base ten.

Counting in binary

To understand how to count in binary, imagine the odometer of an automobile, which records the total mileage traveled in base ten. It usually consists of a row of adjacent wheels turning on a spindle. Each wheel has the digits 0 to 9 around

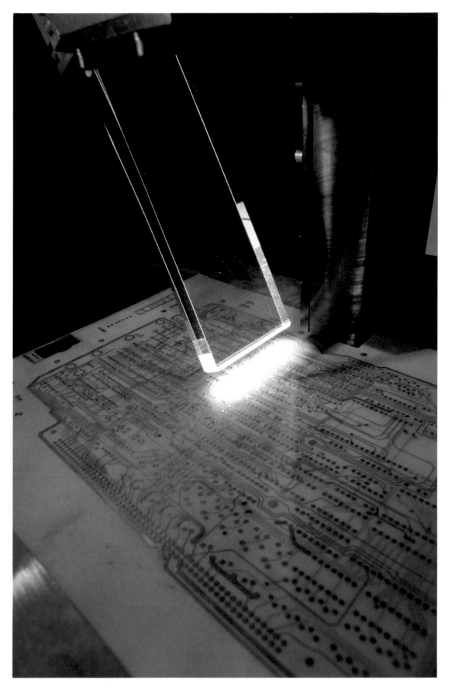

its circumference. When the car moves, the right-most wheel turns. When it reaches 9 and begins to show 0, the wheel on its left is dragged along and made to advance by one notch. In this way, a ten is carried to the left-hand wheel. Similarly, when the left hand wheel reaches 9 and begins to show 0, the wheel to its left is dragged along and made to advance by one notch. In this way, a hundred is carried, and so on.

Now consider a binary odometer. If such a device were to exist, its wheels would carry only the digits 0 and 1. In a binary odometer, whenever a wheel reaches 1 and begins to show 0, the wheel on its left is made to advance by one notch. This is the way to count in base two, or binary.

(v) Here are some examples of binary arithmetic and beside them the base-ten equivalents:

▲ A digital computer can handle numbers, text, or graphics, but it works in binary. It can accept binary digits stored as levels of magnetism on program disks or stored temporarily as voltages in the random access memory (RAM). These instructions switch circuits on the microchip on and off.

a) 1001 + 101 = 1110; 9 + 5 = 14
b) 11101 − 1001 = 10100; 29 − 9 = 20
c) 101 x 11 = 1111; 5 x 3 = 15

Converting a binary number to decimal, base ten, is just a matter of thinking about what a binary number means. Look back to example (ii) and see how it was done. Converting a decimal number to binary is slightly more tricky. In principle, all that needs to be done is to express the decimal number as a sum of units, twos, fours, eights, and so on.

For example: 63 = 32 + 16 + 8 + 4 + 2 + 1
So, 63 = 111111 in binary.

This is not always easy to do. Fortunately, there is a useful trick to help convert a number from decimal to binary. Keep dividing the decimal number by two and writing down the remainder.

(vi) Take, for example, the decimal number 39; r. is the remainder.

2	39	
2	19	r.1
2	9	r.1
2	4	r.1
2	2	r.0
2	1	r.0
	0	r.1

Stop dividing by two when there is nothing left and read the remainders from bottom to top. So, in this case 39 in base ten is 100111 in binary.

John von Neumann, the U.S. mathematician, born in Hungary, was the first to realize the advantages of using binary to represent numbers inside a computer. A computer consists of banks of tiny electronic components, each of which can be in one of two states: "on," letting an electric current flow, or "off," allowing no current to flow. These states can represent the 1 (on) and 0 (off) of a binary digit (or *bit* in computer jargon). Unfortunately, binary is a very unwieldy code to handle—it would take eight binary digits to represent a three digit decimal number such as 255 and nine to represent 256. As eight bits make up one byte of computer memory, it would require a surprising amount of memory just to store the numbers 1 to 1,000 in binary.

Hexadecimal system

To overcome this problem, another number system is used. Hexadecimal uses base 16, which has the advantage of being very compact; also it is easy to convert it into binary, and vice versa. In addition to the digits 0 to 9, it uses the letters A, B, C, D, E, and F. The letters represent the decimal numbers 10 to 15, respectively. When writing hexadecimal numbers, programmers put a 0 at the beginning of the code to make it easy to translate into binary and an H (or h) at the end of the code to indicate that it is base 16. Sometimes 0x is used instead of an H. Thus, the decimal number 1,970 can be written as either 07B2H or 0x7B2 in hexadecimal.

Converting hexadecimal into binary can be carried out using the table (*see* p.247) Each hexadecimal number corresponds to a four-bit binary code. So the number 07B2H would read

0111 1011 0010

in its binary equivalent. Similarly, the binary number 011010011101 easily translates into hexadecimal by splitting it into blocks of four, i.e.

0110 1001 1101
which converts to 069DH.

To turn this into decimal, multiply the value in each position by its hexadecimal weight and add them together. For the example 069DH:

6 x (16 x 16)
+ 9 x (16 x 1)
+ 13

gives a value of (1,536 + 144 + 13) = 1,693 in base ten.

Hexadecimal is used as an assembly language by computer programmers. It acts as an intermediate level of instruction between the high-level languages used to create software programs and the machine language (off-on binary switching) that the hardware understands. Every type of computer, such as IBM, Apple, or Unix, has its

▼ The use of high-level languages allows even inexperienced users to communicate with a computer, without ever having to understand binary notation because the computer acts as an interpreter.

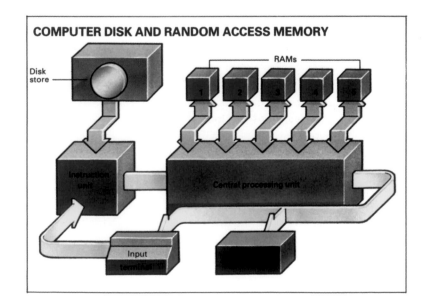

COMPUTER DISK AND RANDOM ACCESS MEMORY

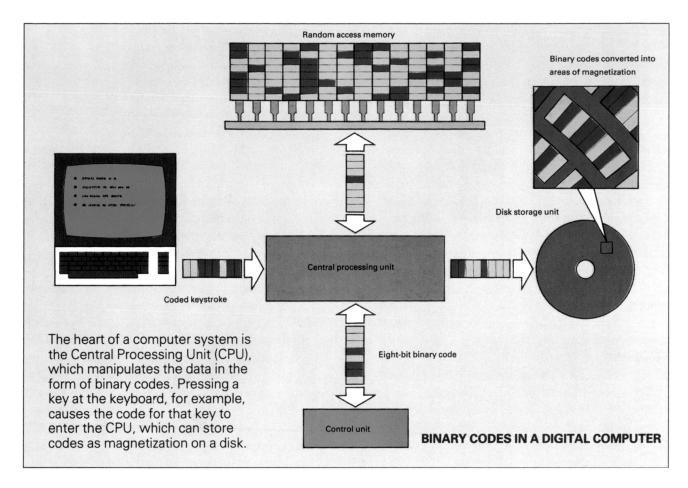

The heart of a computer system is the Central Processing Unit (CPU), which manipulates the data in the form of binary codes. Pressing a key at the keyboard, for example, causes the code for that key to enter the CPU, which can store codes as magnetization on a disk.

BINARY CODES IN A DIGITAL COMPUTER

own machine language. Programs therefore have to be rewritten to run on different systems.

One example of how a computer uses hexadecimal is the ASCII code, which stands for American Standard Code for Information Interchange. This is a set of 128 numerals, characters, and symbols that have been standardized in hexadecimal so that different computers can open simple documents without the need for complicated translation software.

The ASCII set is divided into four groups of 32 characters. The first group uses the hexadecimal codes 00H to 01FH and is used for nonprinting control characters. These include the carriage return (0DH), the line feed (0AH), and the backspace (08H). The second group includes the numerals 0 to 9 (030H to 039H in ASCII), and the space character, 020H.

Upper- and lowercase letters are controlled by the third and fourth group of ASCII characters. Capitals A to Z are covered by the hexadecimals 041H to 05AH, and lowercase by 061H to 07AH. As there are only 26 letters in each group, the remaining codes are used for special symbols.

Each character in the ASCII code occupies eight bits in binary code, and bits are numbered zero to seven. Because bit seven (the character farthest left in the sequence) is always set at 0, switching it to 1 creates the option of a further 128 characters, which can be used for interna-

tional letters with umlauts or accents, math symbols, and Greek characters. This extended character set, as it is known, is less standardized than the first 128 characters and may not produce the same letter or symbol on a different computer.

Decimal	Binary	Hexadecimal
00	0000	00H
01	0001	01H
02	0010	02H
03	0011	03H
04	0100	04H
05	0101	05H
06	0110	06H
07	0111	07H
08	1000	08H
09	1001	09H
10	1010	0AH
11	1011	0BH
12	1100	0CH
13	1101	0DH
14	1110	0EH
15	1111	0FH

 SEE ALSO: ANALOG AND DIGITAL SYSTEMS • COMPUTER • DATA STORAGE • MATHEMATICS

Binding Energy

Binding energy is the energy required to separate a physical system into its components. The binding energy of an electron in an atom is the minimum energy that will eject it from the atom, also called the ionization potential. The binding energy of a solid is the energy needed to break the solid up into its component atoms or molecules. For a nucleus, it is the energy required to break it up into its component protons and neutrons. It is also the energy that would be released if the nucleus were to be formed from free protons and neutrons. As such, it is the source of both fission and fusion energies, which have had such an impact on the modern world.

The realization that large amounts of energy are available from the nuclei of the atoms followed from precise measurements of nuclear masses early in the 20th century. Using instruments called mass spectrometers, the masses can be accurately calculated by measuring the curvature of the paths taken by charged clusters of particles as they travel through electric and magnetic fields. The measurements reveal something that, taken by itself, seems impossible. The masses of the nuclei are less than the total arrived at by adding the masses of the protons and neutrons of which they are formed.

This enigma can be resolved using the U.S. physicist Albert Einstein's formula $E = mc^2$ (energy equals mass multiplied by the speed of light, squared). Mass and energy are interchangeable, and the mass, which is missing in the sums for the nucleus, is related to the energy that holds the nucleus together. This is the binding energy, also known initially as the mass defect. When a nucleus is formed, energy is given off, and the mass of the nucleus is less than that of the protons and neutrons that make it up.

When the nuclei of all the chemical elements are examined, a crucial fact emerges. Most of the elements have nuclei with a binding energy of about 8 MeV, or 8 million electron volts, per particle—nearly a thousand times the energy of the electrons striking the screen in a television picture tube. The lightest and heaviest elements, however, have less binding energy per particle on account of the structure of their nuclei. The amount of mass that is missing is greater for the elements near the center of the periodic table; if the light or heavy elements can be converted into these central elements, some mass can be liberated as free energy.

To take a specific example, a helium nucleus is built up of two protons and two neutrons. The mass of a proton (the nucleus of the normal hydrogen atom) is about 1.7 millionth of a millionth of a millionth of a millionth of a gram. This is a rather clumsy unit with which to calculate; using the mass–energy equivalence, the nuclear physicist usually handles the proton mass in units of energy—a proton is 938 MeV, and a neutron is slightly heavier with 939.5 MeV. The helium nucleus is, however, 3,727 MeV, or 28 MeV less massive than its constituents: 28 MeVs worth of energy can be released in the formation of a single nucleus. Compared with conventional sources, this is a colossal amount of energy.

Conventional energy uses, say the burning of oil, involve electron binding energies—they are chemical reactions in which the binding of the electron clouds surrounding the nucleus changes. Here also, the release of energy is connected with the conversion of mass—the products of the burned oil have very slightly less mass than the oil itself—but nuclear energy sources, which bring the center of the atom into play, are several million times more powerful.

This process of joining light elements together to form heavier ones is known as fusion, and it is the process that powers the H (hydrogen) bomb, the Sun, and the stars. There is a great deal of research under way in an attempt to master fusion in the laboratory so that it can be used in power plants. Progress has been slow because, in order to overcome the natural repulsion between positively charged hydrogen nuclei, temperatures as high as ten million degrees must be sustained, and it is difficult to confine any material that hot.

At the other end of the table of elements, the breaking up of heavy nuclei such as uranium is another source of energy. This process is known as fission. A uranium nucleus usually breaks up into two almost equal parts, ending up, for example, as nuclei of barium and strontium.

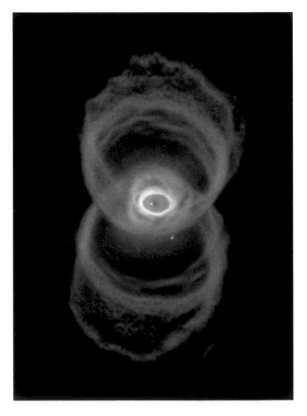

▼ The Hourglass nebula is a dying star that is shedding its stellar matter. The shock wave produced by the exploding star has provided enough energy to strip electrons from its atoms, revealing a significant quantity of ionized nitrogen (red), hydrogen (green), and doubly ionized oxygen (blue) in its chemical composition.

SEE ALSO: ATOMIC STRUCTURE • FISSION • FUSION

Binoculars

A pair of binoculars is essentially two telescopes mounted side by side. Since both eyes are used to look at a scene, a stereoscopic view is obtained so that nearby objects are seen in depth, and there is less eye strain than with a single telescope.

The simplest binocular instrument uses two Galilean telescopes, each of which has just two lenses. Known generally as an opera glass or field glass, this instrument has a rather small field of view—like looking through a tube—and a low magnification, rarely more than four times.

Better telescopes usually have achromatic lenses and are much longer and heavier than the Galilean type. To make a powerful pair of binoculars using ordinary telescopes without any modification would mean that they would be very long and clumsy. But by using a pair of right-angled prisms in each optical system, the light can be folded so that the distance it travels between the front object glass and the eyepiece is lengthened quite considerably without lengthening the body of the instrument. This also allows the object glasses to be offset so that they can be farther apart than the viewer's eyes, giving a greater stereo effect and allowing larger lenses to be used

▶ An operative using a binocular-based laserguide rangefinder. This is a highly specialized application of binocular vision, but the principle is not unlike the one used on the once popular rangefinder cameras.

▼ The light through a binocular is reflected an even number of times, so the image is viewed upright, unlike a telescope, in which the image is normally viewed upside down.

without touching at the center. The basic telescope design gives an upside-down image, but the prisms turn it the right way up so no extra lenses need be used.

Focusing is usually carried out by a central wheel on a bridge that links the two eyepiece tubes. Turning this wheel moves the two tubes in or out simultaneously. There are often differences in strength between an individual's eyes, so a separate twist-focusing thread is provided on the

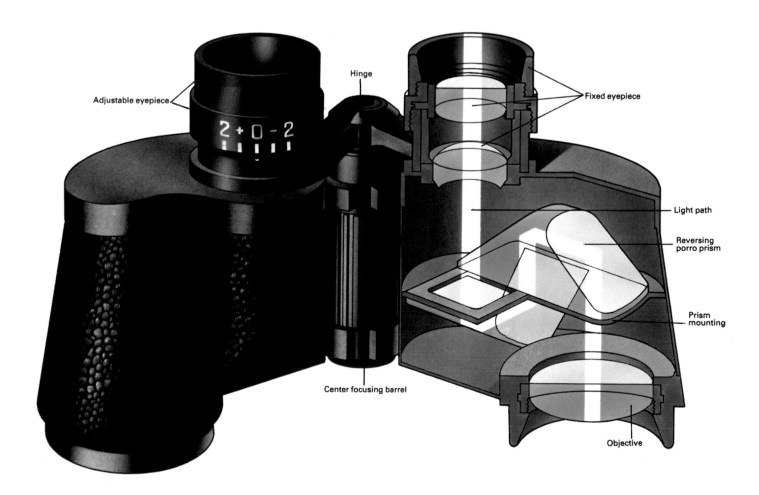

Adjustable eyepiece

Hinge

Fixed eyepiece

2 + 0 - 2

Light path

Reversing porro prism

Prism mounting

Center focusing barrel

Objective

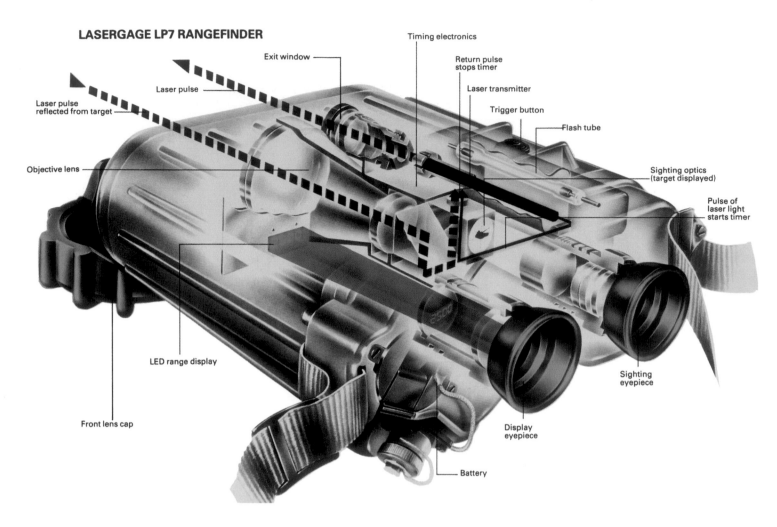

LASERGAGE LP7 RANGEFINDER

Timing electronics

Return pulse stops timer

Laser transmitter

Trigger button

Exit window

Laser pulse

Flash tube

Laser pulse reflected from target

Objective lens

Sighting optics (target displayed)

Pulse of laser light starts timer

LED range display

Sighting eyepiece

Front lens cap

Display eyepiece

Battery

right-hand eyepiece to allow for this. These center-focus (CF) models can be quickly focused on objects at different distances, and so are popular for ordinary use. They are not as robust as independent-focusing (IF) models, however, in which each eyepiece is fitted directly to the main body and has to be focused separately. Binoculars intended for military or marine use are of the independent-focus type.

The two halves of a pair of binoculars are hinged, so that they can be altered to suit the distance between the user's eyes. A scale marked on the bridge shows this separation in millimeters. A value of 2.5 in. (64 mm) is common.

If the two light paths of the separate halves of the binocular are not parallel, a double image will be seen. Even a slight misalignment is noticeable, if only by the discomfort produced when the eyes try to bring the image together. This is actually bad for the eyes; binoculars should always be perfectly collimated so that the beams are parallel.

The prisms are held in place in recesses by metal straps and are adjusted to collimate the beam by using wedges or screws. Fine adjustment is carried out by rotating the cells, which carry the object glasses. These cells are made so that the lens is slightly off center; the screw thread they fit

into is also slightly off center so that by turning one inside the other the lens can be brought to any position, including dead center.

Cheap binoculars, though they may at first appear to be every bit as good as more expensive ones, often have poor prism mountings. Usually, the prisms can be knocked out of alignment easily and thus ruin the instrument.

Early binoculars tended to be large and heavy because of the weight of the lenses and prisms needed to give a good magnification. New optical developments such as plastic and high-index lenses mean that binoculars can now be made much smaller and are often compact enough to be carried in a jacket pocket. Lenses and prisms in all binoculars are coated to reduce scattered light, increasing the brightness of the image and reducing glare. Binoculars made for use at night take account of the user's pupils dilating to let in more light. This objective is achieved by making the exit pupils bigger.

A binocular form of telescopic night sight is also available to fit rifles and similar high-performance weapons.

▲ A binocular laser rangefinder combines the advantages of compactness and ease of use.

 SEE ALSO: IMAGE INTENSIFIER • LASER AND MASER • LENS • LIGHT AND OPTICS • PRISM • TELESCOPE, OPTICAL

Biochemistry

Biochemistry can be simply defined as the science that deals with the chemistry of living organisms. It seeks to explain the properties of living organisms, whether a microbe or a human, in terms of the chemical substances that they contain. Cells consist of extremely complex components: proteins, nucleic acids, carbohydrates, lipids (or fats), and a host of other smaller molecules often present only in trace amounts. Moreover, thousands of chemical reactions are occurring in living cells simultaneously in a carefully controlled and regulated way. The outward manifestation of these reactions is life itself.

Biochemists use a number of scientific methods to help them understand the paths by which the body takes up and uses chemical compounds. These include chromatography, which is used to separate and identify organic compounds such as amino acids, the compounds that make up proteins. Proteins themselves can be isolated by electrophoresis, which is also useful in detecting changes in the molecular structure of blood caused by certain diseases. Radioactive isotopes are often used to "label" molecules of an organic compound so that its passage round the body and incorporation by metabolic processes can be discovered.

Living cells are separated from their environment by a membrane composed of a double layer of lipid. Embedded in this are a variety of membrane proteins that perform a variety of tasks. Some are selective channels for ions and solutes such as glucose, while others are part of the complex communication system between cells characteristic of multicellular organisms. The messages are initially carried around the body in the form of small molecules, called ligands, that diffuse through the intracellular medium and interact with larger molecules, for example, proteins. If a ligand such as a hormone interacts with a protein bound to the membrane (the hormone's receptor) that recognizes it, then a second intracellular messenger is generated. This in turn may lead to a change in the cell's metabolism. Two such second-messenger systems have been identified.

The first, cyclic-AMP, was discovered by Earl Sutherland in 1972. It is formed from ATP—an all-purpose energy molecule—by the activation of an enzyme, adenylate cyclase, that is bound to the membrane. The cyclic-AMP then activates enzymes called kinases that in turn can transfer phosphate groups to key metabolic enzymes, switching them on or off as appropriate. The challenge has been to discover how the binding of a ligand to a receptor on the outer membrane of the cell activates the adenylate cyclase.

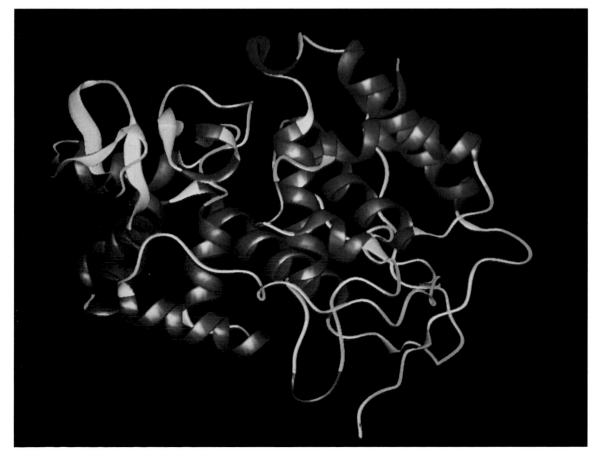

◄ The structure of an enzyme called CCP, displayed by computer. The ribbons represent chains of amino acids and actually involve hundreds of individual atoms. The model shows how these fold to create a unique tertiary structure.

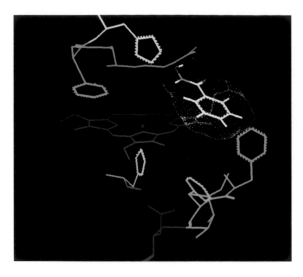

A powerful tool in working out this process has been the development of analogs that mimic the activity of the natural ligands, termed agonists, and others that block the activity of the natural ligand, termed antagonists. In fact, some of the most effective drugs for asthma, hypertension, and stomach ulcers work at their respective receptors in this way. For example, a beta-2 adrenergic receptor agonist (salbutamol) activates the appropriate receptor to cause a dilation of the bronchi to relieve asthma.

Researchers have found that the intermediate between the ligand-receptor complex and the adenylate cyclase is a group of proteins called G proteins (G because they bind guanosine diphosphate). When a chance mutation switches them permanently on, these may be involved in causing some cancers. The ras oncogene, for example, behaves as a permanent stimulus for growth and proliferation, leading to a tumor.

A development in the 1980s was the discovery of the phosphoinositide system by Michael Berridge in the United Kingdom and Yasutomi Nishizuka in Japan. This second "second messenger" system controls intracellular calcium levels. Two "second messengers," diacylglycerol and inositol triphosphate, are generated by the binding of an agonist. The latter causes the release of intracellular calcium stores, while diaglycerol activates protein kinase C, which requires the released calcium for its activity and in turn transfers phosphate groups to key proteins, switching them on to give a cellular response.

The folding problem

Essentially all proteins and enzymes are composed of 20 basic building blocks called amino acids common to all forms of life on Earth. The unique sequence of amino acids that makes up a protein or polypeptide chain contains all the information it needs to take up its correct three-

dimensional shape. This shape, or tertiary fold, is crucial for biological activity. However, the precise shape of a protein cannot yet be predicted from its primary amino acid sequence alone. This is because the laws that govern the "folding" of polypeptide chains are not understood. Recently, biochemists have discovered that the folding process is often aided, and its efficiency increased, by helper proteins called chaperonins.

As X-ray crystallography or nuclear magnetic resonance (NMR) spectroscopy revealed more protein structures and amino acid sequences, biochemists came to realize that proteins and enzymes can be grouped into "superfamilies" with essentially the same tertiary fold. Over 800 enzyme superfamilies had been identified by the beginning of the year 2000.

It is also possible to model unknown protein structures using appropriate building blocks chosen from the wide range of known structures. The tools for this modeling process, increased availability of computing power coupled to high-resolution computer graphics, will eventually allow biochemists to design enzymes from scratch for specific purposes.

▶ A child uses an inhaler to take the drug salbutamol, which uses an agonist to activate the appropriate receptor to cause a dilation of the bronchial muscles in order to relieve asthma.

 SEE ALSO: AMINO ACID • CELL BIOLOGY • CHROMATOGRAPHY • CRYSTALS AND CRYSTALLOGRAPHY • ENZYME • HORMONE • MOLECULAR BIOLOGY • PROTEIN

Bioengineering

▲ By using standard parts, a range of limbs can be provided to suit individual needs. Limbs are often made of carbon fiber, which can be cut to length. The structure of the prosthesis can be effectively disguised using a plastic sheath. This man's left leg is completely artificial.

Bioengineering, often confused with biotechnology, can best be described as the application of engineering practices, principles, and thought to biological problems. The vast majority of bioengineering, sometimes also called biomedical engineering or even the rather science fiction-like bionics, is applied to medicine and medical research.

Some forms of bioengineering rank among humankind's oldest skills. When primitive humans injured or lost a leg, they probably used a stick or a crutch or extended the shortened limb with a piece of wood or bone. A substitute for any part of the body is called a *prosthesis*. In modern medicine, external prostheses are available for limbs, hands, and feet, while internal prostheses can be made for most joints, short sections of larger blood vessels, and some bones, including those of the face and skull.

A body part may have been injured in an accident, or removed because of disease, or perhaps had to be reshaped because it was the wrong shape at birth or failed to grow properly. Both types of prostheses have benefited enormously from the availability of modern materials that are light and strong, such as plastics, sometimes reinforced with carbon fiber, titanium, and ceramics.

Artificial limbs can be broadly categorized into two groups, upper and lower extremities (arms and legs). The problems encountered by the prosthetic designer for each of these levels are quite different. In the upper extremity, the major problems are associated with manipulation and control of many joints, whereas in the lower extremity the problems are of a structural engineering nature, requiring components of very high strength that are not prohibitive in weight.

Artificial legs

An example of the best engineering and use of materials is the modular artificial leg. While the socket is made from a precise plaster cast measured to fit the patient, the structure and mechanism are built up from a series of modules that are manufactured just like the components of a car engine. These modules are made in a range of sizes and different characteristics and then custom-assembled to suit the wearer.

Air-pressure casting is one of the modern techniques routinely used today to achieve an accurate impression of the arm or leg stump. The latest research uses laser holography to scan the stump and build a three-dimensional computer model, the surface of which may then be topologically modified for weight bearing. This computer-generated shape is then manufactured in hard wax to produce the socket, which must be carefully and individually fitted to the stump. Areas that are sensitive or tender must be skillfully relieved of pressure.

On the basis of the confidence and ability of the patient, different kinds of knees can be fitted, some with a brake so that the lower leg can swing free until a load is applied, when it locks securely. Knee stability can be achieved simply by carefully positioning the knee joint in relation to the load line through the limb. This technique is referred to as alignment stability. Alternatively, a friction brake-type device can be used. Polycentric mechanisms and linkages are often used, as are hydraulic systems. Swing-phase controls can be either simple friction or pneumatic or hydraulic dampers. The latter permit the amputee to walk at different speeds (they are velocity sensitive) without the need to readjust the mechanism. With a mechanism like this giving security and

▼ An artificial leg (below) does not appear readily obvious once the user is fully dressed, and although its mechanism (bottom) is simpler than that of the artificial hand, its design is just as challenging.

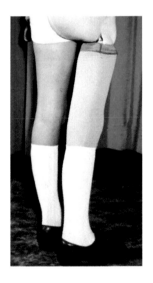

confidence, many amputees are able to run, dance, play golf, and enjoy a full and active life.

The latest modular hip joints incorporate an alignment device such that the joint can be positioned on the anterior/distal (frontal end) aspects of the pelvic socket. This enables the amputee to adopt a very natural sitting position and helps with the stability of this very high-level artificial leg. Most prostheses for this level also incorporate a stride adjustment to control the angle of hip flexion movement. For the patient to sit down, this control must be overridden. When the patient stands up, however, the mechanism will automatically reset itself to the walk mode.

The simplest replacements for the foot consist of molded polyurethane components, which are light and robust and are manufactured in standard shoe sizes. The inherent flexibility of the material is carefully controlled so that the required toe-joint movements and stiffness are simulated. A plastic foam sheath, shaped like a natural leg, surrounds the bare components, while a skin-colored stocking gives the whole thing a very natural appearance.

An advance announced in 1992, the "intelligent prosthesis," uses microprocessor control to adjust the pneumatic damping of the artificial leg

▼ Power for this motorized hand is supplied from a battery pack mounted at the wrist. Sensors pick up the electrical impulses from the wearer's remaining nerves and amplify them to drive the fingers. With practice, the user can operate the hand just by willing it to move.

to suit the wearer under a wide variety of conditions. Normally, the damping is set for a particular speed or gait, often resulting in a tiring limp at other speeds. But with active control, the limp can disappear and the wearer can become more agile.

Artificial arms

Currently, almost all artificial limbs are passive; that is, they are operated by the wearer's remaining muscle power rather than by any internal power source. There are two reasons for this. First, it is difficult to store enough energy in a limb to substitute, even for short periods, for the energy that would have been supplied by the muscles. Second, if the limb is to be moved unconsciously, rather than deliberately, it is difficult to obtain a sufficient number of control signals, perhaps from the electrical activity of muscles in the stump, to manage complex movements. An exception is the hand; there are powered versions of the hand because the power requirements are modest and control signals can be obtained from the forearm.

Body-powered limbs are so called because they rely on body movement elsewhere for their function and control. The hand, for example, is

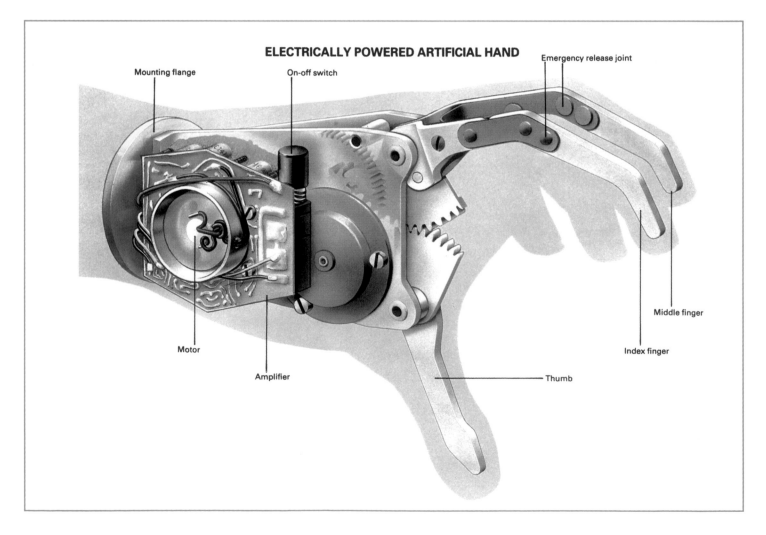

ELECTRICALLY POWERED ARTIFICIAL HAND

Mounting flange

On-off switch

Emergency release joint

Middle finger

Index finger

Motor

Amplifier

Thumb

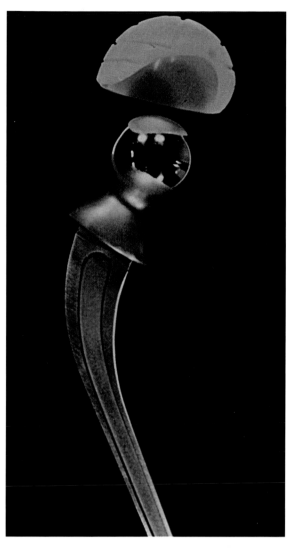

◄ A complete hip joint made from stainless steel. The socket, into which the ball fits in the pelvis, is made of polyethylene. Friction is minimized by giving the ball a high polish.

◄ A complete hip joint made from stainless steel. The socket, into which the ball fits in the pelvis, is made of polyethylene. Friction is minimized by giving the ball a high polish.

Movement and control are provided by the remaining muscles in the stump, or from the shoulder, transmitted through a simple harness system and operated by cables. For amputations above the elbow, the prosthetic elbow unit is one of the most important components. It must permit bending of the forearm and provide locking of the joint at will.

Endoprostheses

Endoprostheses are required where bone and joint tissues are beyond repair. There are many types of joints in the body, each adapted to a particular function, degree of movement, and control required. Usually, the two bone surfaces forming the articulation are covered with a layer of cartilage, a tough yet pliable matrix of fibers with a glassy, smooth surface. Sometimes there is a further layer called the fibrocartilage or meniscus. The bones are tied together with very tough bands or capsules of fibrous tissues called ligaments, and the whole joint is partially lined by the synovial membrane, which secretes a transparent, yellowish-white or reddish fluid called synovia. If the synovial fluid either is not produced or crystallizes or the articular cartilage loses its smooth properties, the joint becomes stiff and painful and can even seize up completely. This can result in the replacement of the whole or part of the

an extremely intricate and versatile instrument that presents a tremendous challenge to the designer. Not only must the replacement be functional, but its cosmetic appearance must also be pleasing—not just to the patient, but also to others.

A simple spring mechanism enables the patient to grasp and hold an object—the most fundamental use of the hand—and is termed *prehension*. The force provided by this simple spring, however, cannot easily be used both for strong grips and for delicate, precision movements.

The other, more practical, approach is the simple hand substitute—the split hook. This is light, cheap, and surprisingly functional for an experienced user. Many different attachments for varying requirements can be speedily interchanged. The big disadvantage, however, is that it is rather ugly.

Where the arm has to be replaced, correct length, weight, and comfort are very important factors for a well-balanced replacement. Much use is made of composite materials, such as fiber-reinforced polyester resin, that combine strength and stiffness with lightness and ease of shaping.

► Artificial limbs, particularly legs and feet, have to undergo rigorous testing to ensure they can withstand prolonged use and impact pressures.

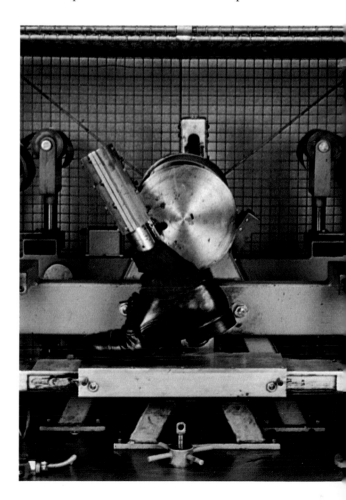

joint. Hip-joint replacement is by far the most common of the implant operations.

The particular problems here are to find very hard-wearing materials that have a low coefficient of sliding friction. Research has shown that a microthin layer of nitrogen atoms may extend the life of such joints. This ion implantation process yields a device that is extremely resistant to mechanical wear and body-fluid corrosion and that minimizes the release of metal particles into the surrounding tissue.

Metal alloys are used to reduce the problems of corrosion and fatigue that render pure metals useless as bone substitutes. Alloys, however, will never eliminate all problems. Vitallium is an alloy consisting of 65 percent cobalt, 30 percent chromium and 3 percent molybdenum with traces of manganese, silicon, and carbon. Unfortunately, this material is so hard that it cannot be machined and has to be cast to the exact shape required.

Titanium is another metal increasingly used for joints as well as bone plates and screws. It is unique among structural metals in that 99.8 percent pure metal (commercially pure) can have varying degrees of strength and ductility by altering the amount of oxygen and nitrogen gas dissolved in solid solution. The proportion varies from 0.04 percent to 0.08 percent. Titanium, however, must not be used in contact with itself because it welds cold.

Implants, particularly femoral head implant prostheses, can be cemented into the femur using cold-setting acrylic cement, commonly used as dental cement. Such cement is slightly exother-mic in setting, which means that heat is generated as it cures. This heat does not destroy too many bone cells, and the hardened cement distributes the stresses fairly evenly to the surrounding bone, which can then regenerate itself unhindered.

Recent research indicates that the stem of bone implants can be finely coated with ceramic materials into which calcified bone will grow, so there is no need to cement the joints. In another development, small sections of sterilized coral, which is light and has a porous structure similar to bone, can be implanted. This acts as a support stucture to regenerative cells called osteoblasts, which lay down new bone around the coral implant. It is sometimes used between deliberate breaks in bones that need lengthening, or carved into shape to replace facial structures.

Bone is piezoelectric, which means that its electrical characteristics change as a function of the forces applied to it. By inducing minute electrical potentials in the bone, the regenerative process can be accelerated. These modern techniques often result in speedier recovery. The tiny currents are induced by electromagnets, and the procedure is termed electromagnetic bone stimulation.

Artificial hearts

The search for a permanent mechanical heart device has been going on for many years. One device, the Jarvik-7 heart, which has been used in human implantation surgery, was first implanted in calves for initial testing. It consists of two pneumatically driven ventricles sewn to the atria of the natural heart and connected to an external control and pumping unit via air hoses. A flexible diaphragm separates the air from the blood; varying the air pressure causes it to move up and down, pumping blood as it does so.

A problem with these artificial hearts is that recipients need to be hooked up to a control apparatus, which severely restricts them from living a normal life. For an artificial heart to be anything but a temporary measure before a human heart is available, it must be totally self-contained. Tests have been carried out on animals with battery-powered devices, but the search is on for a powering mechanism that will run for many years without replacement.

An interim measure that has been approved for use in the United States is the left ventricular assist device (LVAD). These have been used by people with severe heart failure to take over the heart's pumping action until a donor heart becomes available. The pump is implanted in the patient's abomen and connected to the left ventricle. A cable attached to the pump runs out

◄ Finishing the manufacture of a Jarvik-7 artificial heart. The body of the heart is made of layers of polyurethane biomer and glass-fiber fabric. The manufacture of a single heart takes 10 days.

BIONIC EAR

Many totally deaf people can now be given some hearing with a cochlear implant, which directly stimulates the nerve fibers of the inner ear in response to sound picked up by an external microphone. The sound quality is often restricted, however, and people who have never had hearing may be unable to decipher the unfamiliar sensations. The sound quality is not perfect, but combined with lip reading it can enable some deaf people to communicate more easily with the hearing world.

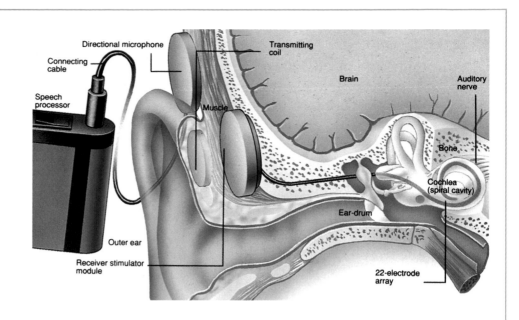

through the skin and is connected to a small electrical or battery-powered computer worn around the waist. Patients are shown how to control the device and can leave the hospital as little as three weeks after implantation. It leaves them free to move around and build up strength for transplant surgery. More data is needed on long-term use of LVADs, but it is thought they may provide a solution for patients who have been turned down for transplant surgery.

Rejection of foreign material by the body continues to be a problem. Drug therapy helps minimize the risk, but research into blood-material reactions to find suitable alternatives is ongoing.

Nonmechanical devices

Not all prostheses are mechanical. Some provide a substitute for a signal. The best known of these is the cardiac pacemaker. The heart's own natural pacemaker is a small piece of excitable tissue that, when modulated by nerve signals, controls the rate at which the heart beats. It is located between the atria and the ventricles. The electrical impulse it generates first causes the atria to contract and is then conducted by a specialized short piece of nervous tissue to the ventricles, which perform the real work of pumping.

Implantable pacemakers are now the norm. The early models used comparatively primitive timing circuits, but pacemakers have now become smarter in a number of ways. Some emit pulses only when they recognize that the heart is not beating spontaneously at the correct rate, while others sense the weak pulse that the natural pacemaker produces in the atrium and use that to trigger the main pulse. Many can now be adjusted by telemetry from the outside to give optimum

matching to the patient, and they can also report their own performance to an external receiver, having kept a record of possibly a few million recent heartbeats.

Helping the blind to see

People who are blind because of damage to the retina of the eye or the optic nerve connecting it to the brain may still have a perfectly good visual cortex, the surface of the brain at the back of the head where something like an electrical representation of the image appears. Work has been done by the Medical Research Council in the United Kingdom to stimulate the cortex directly with electrical signals. A silicone-rubber mold carrying a 16-by-16 grid of electrodes is implanted underneath the patient's skull. The electrodes are in direct contact with the surface of the cortex and can each be addressed individually by a form of radio receiver.

Signals are transmitted by induction from a coil outside the head, as is the power needed to operate the receivers. The external transmitter can be connected to a television camera, which also breaks up the pictures it sees into a 16-by-16 grid. The wearer experiences an arrangement of bright flashes that would, for example, allow single letters to be recognized.

The technical difficulties to overcome in constructing such a prosthesis, for example, preventing water from the tissue fluid from getting into the electrodes, have in principle been solved, and a number of these devices have been transplanted.

SEE ALSO: ALLOY • BONES AND FRACTURE TREATMENT • HEART PACEMAKER • HEART SURGERY • SURGERY • TRANSPLANT

Biofuel

Biofuel is a term used to describe all fuels of organic origin. Coal, natural gas, and oil are biofuels found underground that were formed by the decomposition of plants millions of years ago. Plant material trapped between layers of sediment was subjected to temperature and pressure changes by movements of Earth's crust, which converted it to carbon and hydrocarbon compounds. Because of their age, such materials are known as fossil fuels and are nonrenewable. More recently, the term *biofuel* has been used to describe renewable sources of energy derived from wood, waste materials, and crop plants.

All plants contain stored chemical energy in their cells that can be converted into useful forms of energy, such as heat. The process of converting organic material, or biomass, into energy is called bioconversion. Energy can be released from biomass by a number of processes—burning, fermentation, or chemical or bacterial breakdown. Burning provides heat that can be used directly or to drive turbines to produce electricity. Fermentation converts plant sugars into carbon dioxide and ethanol, which can then be used as a liquid fuel. Chemical breakdown can provide synthetic gases and fuel oils, while bacterial processes can be tailored to produce methane, alcohols, and a range of other chemicals.

Wood and charcoal

Wood is the world's oldest fuel and is still the main source of energy for cooking and heating in developing countries. Its use in industrialized nations has been increasing since the 1980s, when massive rises in the price of oil and improvements

▲ In the tropical rain forests of the Amazon, wood is cleared and turned into charcoal for fuel. Charcoal burns more efficiently than wood, and in some countries it is used in industrial manufacturing. Nearly 40 percent of the energy used in steel making in Brazil is obtained from charcoal.

in wood-burning stoves made it an attractive proposition to rural homeowners in countries including the United States. Industry, too, is reverting to wood at a growing rate. Furnaces burning sawdust, wood chips, or special wood pellets are becoming very popular since the introduction of a new type of burner, the fluidized bed combustor, which is extremely efficient and can even burn wood that is wet.

Electric power plants also burn wood, and in many areas where there is no coal and nuclear power plants are too expensive to build, it is still the best fuel. Small power plants, of about 50 MW output, can supply rural communities with electricity economically by burning wood chips. The Vermont Gasifier in Burlington, Vermont, uses a low-pressure process to turn wood chips into gas that is then fed to high-efficiency turbines that convert it to electricity. Burning wood can cause pollution problems—the smoke from some wood fires contains many substances that may cause illness, even cancer. However, wood contains little sulfur, so the acid rain that is caused by the release of sulfur oxides from coal and oil does not occur with wood combustion. Where wood is the only cheaply available fuel, as in less-developed countries, this advantage may be counterbalanced by the destructive environmental effects of deforestation.

More promising is the conversion of wood to wood alcohol, better known as methanol or methyl alcohol. Being liquid, it is suitable for powering aircraft and motor vehicles that currently run on oil-based products. Motor cars will run satisfactorily on methanol, and diesel engines will work well on a mixture of 95 percent methanol and 5 percent oil. Blends of methanol and gasoline are already in use in Europe and many other countries are considering methanol-from-wood pilot plants. When engines are fueled with methanol, no lead is added and much less pollution is produced than when they are fueled by gasoline or diesel.

Charcoal is another fuel made by burning wood in a much reduced air supply. This process converts the complex chemicals in the structure of wood into simpler ones that burn more easily.

Fermentation

Other useful biofuels are the alcohols produced by fermentation. Fermentation is a microbial process where bacteria or yeasts break down a carbon-containing substance, or substrate, in the absence of oxygen. Typical carbon sources

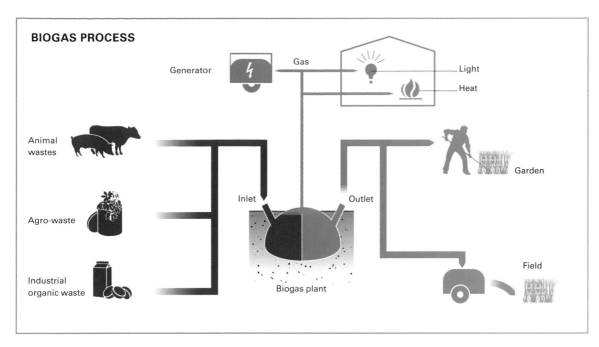

BIOGAS PROCESS

Generator — Gas — Light — Heat

Animal wastes

Agro-waste

Industrial organic waste

Inlet — Outlet

Biogas plant

Garden

Field

◀ Biogas is a useful product of the breakdown of organic matter by bacteria. Complex molecules, such as carbohydrates, proteins, and lipids found in agricultural wastes, are broken down into low-molecular-weight compounds, including methane and carbon dioxide. Methane can be collected and used for heating, lighting, and conversion into electricity by a generator. The material left by the biogas process can be used as a useful fertilizer, as it is rich in nutrients. Any harmful pathogenic organisms present in the waste are killed by the heat generated during digestion.

include grains such as corn and barley, residues from other commercial processes, particularly molasses from sugarcane; and agricultural wastes like straw, chaff, and rice husks. Nearly 95 million tons (86 million tonnes) of agricultural waste are generated every year by the United States, making it the largest potential feedstock for biofuel.

Ethanol is the most widely produced artificial biofuel, and more than 1.5 billion gallons (5.7 billion l) are added to gasoline in the United States annually. It is used to increase the octane rating and improve the emission quality of exhaust gases. Most ethanol comes from fermented cornstarch, but a major research program is underway to increase the amount derived from agricultural waste. This type of ethanol is called bioethanol. A major drawback to its production is the non-uniformity of the feedstock, which can contain complex compounds such as pectins, hemi-celluloses, and lignins. Traditional yeasts used in fermentation can only make use of 6-carbon atom sugars like glucose, so new systems of enzymes that can chop these compounds up into usable sugars are being developed. Experiments are also taking place to genetically engineer organisms that can produce ethanol from multiple substrates.

Another gasoline replacement, biodiesel, is an ester (an acid derivative) rather than an alcohol. It can be made from oils such as soybean, rapeseed, and vegetable oil or from animal fats. The conversion process is called transesterification and involves mixing the oil with alcohol to form fatty esters such as methyl or ethyl ester. These compounds can be mixed with ordinary diesel fuel or used neat. Current production in the United States is 30 million gallons (113 million l)

per year and looks set to rise, particularly in areas where people are heavily exposed to diesel fumes such as at airports or in workplaces with diesel machinery.

Biogas

Biogas is the term used to describe the gas produced by bacteria as they break down organic material under anaerobic (unoxygenated) conditions. These methanogens (methane-producing bacteria) are the last in the chain of microorganisms that degrade organic compounds to their

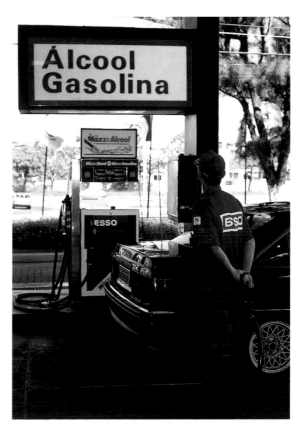

◀ Gas stations selling fuel that has had a biologically derived alcohol added to it are becoming increasingly common throughout the Americas. As well as reducing the consumption of fossil fuels, adding alcohol results in cleaner exhaust emissions.

GROWING FUEL

With the growth in the use of biofuels has come the need to grow crops for specific purposes in so-called energy plantations. One such crop is the physic nut, *Jatropha curcas*, which is being grown in Nicaragua to provide a source of biodiesel.

Nicaragua has no petroleum reserves of its own and lacks the infrastructure to refine crude oil. Importing diesel to meet its energy needs consumes 59 percent of its export income, so the search began for a biological alternative. The physic nut is a native species, grown mainly for shade and hedging. Interest in it as a fuel began during World War II, when the Germans investigated its oil, curcas oil, as a possible substitute for petroleum-based fuels.

A trial plot of nearly 2,500 acres (1,000 ha) was planted in 1994 and is now producing 36,000 tons (33,300 tonnes) of fruit per year. After depulping, the fruit yields 5,500 tons (5,000 tonnes) of dry seed, which is heated, steam dried, and pressed to give a crude oil. About 1,750 tons (1,600 tonnes) of oil is extracted for the next stage, transesteri-fication. The raw oil is mixed with methanol, and potassium hydroxide is added as a catalyst. The mixture separates into methyl and ethyl esters, and a small quantity of glycerine. After removal of the glycerine, the esters are washed to remove traces of alcohol or potassium hydroxide. Nearly 98 percent of the curcas oil is turned into fuel.

With the trial now providing 0.3 percent of the national diesel market in Nicaragua, there are plans to scale up production, providing jobs and reducing the need for expensive imports. The local environment benefits because contour planting the

◄ Seeds and fruits (below) of the physic nut tree, *Jatropha curcas*. Species of this tree are common in many parts of the world, which opens the possibility for many countries with no natural reserves of petroleum to grow their own supplies of diesel.

trees stabilizes the soil and makes the best use of water resources; also, sulfur emissions from petroleum-based diesel are reduced.

simplest constituents, usually gases like methane and carbon dioxide. In theory, any type of organic material can be fermented or digested, but most biogas plants use diluted animal manures or sewage. Wastes from food-processing industries or slaughterhouses can be used if they are homogenous and in liquid form.

The process takes place in a digester, or fermentation tank. The size and operation of the tank depend on local conditions, the material to be digested, and how much gas is required to meet energy needs. Most plants are of the continuous type and are fed and emptied all the time, emptying through an overflow when new material is added. They are suitable for rural households as maintenance can be done as part of the daily routine, and gas production is constant.

On the basis of the substrate used, the tank may need several days or weeks to achieve stability. Agitating the slurry helps digestion, and some extra heat may be needed in cold climates. Once stabilized, gas production becomes steady and the output can be stored in a gas holder for use in heating systems or cooking. Biogas systems could be of value in developing countries, especially those that currently burn wood and are beginning to suffer deforestation. Another benefit of the process is the sludge that is left after digestion, which provides a valuable fertilizer for crops as it is rich in nitrogen, phosphorus, and potassium.

SEE ALSO: ALCOHOL • FERMENTATION • GASOLINE, SYNTHETIC • WASTEWATER TREATMENT

Biophysics

Biophysics is the application of physics techniques and physics "ways of thinking" to biological problems. One area where there has been a great deal of development is in molecular biophysics. What can the application of physical methods teach scientists about the molecules of which we are built?

Some of the most significant biological molecules are very large, up to 1 million times the size of a water molecule, and contain hundreds or thousands of atoms (water, H_2O, has only three atoms). Two of the major classes of these macromolecules are proteins (such as hemoglobin and collagen) and nucleic acids (DNA—deoxyribonucleic acid). It is the nucleic acids that store genetic information sufficient to determine our individual identities. Proteins are assembled using information carried by the nucleic acids to fulfill a variety of roles, including as enzymes speeding up biochemical reactions, as structural molecules (in skin, bone, tendons, and hair), and as part of molecular machines such as muscle.

One of the great physics achievements of the 20th century was the invention of methods to determine how the atoms in proteins or nucleic acids are organized. These structures, in turn, have revealed how the molecules function. For example, the structure of DNA, discovered in

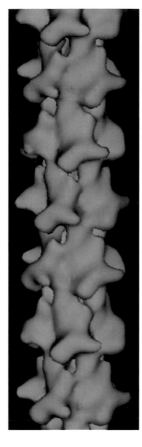

▲ A computer-generated view of a helical protein filament taken from a muscle that enables giant water bugs to fly.

◀ The structure of the foot-and-mouth virus, which was discovered using synchrotron radiation. The nucleic acid complex, seen in the center in pink, is surrounded by protein complexes. By determining the structure of the virus, scientists are moving toward finding a cure for this disease, which can have a devastating effect on farm livestock.

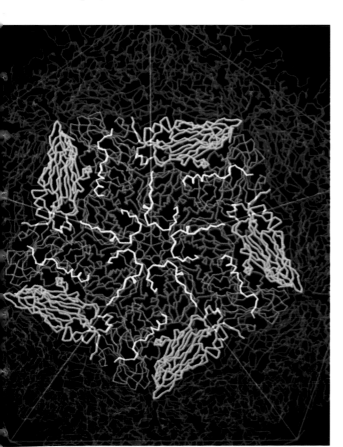

1952, showed how genetic information in a cell could be duplicated and transferred to two identical daughter cells during cell division. It also showed how the information (the genetic message) needed to define a particular protein was actually stored. But how are these structures determined?

The level of detail that can be seen in an ordinary microscope depends on the nature of the light illuminating the specimen. With visible light (wavelength about 1/65,000 in.), the largest objects that can be seen are about 1/150,000 in. Molecular dimensions are about 100 times smaller than this. In order to study such objects, it is necessary to use very short wavelength radiation—such as X rays, electrons, or neutrons.

X rays have great penetrating power, and appropriate "lenses" are very hard to make. But X rays can interact with regular structures at the atomic or molecular level to give so-called diffraction patterns. In 1913, not long after X rays were discovered (1895), it was found that they could be diffracted by crystals such as rock salt (NaCl) to give beautiful diffraction patterns. In the 1930s, it was found that proteins could also produce crystals. One of the tremendous achievements of the middle part of the last century was the invention of methods that could interpret diffraction patterns from protein crystals to solve the structure of the protein molecule. Today, the structures of over 1,000 macromolecules are known from X-ray crystallography, and more are solved each week.

The best information from crystals of biological macromolecules is usually obtained if the X-ray beams are very intense. The most intense beams available for such studies are currently produced by large circular particle accelerators known as synchrotrons, but there are not very many of these. In the United States, they are located at major research centers such as those at Brookhaven, Stanford, and Cornell. The high intensity of the X-ray beams allows increasingly complex structures to be studied. For example, one success at the Daresbury Laboratory in the United Kingdom has been the determination of the structure of the foot-and-mouth-disease virus (FMDV)—a complex of nucleic acid, surrounded by an outer spherical "shell" of protein. One of the benefits from knowing such a structure is that it is possible to use computer displays to help in the design of drug molecules that will interact with particular parts of the virus and so block its action. In the case of FMDV, the potential benefits to agriculture are clearly enormous. The structures of a number of other medically important viruses have also been solved.

As well as X rays, it is possible to use electrons to study molecular structures. The great advantage of electrons is that they carry a charge and so can be focused by electromagnetic "lenses" to produce images of the object. However, electron microscopes can only operate if they contain a vacuum; under such conditions, and with substantial electron irradiation, biological specimens are easily damaged. Much effort has gone into preserving molecular structures so that they can be observed in electron microscopes before they are destroyed. The images obtained are then often computer processed to provide more reliable information.

With modern electron-microscope methods, it is possible to view the internal structure of protein molecules. Soon, for particular types of specimens, such as two-dimensional crystalline sheets of molecules, the resolution obtained will be comparable to that achieved with X-ray crystallography.

Observing molecule changes

One of the ambitions of many biologists is not just to determine molecular structures but also to be able to see changes in these molecules as they go through their normal activities. Muscle is a molecular machine in which protein molecules move on a time scale of milliseconds or less to produce muscular force. Using synchrotron radiation, it is possible to record the pattern produced by muscle molecules in about five milliseconds. If the muscle is stimulated to produce force, the X-ray diffraction pattern changes as the molecules move. Biophysicists are currently following changes in these patterns to determine the nature of the movements involved so that the origin of muscular force can be determined at the molecular level.

Size ratios

An interesting discovery in biophysics has been the relationship between the size of an organism and its metabolic rate. As the body size of a species gets bigger, its metabolic rate falls, so the animal becomes more energy efficient. Larger species need lower metabolic rates or they would get too hot. First observed in the 1930s by a U.S. veterinarian, Max Kleiber, this relationship has been found to hold true from the smallest microorganism to the largest animal, the blue whale. What makes this surprising is that, under the rules of three-dimensional geometry, the scaling relationship between body mass and metabolic rate should be a two-thirds power. In fact, it turns out to be a three-quarter power.

In 1997, a group of researchers from New Mexico in the United States developed Kleiber's law by looking at plant nutrient networks and found the same scaling ratio held true for plants. They reasoned that to deliver nutrients with maximum efficiency to cells, plant and animal networks must have a fractal structure, which effectively creates a fourth spatial dimension. This ability to exploit another dimension could well be the source of biodiversity. If scaling did not exist, all organisms would operate at the same level of energy efficiency. Because species vary in their energy efficiency, they eat different quality foods, creating niches for a wide variety of species to develop and adapt in the course of evolution.

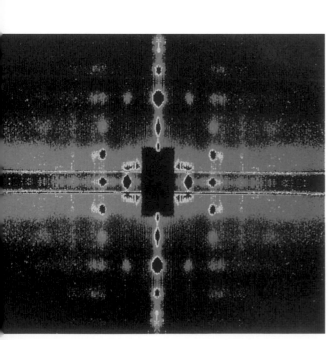

◀ A diffraction pattern, obtained through synchrotron X ray, of a turbot's fin muscle. The regular pattern shows that the muscle is highly organized at a molecular level. In the image on the left, the muscle was at rest, while the image below—in which the molecules have moved—was taken while the muscle was producing a force. Each pattern was recorded in about five milliseconds.

SEE ALSO: BIOCHEMISTRY • CRYSTALS AND CRYSTALLOGRAPHY • MICROSCOPE, ELECTRON • MOLECULAR BIOLOGY • PHYSICS

Biotechnology

In the three decades since scientists first learned how to cut, splice, and recombine genes, the use of living organisms in the manufacture of new products has become a major industry. Genetically modified bacteria, yeasts, and other one-celled creatures are being used to create new drugs, vaccines, and industrial chemicals, with annual sales in billions of dollars. Meanwhile, modified plants and animals are increasing yields and reducing costs for farmers.

There is nothing new about using living organisms in industry. For centuries, we have made beer and wine by fermentation and cheese by the action of natural enzymes on milk. Yeasts have been used to make bread rise. For decades, pharmaceutical companies have used microorganisms to produce antibiotics. Usually, however, the term *biotechnology* is used to refer only to the manipulation of life at the molecular level.

Most of these technologies grow out of our understanding of how deoxyribonucleic acid (DNA) directs the manufacture of proteins. Each protein is a unique chain of amino acids, and a single gene—a segment of the long strand of DNA that makes up a chromosome—codes for that particular amino acid sequence. Biotechnology came into being when scientists learned how to insert a foreign gene into a living cell in such a way that it would be "expressed"—that is, so that the cell would make the protein for which it codes.

Perhaps the best-known product made in this way is human insulin. Others include human growth hormone, used to correct dwarfism; several forms of interferon, used to stimulate the immune system; and tissue plasminogen activator, used to dissolve blood clots to minimize the damage from a heart attack. These products

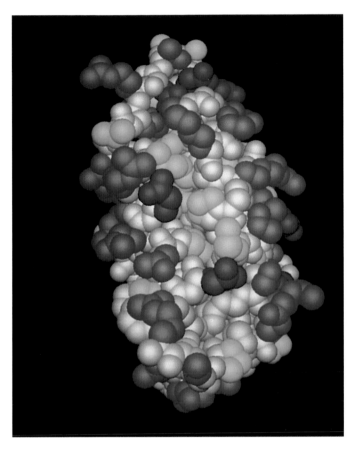

▲ Computer image of a biomanufactured protein, known as GM-CSF. Found naturally in the body, it is used to treat blood disorders.

▼ An immunosuppressant drug (yellow), showing how its shape fits an immune system protein.

are all substances that occur naturally in the human body; biotechnology has made it possible to produce them in large enough quantities to use as drugs.

Engineered bacteria

The technique most often used to make these products depends on the fact that the DNA in a bacterial cell is in the form of rings, called plasmids. Plasmids are removed from the cell, genes for the desired product are inserted in the ring, and the plasmids returned to cells. While producing all the other proteins normally needed in the course of bacterial life, each modified cell also manufactures the protein for which the inserted gene codes.

The most commonly used bacterium is *Escherichia coli* (*E. coli*), found in the human intestine. To avoid any possible side effect should the modified bacteria be released into the environment, most workers use a weakened strain called K-12, which grows in artificial cultures but cannot survive in humans or animals. Other simple organisms, including yeasts and fungi as well as animal cells in culture, have been used.

Cells that take up and express the new gene are separated, grown in large quantities, and harvested, and the product is extracted from the soup of chemicals that results. Usually, this is done by chromatography (by which the mixture is pulled through a porous material that separates substances by their molecular weight) or by forcing the mixture through membranes that select molecules by size. Because contaminants might remain, the resulting product has to be rigorously tested for purity.

It is possible to insert genes in higher animals, but the process is much more difficult. Usually fertilized eggs are surgically removed, the new genes inserted through the cell wall,

▲ Transgenic ewes are raised not for their wool or meat but for an enzyme that they produce in their milk, which is used to treat emphysema. Similar research is being carried out in cows to obtain the human serum albumin, used in the treatment of burns, demand for which currently stands at over 660 tons (600 tonnes) each year.

and the eggs reimplanted in the original or surrogate mothers. It may take hundreds of tries before the inserted gene is expressed. So far, this sort of work has been confined to the laboratory; though many companies have obtained patents on genetically modified, or transgenic, animals.

Perhaps the biggest breakthrough in this selective breeding process has been Dolly the sheep, bred at the Roslin Institute in the United Kingdom. Dolly is a clone, that is, she is an identical replica of her donor mother. All her nuclear DNA originated in a cell from an adult sheep's udder tissue, which was put together with an oocyte that had its nucleus removed, and subjected to an electric current. The two cells became fused as one and were allowed to divide until they became a small embryo, which was then implanted into a surrogate mother.

Cloning animals in this way would make it possible to produce a number of genetically identical offspring from an animal with superior physical or biological characteristics. These animals could be further modified at the egg-culturing phase by

inserting genes for disease resistance or other desirable traits. The reality is that cloning is at present a very difficult process, requiring large numbers of donor eggs, and it has a considerable ethical dimension to be debated.

Safer vaccines

Genes have also been inserted into viruses to make vaccines. A virus has a protein coat that enables the virus to penetrate the outer membrane of a cell plus DNA (or RNA), which codes for the proteins. Once inside a cell, the viral DNA uses the machinery of the cell to make copies of itself and of its protein coat, which reassemble into more viruses.

To defend against a virus or any other foreign invader, the immune system creates antibodies: complex molecules designed to fit the exact shape of a part of the virus protein coat—called an antigen—and attach to it. The purpose of a vaccine is to stimulate the immune system to make antibodies without forcing the body to experience the disease. One way to do this is by killing or attenuating the virus so it cannot reproduce. Unfortunately, if the virus is not completely deactivated, the vaccine may cause the disease it was designed to prevent. Bioengineered vaccines are made by inserting the gene for an antigen into the DNA of an otherwise harmless virus, such as the *Vaccinia* virus used to immunize against smallpox. It is possible to add several genes to a single virus, producing a vaccine that protects against several illnesses at once.

GENETIC ENGINEERING

The basic technique of genetic engineering takes DNA from plasmid rings in bacteria. These are then spliced using enzymes, and a fragment of the desired DNA is inserted back into the cell. Those bacteria that express the gene by producing the required proteins can then be cultured on a large scale.

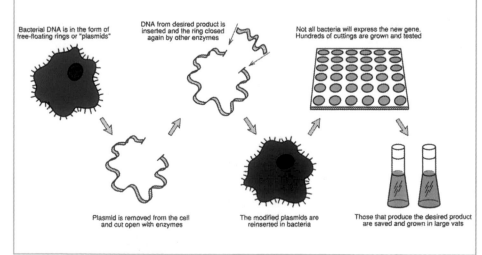

Bacterial DNA is in the form of free-floating rings or "plasmids"

DNA from desired product is inserted and the ring closed again by other enzymes

Not all bacteria will express the new gene. Hundreds of cuttings are grown and tested

Plasmid is removed from the cell and cut open with enzymes

The modified plasmids are reinserted in bacteria

Those that produce the desired product are saved and grown in large vats

Another use of this type of gene therapy may be to produce a vaccine for cancer. Investigations are under way into using genetically modified tumor cells to express a protein that appears to protect against an agressive form of skin cancer (melanoma) in animals. The protein—granulocyte macrophage colony stimulating factor, or GM-CSF—is a naturally occurring compound with the ability to enhance the immune system's recognition of antigens on the surface of tumor cells. Early results have shown that a prototype vaccine can lead to rejection of an established tumor in animals, but it will take many years before a vaccine suitable for human cancers is approved for use.

Monoclonal antibodies

Biotechnology has provided a way to make antibodies to order. In the classic procedure, a foreign antigen is injected into a mouse (or other animal), causing the mouse's immune system to create cells called B lymphocytes, which produce antibodies to that antigen. A few days later, B lymphocytes obtained from the mouse are fused with cancer cells, creating immortal cells called hybridomas. The hybridomas that produce the desired antibody are separated out and grown in a cell culture to make large quantities of just that antibody; since the antibodies are all alike they are called monoclonal.

Monoclonal antibodies are widely used in clinical tests, such as those used to detect the

▲ The larger mouse, the first transgenic animal, has a gene for rat growth hormone. It is 50 percent bigger than its normal-size brother. Even larger mice have since been bred that are twice as big as normal and more muscular.

presence of drugs or the AIDS virus. These tests use an antibody that will attach to the substance to be detected; this antibody is chemically linked to a radioactive or fluorescent tracer or to an enzyme that will produce a color change in another chemical. A solution of these antibodies is mixed with a sample of blood, urine, or other body fluid or tissues, then treated to separate out only antibodies that have attached to a target. The presence of the tracer then signals a positive test. The most familiar example of this technology is the home pregnancy test.

Since it is now possible to synthesize DNA in any desired sequence, strands of DNA (or RNA) are in use as drugs and research tools. When the ladderlike double helix of DNA is split into two complementary chains, a short segment of DNA that is designed to be complementary to a gene will bind to that gene. Such "DNA probes" can be used to test for the presence of a particular gene in a DNA sample. Similarly, a strand of DNA or RNA can bind to a complementary gene in a living organism, inactivating it. A strand of nucleic acid used in this way is called an "anti-sense" drug. Such drugs may turn off the oncogene that causes a cancer cell to reproduce indefinitely.

Biotech in the chemical industry

The industry making the most use of biotechnology is of course the one that already deals with living creatures: agriculture. Plant breeders may now shorten the tedious process of crossing and recrossing

---

MONOCLONAL ANTIBODIES

Monoclonal antibodies are produced by stimulating a mouse's immune system to produce antibodies. The lymphocytes produced are then fused with cancer cells to create hybridomas. Hybridomas that produce the right antibodies can then be separated and cultured to create more identical copies of the antibody. These antibodies can then be used to trace substances in the body.

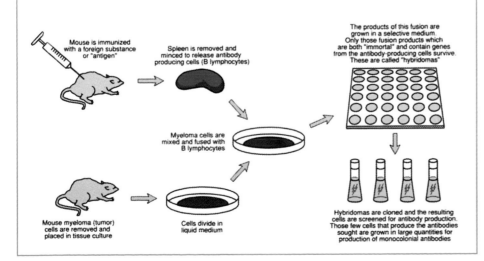

Mouse is immunized with a foreign substance or "antigen"

Spleen is removed and minced to release antibody producing cells (B lymphocytes)

Myeloma cells are mixed and fused with B lymphocytes

Mouse myeloma (tumor) cells are removed and placed in tissue culture

Cells divide in liquid medium

The products of this fusion are grown in a selective medium. Only those fusion products which are both "immortal" and contain genes from the antibody-producing cells survive. These are called "hybridomas"

Hybridomas are cloned and the resulting cells are screened for antibody production. Those few cells that produce the antibodies sought are grown in large quantities for production of monoclonial antibodies

■ *The future of pharmaceutical manufacturing may lie not in vats of bacteria but in "biopharming" of higher plants and animals. Scientists have created transgenic (genetically modified) plants and animals that produce useful drugs.*

■ *Pharmaceutical Proteins Ltd. in Edinburgh, Scotland has raised four transgenic ewes whose milk contains an enzyme called alpha-1 antitrypsin; persons lacking this enzyme run a particular risk of contracting emphysema. Five liters of milk from one ewe yielded enough of the enzyme to treat one patient for a year.*

■ *Gene Pharming Europe B.V., a company in Leiden, the Netherlands, has reported creating cows whose milk contains lactoferrin, an antibacterial agent. Cows are considered the ideal animals to use as biofactories because they produce far more milk than sheep or goats, but the surgery to remove their eggs is much more difficult and expensive. The Dutch workers got around this by collecting eggs from a slaughterhouse and fertilizing them in a test tube.*

■ *A Japanese company has engineered silkworms to produce a vaccine for hepatitis B. The worms are squeezed to harvest the product.*

■ *With the successful birth of Dolly the sheep has come the question of whether it is now possible to clone humans. The answer is probably yes, but many countries have moved to ban such attempts on ethical grounds. In practice, it took 277 attempts at fusing cells to produce Dolly and required 400 unfertilized eggs from donor ewes. Many of the fetuses were spontaneously aborted and found to have severe deformities. Current human in-vitro fertilization can only recover 5 to 10 eggs at a time, so it would take at least 40 donors for each prospective baby—and sheep are between 3 and 10 times more successful at establishing a pregnancy.*

plants by simply inserting desirable genes for such traits as disease resistance into already successful crops. Bioengineered drugs and vaccines have enhanced the health of farm animals, and biomanufactured hormones promise to increase the yield of meat and milk.

A future goal of biotechnology is to make proteins that do not already exist in nature. The biological activity of a protein is determined by its shape. The complex shape of an enzyme interlocks precisely with other molecules, causing them to react; the shape of a hormone connects with a receptor on the surface of a cell, and so on. By designing molecules with new shapes, we might be able to cause new reactions or enhance existing ones.

▲ A large scale fermenter used for producing monoclonal antibodies on a commercial scale in batches of 525 gallons (2,000 l).

Preserving biodiversity

As well as creating new species and substances by manipulating genes, biotechnology is playing a key part in preserving existing characteristics of plants and animals. Techniques such as in-vitro culturing are useful in maintaining the germ plasm of plants that propagate asexually, such as bananas and onions, or that are difficult to keep as seeds. Animal semen, embryos, and even hair follicles from rare species and indigenous breeds can be kept frozen to preserve characteristics like hardiness, heat tolerance, and disease resistance that may be threatened by imported flocks.

SEE ALSO: AGRICULTURAL SCIENCE • GENETIC ENGINEERING • IMMUNOLOGY • MOLECULAR BIOLOGY

Black Hole

◀ Black holes are thought to grow by the process of accretion. The gravity of a black hole is so strong that it can drag matter from a nearby star, heating it to such high temperatures that X rays and gamma rays are given off just before the material crosses the event horizon. Emissions like these are often the only indication to astronomers that there may be a black hole lurking in a region of the Universe.

A black hole is a region of space where gravity is so immensely strong that even light cannot escape it. Although black holes cannot be seen directly, they have some extraordinary properties, and there is increasing evidence that they really do exist.

Observations have given rise to the idea that there are two types of black hole: those formed by the collapse of a massive star and supermassive or galactic black holes with a mass of about 10 to 100 billion times that of our Sun. It is also possible that some black holes may have been formed in the Big Bang. Stellar black holes have masses of between 4 and 15 Suns and are believed to be formed when a star dies in a huge explosion called a supernova.

Gravity is responsible for both the birth and death of stars like our Sun. A star is born when a huge and diffuse cloud of hydrogen gas collapses under gravity. For a time, nuclear fires at the heart of a star provide a pressure that counterbalances gravity and holds up the surface layers of matter against further contraction. Our Sun is at this stage. Its core is generating heat like a huge, continuously exploding hydrogen bomb.

Eventually the nuclear fuel of a star will run out. When this happens—and this should not happen to our Sun for many billions of years—gravity will prevail again. If a star contains more matter than about three Suns, then there is no known force in the Universe that can stop it from collapsing to a point where it has no volume but infinite density, creating something called a singularity. This becomes the center of the black hole. At this point, space reaches its maximum curvature and gravitational tides diverge, stretching matter to an infinite thinness; theoretically, no solid object could survive hitting a singularity.

Surrounding the center of the black hole is a region called the event horizon. This is effectively a point of no return for anything approaching a black hole. Once the event horizon has been crossed nothing, not even light, can ever escape. The collapsing star finally falls through its own event horizon and vanishes abruptly from sight.

Supermassive black holes

Not all objects thought to be black holes represent the end stage in the life of a giant star. Observations of "active" galaxies show that they appear to be emitting more energy than should be present from calculations. These galaxies are known as Seyfert galaxies, quasars, and blazars, and are all thought to be powered by massive black holes.

One theory of how they come to be so big is that a small seed black hole in a very dense galactic nucleus begins to swallow up gas and nearby normal stars. If the conditions are right, the black hole can grow to billions of times the mass of the

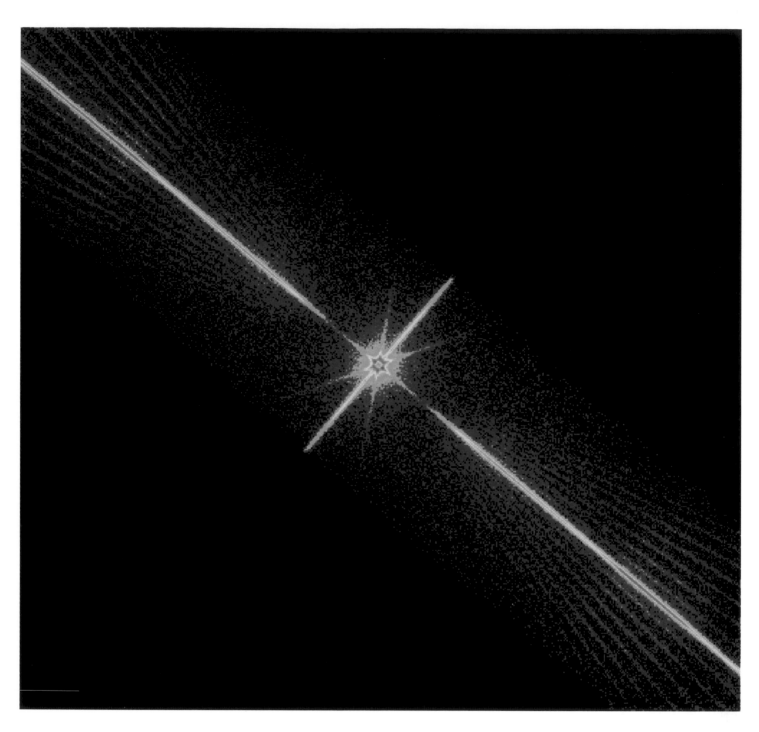

Sun in an extremely short period of time. Another possibility is that gas in a dense galactic nucleus becomes so concentrated that it forms a super-massive star that undergoes its life-cycle at a rapid rate, collapsing into a massive black hole.

Spotting a black hole

Because light cannot escape from a black hole, finding one out in space is very difficult. Proof of their existence is coming instead from observations of X-ray and gamma-ray emissions from stars with hidden companions. When a black hole passes through a cloud of gas or is close to an ordinary star, it begins to pull matter toward it, forming what is known as an accretion disk. As the matter falls toward the center, it gains kinetic

▲ The X-ray spectrum (the bright strip running top left to bottom right) of a possible black hole, as captured by the Chandra X-ray Observatory. The X rays are produced by particles in the accretion disk as they are about to cross the event horizon and vanish into the black hole. From this data researchers can estimate how far inward the accretion disk extends.

energy and is squeezed by tidal forces that heat the atoms, which become ionized. When they reach a temperature of several million degrees, they emit gamma and X rays. These escape into space before the matter crosses the event horizon and can be detected by astronomical instruments.

Searches among binary star systems emitting X rays have come up with a number of likely prospects. The mass of a black hole can be determined by observing changes in the spectral emissions of the companion star. Depending on how big this "wobble" is, astronomers can tell whether it is being orbited by a black hole or a neutron star. Another clue comes from variations in X-ray intensity: matter falls into a black hole sporadically rather than steadily. In fact, these binary systems can turn off for decades at a time. Astronomers also look for periodic cutoffs in emissions when the source is eclipsed by its companion star.

One binary system that has been investigated is Cygnus X-1. The companion star is a supergiant with a surface temperature of about 31,000 K. Because it is a source of irregular and variable X rays, it was thought to be a prime candidate for having a black hole with a mass equivalent to seven Suns orbiting it. However, difficulties in calculating the mass of the companion star and how far apart the binary is have led astronomers to think that the unseen component is a much smaller neutron star.

Einstein and Newton

A proper understanding of black holes had to wait until the U.S. physicist Albert Einstein improved the law of gravity put forward by the English mathematician Isaac Newton. Newton's law describes the pull one material's body exerts on another. Earth's gravity, for example, holds our feet on the ground and the Moon in its orbit. But Newton's law applies only when gravity is weak; around a black hole gravity is very, very strong indeed.

Einstein's theory predicts that a black hole will strongly distort space and time in its neighborhood. We can begin to understand this by thinking of space as a rubber sheet. Any mass, a star or planet, for example, creates a small gravitational dimple in the sheet. In this scenario, a black hole warps space into a bottomless well, down which

BIRTH OF A BLACK HOLE

Most black holes are thought to form when a massive star burns up all its fuel and can no longer support the weight of its outer layers. This is the point at which the star starts to collapse (left). As it does so, its density and surface gravity increase. The star begins to contract, and the amount of light (blue arrows) it gives off slowly decreases (center).

Eventually, the star collapses to a critical volume, where its gravitational forces are too strong for light to escape. This is called the event horizon (right). The only indication of a black hole's existence is the presence of high-energy radiation, emitted when particles of interstellar dust or gas are dragged into the black hole by gravity.

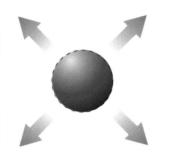  

matter and light fall and out of which nothing can ever climb. Artistic representations of a black hole make it look flat because it is impossible to portray the fourth dimension, time.

The steeply curved space surrounding a black hole can cause some very odd things to happen. If an astronaut were to fall feet first into a black hole and we were to watch, we would witness the fol-

NOAO

HST

◀ The Centaurus A galaxy, the closest example of an active galactic nucleus to Earth, is only 10 million light years away. In this complex region, a hidden, massive black hole at the center of the galaxy is thought to be feeding on a smaller galaxy that has collided with it. Astronomers have found a twisted disk of hot gas being swept into the black hole that has not yet aligned itself to the black hole's spin axis. This may be because the gas disk has only recently formed, or because of the gravitational pull on the material of the bigger galaxy.

lowing. First, although his watch would tell him that the fall to the center of the black hole takes only a short time, to us the astronaut's fall would seem to take forever. Then, as he got closer and closer to the event horizon, the astronaut would begin to fade from sight as it became more difficult for light to escape.

There would also be other bizarre occurrences. Close to the event horizon, the astronaut would see stars and constellations beyond the black hole, which would begin to shift and distort; the intense gravity of the hole would be bending starlight. There would even come a time when the astronaut would see the back of his own head when he looked toward the black hole. Light reflected from his head would be bent once around the hole before striking his eyes.

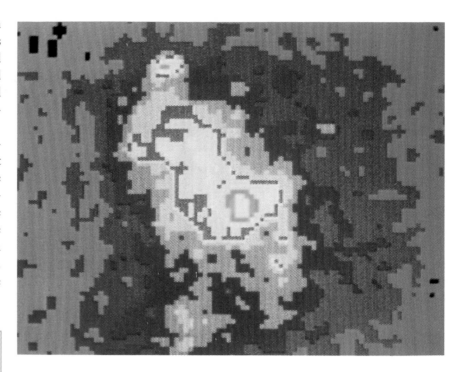

FACT FILE

- *Karl Schwarzchild was the first astronomer to use Einstein's theory of gravity to calculate how small a star, or sun, must shrink so that its gravity becomes strong enough to trap light. Schwarzchild found that if our Sun were to become a black hole, it would have to contract until it was just 4 miles (6 km) across; that would make it less than one thousand million millionth of its present volume.*

- *There is even evidence that a supermassive black hole lurks at the heart of our own galaxy. Astronomers have observed material falling onto an unseen object near one of the stars in the constellation of Sagittarius. Estimates of its size put it at one million times the mass of our Sun.*

- *The method of gaining mass by accretion makes black holes more efficient at releasing energy than nuclear processes such as fission or fusion.*

- *Black holes need not be accompanied by enormous gravitational forces. It is only with the creation of star-sized black holes that matter is squeezed so small that intense gravity results. A supermassive black hole need only be as dense as air. And a black hole with the mass of the Universe might have just the density astronomers observe around us. So, at this moment, we may be living inside the largest black hole of all.*

Quantum mechanics

The British physicist Stephen Hawking has modified the theory of black holes and shown that they may not be as entirely all consuming as was thought. Quantum mechanics allows black holes to emit particles contrary to the laws of classical mechanics. Tiny particles such as electrons are continually popping into existence then popping out again before the laws of physics can protest that something is being created from nothing. Each particle is created together with its antiparticle, a sort of mirror image of itself, and each particle can only disappear again by colliding with its antiparticle.

Hawking has pointed out that if a particle and its antiparticle should pop into existence close to the event horizon of a black hole, one particle might fall into the black hole while its partner escaped. A collision between the two resulting in their destruction could then never occur; matter would have been permanently created. Einstein showed that mass and energy are the same thing, so the black hole would have to lose mass, or energy, to pay for the newly created particle. In short, the black hole would begin to "evaporate," or gradually lose matter. In practice, the rate of particle escape would be negligible and it would take billions of years for it to be noticed. The microscopic particles leaked by the black hole are now referred to by physicists as Hawking radiation.

▲ An X-ray image of our galaxy reveals an intense X-ray source in a compact region at the center. Any X-ray source in space is of interest to astronomers because it could be associated with a black hole. Astronomers also believe that quasars, distant and powerful radio sources, may be powered by black holes, but there is as yet no evidence for the theory.

SEE ALSO: ANTIMATTER • ASTRONOMY • ASTROPHYSICS • ELECTROMAGNETIC RADIATION • GRAVITY • QUANTUM THEORY • RELATIVITY • SUPERNOVA

Blood

Blood is the most essential transport mechanism in the human body. Its main tasks are to carry oxygen and nutrients to tissues and organs and to remove waste materials. Blood is also vital in defending the body against infections, regulating temperature, carrying chemical messages that affect body functions, and repairing the body's vessels to prevent it from bleeding to death.

The average adult body contains 10 pints (4.7 l) of blood, though people who live at high altitudes where there is less oxygen may carry up to 3½ pints (2 l) more. Blood consists of a watery fluid called plasma, and various cells—red blood cells (erythrocytes), white blood cells (leucocytes), and platelets (thrombocytes). New blood cells are produced in the marrow of long bones such as the leg and flat bones like the ribs and vertebrae. Worn out red blood cells are broken down by the liver and spleen, where their components are recycled into new cells or for compounds used elsewhere in the body.

Red blood cells carry oxygen to body tissues and remove carbon dioxide. They are flat and disklike in shape and are thinner in the middle than at the sides. Composed mainly of the oxygen carrying protein hemoglobin, they also transport enzymes and chemicals. White blood cells fight infections by surrounding bacteria and ingesting them or by producing antibodies that render the invading bacteria or virus harmless. Platelets are small cells that stick to the edges of a wound and each other to form a plug, sealing the break and preventing further blood loss.

Blood groups

Although all human blood looks the same, early attempts at transfusing blood from one person to another were often unsuccessful, with the recipient becoming very ill or even dying. It was not until 1901 that Karl Landsteiner, a U.S. pathologist, discovered that there were different blood groups.

Blood typing, or grouping, is carried out before a blood transfusion, to ensure compatibility of the donor's blood with that of the patient. It is also important in forensic medicine, where typing of bloodstains is a routine procedure.

Blood from the vast majority of people is classed in the groups A, B, AB, and O. Identification of these groups is based on the presence or absence of substances called A or B antigens (also called agglutinogens) that occur on the surface of red blood cells. Blood from someone whose red cells carry one of these antigens is

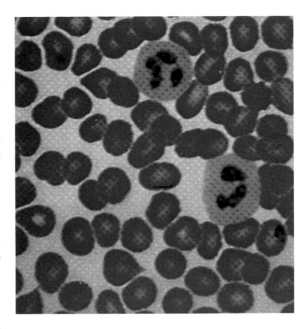

◀ Viewed under the microscope at a magnification of x75, human blood cells are revealed as tiny disks. The larger pink disks are white cells.

classed as Group A or Group B; if both antigens are present, it is Group AB; if neither is present, it is Group O. These antigens stimulate the formation of antibodies (also called agglutines), which are produced by the body as a defence against invading substances or organisms. They work by combining chemically with foreign antigens and making them harmless.

If blood from an incompatible group is transfused into a patient, the resulting agglutination could prove fatal, so cross-matching of the donor's blood with that of the patient is a vital procedure. The adverse reactions from transfusions happen when an antibody in the recipient's blood plasma attacks antigens on donor red cells.

Typing technique

The method used to determine a blood group is fairly simple. Red cells are extracted from the blood with a centrifuge and mixed with antisera containing known antibodies, and the presence or absence of agglutination observed. Comparatively simple apparatus may be used, such as a row of glass tubes or slides, or tiles containing indentations to hold the liquid. The antisera are obtained by repeated inoculation of blood containing a known antigen into animals or human volunteers, whose bodies react by producing the corresponding antibody. Serum from such immunized subjects is then extracted and used for typing.

In 1940, Landsteiner and Alexander Weiner made another important discovery. This was the Rhesus (Rh) factor, so-called after the rhesus monkey, whose blood contains this factor. The Rh factor is an antigen carried by about 85 percent of the population, such blood being typed as Rh-positive. When the Rh-factor is absent, blood is Rh-negative; such blood does not normally contain the anti-Rh antibody.

In transfusion, blood from patient and donor is typed according to Rh-factor and ABO grouping to ensure general compatibility; then, as a final precaution, the donor's red cells and the patient's serum are cross-matched. In theory, a person with group AB Rh⁺ blood could receive a donation from anybody (this blood group is known as the Universal Recipient), while a person with blood group O Rh⁻ (known as the Universal Donor) could donate to anybody. It is unlikely that such transfusions would be given except in the most dire emergency. Many additional groupings are also possible, and in forensic medicine, a dozen independent blood grouping systems are used to enable a blood sample to be identified with a high degree of probability.

Transfusion

Blood for transfusing is collected from live donors after a preliminary screening to find out whether they have any illnesses or infectious diseases. A sample is taken and tested for anemia before donation takes place. Up to a pint (450 ml) is usually taken from the donor from a vein in the left arm and collected in a plastic bag. Bags are bar coded with the donor's details to make the system safe and efficient.

Donated blood is subjected to extensive laboratory tests to make sure no disease-causing agents such as HIV or hepatitis are present. If passed for use, it can either be stored as whole blood or split into its components for specialist treatments. Whole blood can be stored in a refrigerator for up to seven weeks, but plasma can be dried or frozen and kept for several years.

During the transfusion process, the blood flows under gravity into the patient, or it may be pumped if a faster rate is necessary. In rapid transfusions, the blood is warmed to avoid shock to the patient's heart. It also passes through a filter to remove any clots that may have formed during storage that could cause an embolism in the patient.

Artificial blood

A great breakthrough in transfusion technology was the development of separation techniques. It was discovered that the red and white blood cells, and the platelets, could be removed, and the remaining plasma could be persuaded to yield the dissolved residues, the coagulants, albumin, and the proteins that provide immunities. The experimenters also discovered that it is possible to make concentrations of the constituents and administer them in whatever concentrations are required.

This "packed" blood can be richer than usual in red or white cells, or indeed in any constituent, and is used sometimes to give a boost to postoperative patients. They claim literally to feel strength and energy flowing back into their bodies. Oxygen starvation of some parts of the body can be very dangerous. Brain activity and heart-muscle action both need constant oxygen supplies. Three minutes without oxygen can cause

FIRST PREGNANCY

Rhesus negative blood in mother

Placenta

Anti-Rhesus antibody

Rhesus antigen (Rhesus positive)

Rhesus positive blood in fetus

SECOND PREGNANCY

Rhesus negative blood in mother

Rhesus positive blood is clumped by anti-Rhesus antibodies

RHESUS BABIES

When a Rh-negative mother conceives a Rh-positive baby, the two blood supplies may mix during delivery and the mother's blood can form antibodies against the Rh-factor. In subsequent pregnancies, she may produce anti-Rhesus bodies that attack the baby's red cells. The highly poisonous pigment released as they break down can attack the baby's nervous system and cause brain damage. A complete change of the baby's blood at birth can result in a healthy and totally undamaged baby.

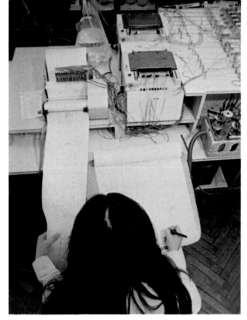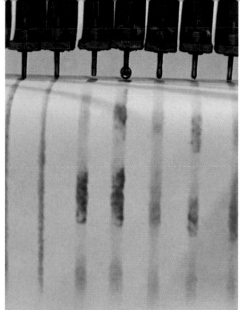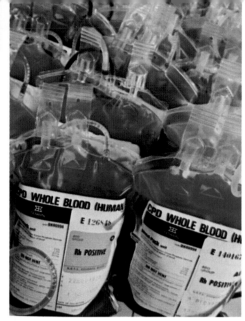

irreversible brain damage. In the event of a heavy loss of blood, it would be particularly useful to be able to inject a temporary blood substitute capable of transporting oxygen, instead of having to wait while the right blood groups are traced through a blood bank.

It would be extravagant, not to mention virtually impossible, to create a completely artifical blood that could perform every single function of real blood and that contained artificial versions of all its constituents. It is a much simpler proposition to design temporary artificial bloods that can carry out limited specific functions for short periods of time—such as during surgery—when the state of the patient may be critical.

At least six artificial blood substitutes have been developed. One is made by a fermentation process from genetically modified bacteria. Another is based on a protein solution extracted from cow's blood. A completely chemical substitute uses perfluorocarbons, an oily by-product from the manufacture of Teflon. These compounds have a great capacity for absorbing gases and are especially receptive to oxygen, hydrogen, carbon dioxide, nitrogen, and the inert gases. A technique developed at the University of Illinois employs blood cells synthesized from human and animal hemoglobin. The hemoglobin is stored in tiny artificial capsules a tenth of the diameter of a normal red cell. Because they can penetrate in a way that ordinary blood might not be able to, these blood cells can be of particular use to some victims of strokes and heart attacks.

Hematology

Hematology is the branch of pathology that deals with diseases of the blood. These range from inherited disorders such as hemophilia and thalassemia to conditions such as leukemia, which can develop in childhood or later life. There are several different types of leukemia. All of them involve excessive production of a certain type of blood cell. The multiplying cells never mature properly, which means they cannot carry out their normal functions, of which one of the most important is fighting infection.

Leukemia is treated with anticancer drugs and sometimes with radiation. The aim of treatment is to kill the leukemic cells while allowing the normal cells to survive. In some cases, bone marrow transplantation can give the patient a better chance of a long-term cure.

Another important breakthrough in hematology has been the development of rapid tests to diagnose inherited disorders of the blood. For example, a test to diagnose sickle-cell disease now takes only 40 minutes. Couples can find out whether one or both partners are carriers of the disease and the likelihood of conceiving an infected child; if they do, they will be offered tests when the woman becomes pregnant.

Growth factors

The discovery of natural chemicals that stimulate bone marrow cells to mature into different types of blood cells allows doctors to give better treatment for cancer and some types of anemia. These growth factors stimulate a particular kind of cell to grow, for example, erythropoietin (EPO) stimulates red cells to grow; another, called GM-CSF, promotes the growth of white cells.

Cancer patients have been among the first to benefit from the use of growth factors, as anticancer drugs can kill blood-forming cells in bone marrow. Doctors can give larger and more effective doses of these drugs if they also give patients growth factors to help their normal bone marrow recover more quickly. When EPO is given to people with kidney failure, they need fewer transfusions for anemia.

▲ After blood is donated, it is first tested by an automatic blood group analyzer (left). Samples are then dripped onto a roll of filter paper (center) to provide a permanent record of the blood. Blood pack units (right) are dated and stored by group type in cold conditions until they are needed for transfusion.

SEE ALSO: Bones and fracture treatment • Cancer treatment • Forensic science • Surgery • Transplant

Boat Building

Until the mid-1950s, wood was the traditional material used in boatbuilding. The development of a new material, glass-reinforced plastic (GRP), brought rapid changes by offering mass production techniques and greater flexibility in hull shapes. Today, most boats in the United States and Europe are constructed in GRP.

Plank construction

Boatbuilding in wood was and still is a skilled craft involving the use of a great many wooden components to build a watertight structure. This structure has to combine stability in the water with the ability to withstand stresses often comparable to those experienced by jet aircraft.

Wood boatbuilding follows two principal styles: clinker (or clincher), using overlapping planking, and carvel (or caravel), where the planking is smooth. The clinker, or lapstrake, technique gives a monocoque, or stressed-skin, construction. The shape of the craft is developed by the addition of successively fastened planks, sometimes using only a single mold or guidance shape amidships. After the planking is completed, light frames are steamed or sawed to shape and added to the interior to strap the planking together as a safeguard against a plank splitting along the grain. This construction makes the boat very light but vulnerable to hard use. The overlapping edges, or lands, of the planking are liable to wear, and it is difficult to keep the planking watertight once it has been disturbed. It is therefore normally used only for small, light craft such as beach boats.

In carvel construction, wooden planks are fitted edge to edge over a completed framework,

▲ The appearance of the Chinese junk has changed little over the centuries because the design of the hull and sails is very efficient.

◀ The simple dugout canoe, here used by the lagoon fishermen of Benin, West Africa, dates back about 8,000 years.

▶ Fishermen on the coast of Orissa, India, use boats that are made by lashing together several roughly-shaped planks to form a canoe.

which determines the shape and forms the structural support of the finished craft. The framework consists of a centerline piece called the keel with a companion piece called a keelson, a stem at the front, which is joined to the keel with a wooden knee (angle piece) called a foregripe. At the other end, the upright part of framing consists of a sternpost with a supporting knee.

The framing across the boat is normally built with timber sawed from branches whose grain lies roughly in the required curves. These frames are

◄ Traditional carvel construction is still used in countries such as Turkey.

▶ Interior fittings and bulkheads are often made of wood, even in boats of glass fiber construction.

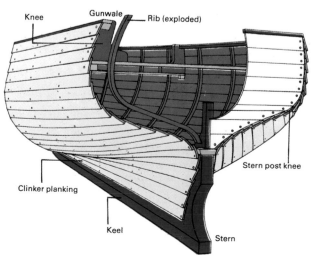

in turn strapped together inside with full-length wooden planks called stringers and at the deck edge with an inwale, or interior plank, which is sometimes called a beam shelf if it has to carry the deck beams. Originally, a number of heavy planks called wales were arranged longitudinally and fastened to the outside of the frame before the skin planking was fitted. Their function was to stop the planking from spreading when the caulking compound was hammered between the planks to make the hull watertight. With modern improvements in planks, fastenings, and building techniques, the wales have now largely disappeared.

There are many variants of the two techniques, and light, steam-bent strap frames are often used to augment and lighten the sawed frame structure. Other common variants include composite constructions, where steel frames are used with a wooden keel and planking; multiple planking, where two or more layers are placed diagonally to make a strong skin that is more watertight, though rather difficult to repair; and strip planking. Very narrow planks are used in the normal way for strip planking but are nail fastened through their thickness to the previous plank as well as being fastened to the frames to form a rigid structure.

To get the best performance from a fast powerboat, a knuckle, or chine (projecting corner), can be built at the division between

▼ A carvel boat (top) is made by fastening planks, edge to edge, over a ribbed framework. In clinker building (bottom) each plank overlaps its neighbor.

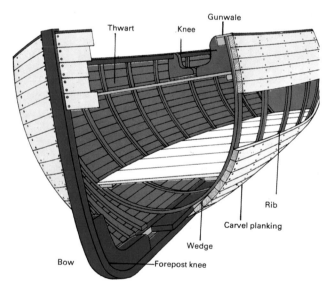

the bottom and sides of the hull. This chine is built like the centerline keel, and the technique is known as a chine construction.

Plywood

During the 1920s, boat-building techniques using plywood were developed, largely in the United States. The invention of waterproof resin adhesives led to the development of water-resistant marine-grade plywood. This quickly became popular for building bulkheads or vertical wall divisions of the hull, and later it became a very common material for the planking skins of inexpensive small craft. This technique, still used in do-it-yourself-built craft, was the first real attempt to use glue to stop water from entering between the components of the hull.

Despite great ingenuity, the shapes that can be constructed from bending flat sheets of plywood are very limited and are invariably angular in appearance. The next step therefore was to make the actual plywood sheets over a curved mold of the required shape. This type of building has been used for high-quality racing yachts, where the high costs involved can be balanced against the strength and light weight. This molded, plywood construction involves the planking of the mold with very thin wood sheets of veneer thickness. These are added in successive glued diagonal layers until a finished thickness approximately half that of a carvel planked hull is achieved. If cold setting adhesives are used, each layer is held down with staples until the glue sets. For hot molded construction, the layers are held in place by air bags or a vacuum press and moved into an oven to give a quick cure to the hot setting glue.

A variation of this construction is the use of laminated structural members. Here the keel, stem, beam, and ribs are built up over a mold to the required dimensions and curves.

Glass-reinforced plastics

The most popular form of construction today uses polyester resin reinforced with glass fiber, generally spoken of as glass fiber, or GRP. The normal building process starts with the construction of a full size solid model of the final boat, called the plug. Over this a hollow mold is

◄ A plastic hull is built on a former, which is similar in appearance to the finished boat but is structurally very weak by comparison. The former is highly polished to prevent sticking.

formed by a similar process to the hull construction. The hull and deck moldings, and even moldings for the interior accommodation, are formed in separate molds.

The materials used in GRP construction consist of polyester resin reinforced with finely spun glass fibers in cut pieces, as a mesh, or made up into a woven cloth.

The mold is first coated with wax or some other release agent to prevent the resin from adhering to the surface. Next a gel or surface coat of resin, usually impregnated with pigment to suit the final color scheme, is sprayed or painted onto the surface of the mold. A very light supporting mat of glass fibers is then placed on top of the resin and pressed in with a roller until completely saturated with wet resin. Subsequent layers of molding resin with heavier glass reinforcement carefully rolled into it are added until the required hull thickness and strength are attained.

The resin hardens in three stages: first to a soft gel, then to a point where the molding can be removed from the mold, and then over a period

▲ A ship's hull made of glass-fiber-reinforced plastic. The mold support rigging is moved along to mold new sections onto the hull. Ships of up to 600 tons (540 tonnes) can be made from GRP.

FACT FILE

- In the sixth century C.E., St Brendan is reputed to have sailed from Ireland to America in a leather boat with a crew of monks. This voyage, detailed in medieval Latin texts, was emulated in 1976 in a specially built boat based on Irish fishing curraghs, constructed from 49 ox hides sewn together with flax threads over a wooden frame, oak-tanned, and treated with wool grease. Propelled by flax sails, the boat took just over a year to cross the Atlantic.

- In 1888, Joshua Slocum, later to become the first man to sail around the world single-handed, built a three-masted sailing boat in Brazil after being shipwrecked. His new canoe, built from wreck timber and forest trees, was 35 ft. (10.7 m) long, 7.5 ft. (2.3 m) in the beam, and weighed 6 tons (5.4 tonnes). The Liberdade was fastened with carriage bolts, copper nails, and wooden pegs. She was rigged with three junk-style sails, based in shape on a Cape Ann dory, and clinker-planked.

- The planks and ribs of the traditional ocean-going Arab trading dhow are stitched together with coir cord made from coconut husks. A large dhow could have as much as 155 miles (249 km) of this cord holding its woodwork together. Every six months or so the coconut rope work is treated with vegetable oil.

◄ The idea of a boat made from concrete seems unlikely, because of the density of the material, but concrete is, in fact less dense than steel.

of weeks it matures to full strength. Bulkheads and reinforcements are added to the molding either in or just out of the mold. Considerable skill and care are necessary in glass-fiber construction to make certain that the resin is properly supported by glass at all corners and edges, that no air is trapped between the layers, and that the glass is thoroughly saturated with resin.

Another method of glass-fiber construction uses a hand-held spray gun to deposit both the resin and chopped glass strands, which leaves a mat of partly saturated fiber that must then be rolled to complete saturation as before. This method involves skilled spraying and accurate control of quantities to ensure uniformity. Glass-fiber construction is also mechanized in other ways, such as with the use of glass mats previously saturated with resin and vacuum or pressure resin saturation of previously laid glass reinforcements.

The main advantage of the glass-reinforced plastics method of construction is the monocoque, or stressed-skin, nature of the hull, without any joins where water might enter. Another benefit is the reduction of maintenance, which can be one-tenth of that for a conventional wooden hull. Further benefits lie in being able to use the molds for production building and the ease of achieving a high finish. The material, however, is fairly heavy (flotation chambers are often included) and inconveniently flexible. One way of correcting these faults is a "sandwich" construction, where another material is placed between the GRP layers to improve stiffness and reduce weight. End-grain balsa wood slabs or foam plastics are commonly used, laid over areas or in patterns as required during the course of the hull molding.

The cost of building a single hull in glass fiber is very high owing to the cost of the plug and mold. To overcome this, some craft are built with a PVC or polyurethane foam core planked over molds like a traditional wooden hull and then

covered with glass fiber inside and out. The outside surface of the hull is ground, sanded smooth, and paint finished.

Other materials

Boats are also built in metal. Steel, for instance, has been a common material for building boats as well as ships. Its strength and weight characteristics limit its use to larger craft, but with welded construction and the new antirust coatings, steel is becoming more popular again for one-of-a-kind larger craft.

Aluminum is also a popular material for high-performance one-of-a-kind yachts, increasing in use as new alloys reduced the original serious corrosion problems of aluminum in salt water. The metal's lightness also makes it suitable for small craft that have to be manhandled. Some small aluminum hulls are made by stretch forming, where a sheet of material is stretched bodily into shape over a hull-shaped former.

Another material used for boat building is concrete, which is strong and economical. Although this material may seem inappropriate for boats, it is sometimes used, particularly by people who build their own boats. It requires a strong reinforcing framework, usually metal rods or piping, with several layers of wire netting around it. This is then completely filled and covered with concrete to the required thickness and smoothness. It makes a tough hull, though the surface finish and durability depend on the concrete plasterer's skill.

► The manufacture of a concrete boat is similar to the method for making a plastic one. First, a mold or former, is prepared, then the concrete is spread onto it evenly to dry.

SEE ALSO: Aluminum • Concrete • Glass fiber • Sailing technology • Ship • Submarine • Warship

Body Scanner

For more than 50 years the simple X-ray photograph was the radiographer's only tool for seeing inside the human body, but since the 1960s, new systems have been developed, capable of picturing soft tissues as well as bone in the minutest detail. These body scanners, as they are known, make it possible to diagnose illness and plan surgery or treatment with greater precision and more quickly and cheaply than ever before.

Body scanners made their debut in 1972. The X-ray Computed Axial Tomography (CAT or CT) scanner was produced by physicists at the X-ray unit of EMI and constituted a major technological breakthrough. A CT machine uses X rays, but in a sophisticated manner. One of the problems with ordinary X-ray machines is that the pictures they give show only the densest body material, such as bone, with any clarity. Less dense material such as muscles, tissue, and tumors show up only vaguely because they absorb very little of the X rays passing through them. Although it is difficult for the human eye to distinguish between these areas of little absorption, a computer can be programmed to do the job much better.

The computer in a CT machine is fed data detailing the amounts of X radiation absorbed by all the types of body material, including water, fat and bone. As a person is scanned by an X-ray beam, it compares this data with the amount of radiation actually absorbed by the material in the person being scanned. In this way, the computer can build up a graphical representation showing the different types of body material in far greater detail than a simple two-dimensional X-ray photograph can.

Rather than exposing a large area of the body to X rays, as in a normal machine, a body scanner looks at only a thin cross section, or "slice," of the patient at a time. This also helps to produce a clearer image of the patient's insides.

In the CT scanner, the X rays passing through the body are picked up by crystal or gas detectors linked to a computer that converts the absorption data into a map of the piece of tissue, visible on a TV screen. The physician builds up a detailed picture of the area with different cross sections, which give almost as much information as if the patient were actually sliced up into many pieces. Today's scanners are capable of examining sections of the body from $\frac{1}{12}$ to $\frac{1}{2}$ in. (2–13 mm) thick, as easily as if they were slices of bread. Seven or eight different slices might be scanned to examine, say, a liver.

No one is quite sure how much damage is done by passing X rays through the body in the amounts needed for CT scanning. Whereas a traditional X ray of the head might require $\frac{1}{10}$ of a rad (a rad is a unit of absorbed radiation), a similar CT scan would subject the patient to about 4 rads. A scan of another part of the body requires about 1 rad. However, while the CT scanner X-rays a different slice of tissue each time, so that each piece receives only one dose of rays, traditional X rays overlap so that a patient may receive six or seven times the basic dose in one area of tissue.

Brain examination

The first CT scanners were used for examining the brain. As well as being much more effective in locating an area producing abnormal absorption values (a tumor, for example) than traditional X-ray methods, the scanners also did away with

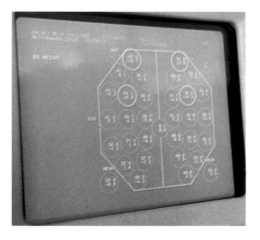

▼ A gamma-ray camera (below) can readily pick up signals from a radioactive tracer in a patient's brain and display the results instantly on a cathode-ray screen (left). The tracer is injected into the patient's blood stream, and the concentration in areas of the brain is studied.

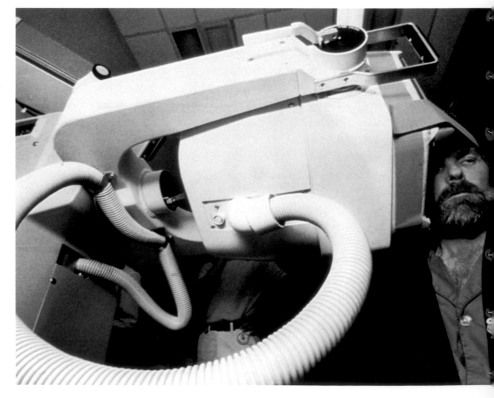

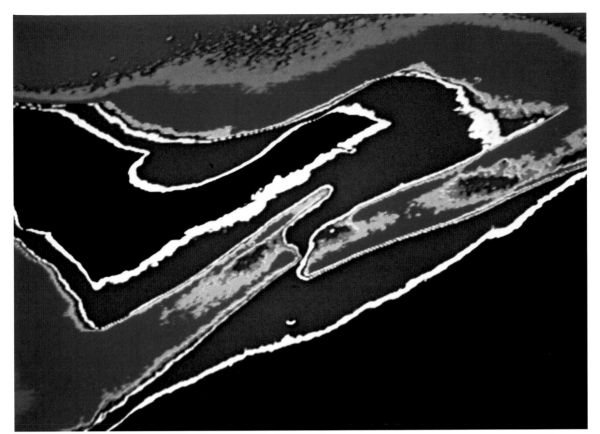

◄ A fracture of the upper arm as revealed by sonography. Sound waves are transmitted through the arm and picked up by the sonograph. Sound intensity reveals tissue density, and the signals are changed into a color display—a safer method than X rays.

the need for so-called invasive techniques to show up blood vessels and tumors on the brain. These techniques depended on the injection of dyes or radioactive material into the blood going to the brain. Not only was this procedure expensive in terms of time and highly skilled personnel, but it was also uncomfortable and even dangerous for the patient.

The system of scanning was later modified so that any area of the body could be placed between the X-ray source and detector. The first scanners could only take pictures of patients lying horizontally, but now they can tilt and make other maneuvers that enable a patient to be scanned from a variety of angles. This is especially useful for scanning organs such as the pancreas, that do not lie flat but are at some other angle.

Scanners are improving in many other ways, too. It usually takes about 20 seconds for a scanner to take a look at each slice of tissue, though the latest machines can reduce this to a mere three seconds. The pictures obtained are a lot more detailed than was possible with the first scanners because a much larger number of absorption points are now plotted. Early scanner pictures were made up of only 80,000 points, but most scanners now produce pictures made up of almost four times that number. One model uses 1.5 million points for each picture to record extra detail.

Modifications to the CT scanner have also enabled doctors to produce a three-dimensional picture of an area of tissue, so that tumors or blood clots can be seen in their true positions. Although scanners can look at tissues from a variety of angles, they can look from only one direction at a time. By taking pictures of adjacent slices of tissue and manipulating them by computer, parts of the body can be viewed from all angles, back and front, and as a three-dimensional image projected on the viewing screen.

Sound waves

CT is not the only method for scanning density variations. Another technique is to use very high-pitch sound—ultrasound. Because the waves used in ultrasound are thought to be completely harmless (unlike X rays, which create a slight radiation hazard), the technique has been used most widely in the field of obstetrics to locate the developing fetus and to check that there are no limb or other visible malformations and also to ensure that the baby is growing normally.

Ultrasound takes advantage of a property called piezoelectricity, exhibited by some crystals, to produce and detect ultrasound waves. In such crystals, an electrical signal will cause vibrations that generate the ultrasound waves, while an ultrasound wave coming into the crystal produces an electrical signal. Frequencies of 3.5 to 20 MHz are typically used. Ultrasound passes through the tissues and, just as sound waves are reflected as an echo from a cave or mountain as the sound passes

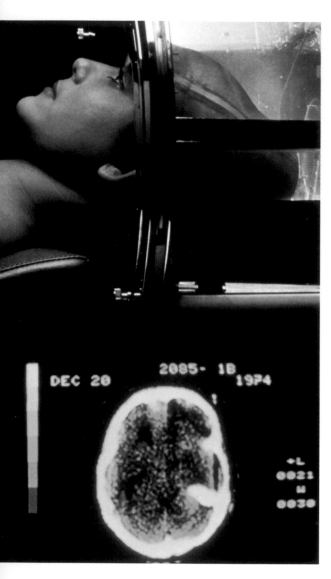

DEC 20   2085- 1B
                1974

◀ A Brain Electric Activity Mapping (BEAM) machine indicates how the brain is working, and its pattern can show up damaged brain tissue.

from one medium to another, so sound waves are reflected as they pass through tissues of varying densities. These reflections can then be converted into a picture showing up the different densities in an area, so that the womb and the fetus, surrounded by its watery bag of amniotic fluid, can be distinguished from other structures in the same area. The reflections appear as bright dots of varying intensity on the ultrasound screen. The equipment can be moved around so that the fetus can be seen from all angles to give a complete picture.

An additional refinement to the system was the introduction of real-time ultrasound in the late 1970s. The part of the machine sending the ultrasound through the tissues, the transducer, can be made up of many small parts, each triggered consecutively to give an almost continuous transmission of ultrasound through the tissues. In this way a continuous picture is obtained, much like a videotape, of the baby as it moves around in the womb.

Ultrasound has also been widely used as a complementary technique to CT scanning to

▶ During a Computed Tomography (CT) scan, the patient is positioned inside a chamber, with the head held steady. The scanner rotates around the patient, building up a scan of the brain by X rays. After computer analysis, technicians receive a readout of each side of the brain.

detect tissue lesions. And real-time ultrasound has proved useful for watching the movement of the heart valves to detect disorders both of the valves themselves and of the heart muscle. It has also been used in liver scanning, where tumors as small as a centimeter or two across can be detected. Malignancies of the kidney and pancreas have also been detected by ultrasound, as have abnormalities within the eye.

Another development of ultrasound is its use in the detection and examination of blood flow. When used in this way, the ultrasound scanner emits an uninterrupted sound beam and the Doppler technique is used to show how the blood is moving.

Ultrasound is also being used to good effect by surgeons to guide their instruments to the right place when they are taking samples of tissue (biopsy) and fluid (aspiration). One drawback of the technique is that ultrasound is highly absorbed by bone and gas, so the brain, or any tissues containing air—the lungs or ears for instance—cannot be examined using the technique.

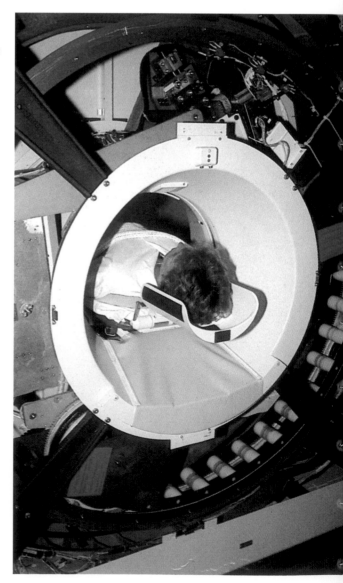

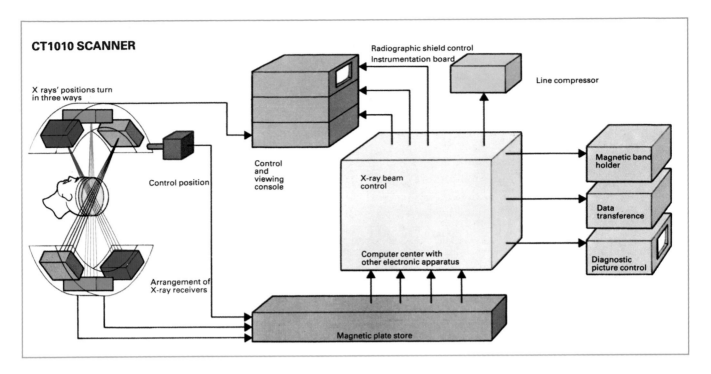

CT1010 SCANNER

Radiographic shield control
Instrumentation board

Line compressor

X rays' positions turn in three ways

Control position

Control and viewing console

X-ray beam control

Magnetic band holder

Data transference

Computer center with other electronic apparatus

Diagnostic picture control

Arrangement of X-ray receivers

Magnetic plate store

Other scanning techniques

Thermography is a technique that measures the differing amounts of heat given off by infrared radiation from separate structures or parts of the body and gives a visual display of them. Mirrors focus the infrared rays given off by the subject onto a sensitive detector that turns the information into an electronic impulse. This is shown on a cathode-ray tube as a thermal map of the parts that have been scanned. Body heat is produced as a by-product of cell activity (metabolism) and passed around the body by the blood and the lymphatic systems. The body gives off this heat by radiation, convection, and evaporation. When thermography is being used, the subject's body is cooled to reduce heat loss by evaporation and convection, as these losses cannot be measured as easily as heat in the infrared part of the spectrum.

Malignant cells give off more heat than normal cells, and so thermography is a useful tool in the location of tumors. It can also pinpoint areas that have either an impaired or enriched blood supply, because the areas with an impaired supply are cooler than those with a normal, enriched supply.

Thermography can also tell a physician how severe burns are. Superficial burns give off a higher level of infrared radiation than deep burns.

Positron Emission Tomography

As well as surveying the structure of the body, scanners can also be used to see how well the body is functioning. Positron Emission Tomography (PET) uses radioactive labeling to track blood flow or important compounds such as glucose around the body, especially in the brain.

Radionuclides give off positrons (positive electrons), which are picked up by a detector. A computer converts this data into a picture that shows the position of the most active regions. Somebody performing a task that involves the brain, like talking or mental arithmetic, creates a surge in blood flow and a demand for glucose to fuel the brain cells involved. This lights up the region on a PET scan, making it possible to pinpoint areas of the brain used for different functions. The quantities of radionuclides used in a PET scan are very small and are rapidly excreted from the body.

A similar method, radionuclide scanning (also called scintigraphy) uses special gamma-ray cameras that show up the distribution of radio nuclides (isotopes) after they have been either swallowed or injected into the body. This technique can be used to scan either the whole body or individual organs, showing up blockages either by an accumulation or absence of radio nuclides. Radionuclide scanning is used more routinely for checking how the body is functioning, but it shows less detail than PET or other scanning methods.

Xerograms

Xerography is a photoelectric process that uses a selenium-coated plate to record the patterns of light and dark of an item, as, for instance, when photocopying a document. The same technique can be used with X rays, rather than visible light, to produce within a short time a paper copy of the X-ray patterns. This method will detect nonmetallic foreign bodies, such as bones lodged in the throat, and will also reveal tumors.

▲ A diagram of an EMI surveillance CT1010 scanner, which is controlled by a computer. Because of the cost of this machinery, it is out of reach for many hospitals, though its X rays of tissue slices would make early diagnoses possible.

Magnetic scanning

An even more sophisticated (and completely safe) technique called magnetic resonance imaging (MRI) has been developed and implemented, particularly in the United States. MRI makes use of the magnetic properties of water in body tissues to draw up a picture of an organ or section of the body. Hydrogen nuclei, which are single protons, behave as small magnets. Their normally random axes of spin become aligned when subjected to a strong magnetic field. When a piece of tissue is placed between magnets and radio waves are

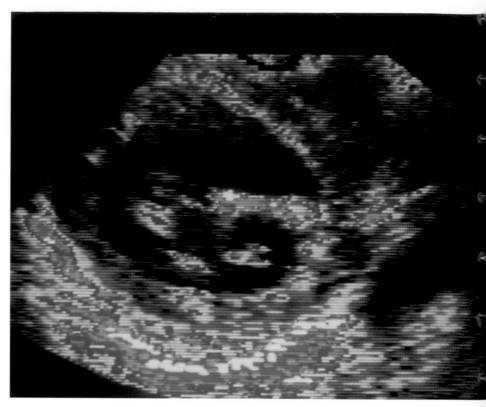

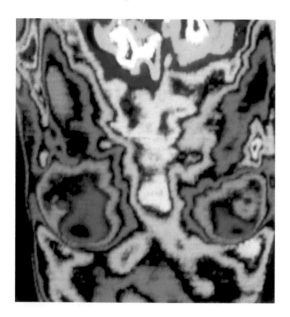

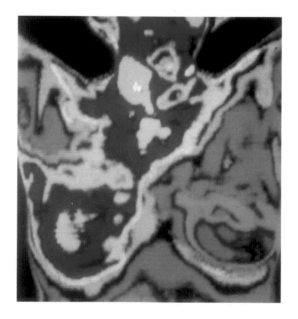

▲ Thermography (heat X ray) is used in cancer detection, using the changes in body temperature between healthy and unhealthy areas to spot cancers. In the top picture, the blue colors of the thermogram show there is no sign of cancer. In the bottom picture, the areas that show up as red in this woman's breasts reveal a change in temperature, which indicate the probable presence of cancer in the region.

passed through the tissue, the nuclei of atoms within the tissue will react with the radio waves. Protons absorb and react to these radio waves differently according to their environment, and so the signal that is received after the radio waves have interacted with the tissue can be converted into a picture of the proton density within specific areas of the body.

American researchers were beginning to investigate the potential of the technique on isolated cells at about the same time that EMI scientists were perfecting the first CT scanners. The nuclei most commonly used are the protons in hydrogen atoms because they give the strongest signal. A particular advantage of proton MRI is that it forms a good image of tissues such as the brain that contain lots of water, and it easily sees through bone, which contains few protons. It is thus useful for tissues that are harder to see using X rays. Other atomic absorption patterns being investigated are those of phosphorus and carbon.

One major drawback of MRI is cost. MRI systems can cost millions of dollars and often require special construction to shield the machinery from stray vibrations and magnetic fields. As a result they are less widespread than other types of scanner.

▲ This color image of a heart mitral valve has been produced using an ultrasound scanner rather than a conventional X ray.

| SEE ALSO: | BRAIN • CANCER TREATMENT • CELL BIOLOGY • ELECTRONICS IN MEDICINE • ENDOSCOPE • NUCLEAR MAGNETIC RESONANCE • ULTRASONICS • X-RAY IMAGING |

Bomb

A bomb is a hollow case filled with explosive or other destructive chemicals and exploded by percussion or a timing device. The outer case may be metal, plastic, concrete, or glass; the shape, size, and contents of a bomb depend on its application.

The term *bomb* was first applied to the short-barreled cannons of the 14th century, which were known as bombards; because the cast iron or stone shot fired from these weapons was lobbed upward in a high arc, the word *bomb* is still used to refer to the ammunition fired from mortars, where the projectile follows a high trajectory. More commonly, the word *bomb* refers to a hollow-cased projectile delivered from the air by an aircraft or a rocket. Sometimes bombs are designed to be placed in position or thrown by hand.

Development of bombing

Shortly after balloons were invented in 1783, attempts were made to deliver bombs from the air. In 1849, during the Austro–Venetian War, the Austrians loaded paper hot-air balloons with small bombs fitted with time fuses and released them so that they drifted toward Venice. Reports say they caused more psychological than material damage.

Strangely enough, the ingenious idea reappeared in the autumn of 1944. The Japanese released on the easterly winds about 1,000 hydrogen-filled paper balloons, each 33 ft. (10 m)

◀ The inside of a typical explosive device. This type of bomb is designed to explode after penetrating the upper floors of a building. As the bomb falls, the propeller screws the firing pin into contact with the booster charge.

▶ Some of the kinds of bomb dropped during World War II. Some cities suffered extensive damage from carpet bombing and incendiary devices, as opposing sides tried to knock out strategic manufacturing or military sites.

in diameter and loaded with a small antipersonnel or incendiary bomb. They were carried toward the United States and Canada, but most fell in remote areas and only 300 or so were recovered.

Throughout the 19th century, there were attempts to use balloons to bomb enemies, but the practice stopped in 1899 when it was forbidden by the Hague Convention. In December 1903, the Wright brothers made their first successful flight in a heavier-than-air machine, and in 1907 the Hague restriction was dropped. Many countries, but mainly the United States and Italy, then began experimenting again with bombs dropped from the air.

The earliest recorded bomb dropping from aircraft was by the Italians in their campaign against the Turks. On November 1, 1911, Lieutenant Gavotti of the Italian army dropped four 4.5 lb. (2 kg) bombs, converted Spanish hand grenades, on the Turkish encampment at Ain Zara in Libya. Although the Turks protested, the Italians quickly pointed out that they had shortly before bombarded the camp with 152 naval shells without eliciting any form of protest. Inevitably, this started a discussion on the ethics of air bombardment. Bombing techniques improved steadily and the advantages over the gun—increased range and greater projectile weight—were realized. During World War I, when both airships and airplanes were used, German zeppelins made more than 200 flights over London, dropping some 200 tons (180 tonnes) of bombs and killing or wounding 1,700 people. In 1923, draft rules for air warfare were drawn up but never ratified.

By the end of World War II, the Allies had dropped about 2 million tons of bombs on Germany and German-occupied territory, and although there has since been much controversy over its value, air bombardment has continued to play a large part in all subsequent conflicts. Nearly 7 million tons (6 million tonnes) of bombs were dropped by the United States on Indo-Chinese targets between 1965 and 1973. The use of so-called smart bombs in the Gulf War and during the Balkans crisis in the 1990s played a strategic part in avoiding ground troop losses and civilian casualties but reopened the debate on sustained bombing as a means of resolving conflict.

The early aerial bombs were ordinary shells with fins and new fuses added. Because they were primed by eye and hand-launched, they tended to be small, about 25 lbs. (11 kg), and inaccurate. During and after World War I, great improvements were made. Mounting racks and aiming devices were fitted to aircraft, and a variety of special-purpose bombs appeared: fragmentation, incendiary, chemical, illuminating, and so on. That bombing had become an important part of warfare was amply demonstrated in the Spanish Civil War (1936–1939) by the German contingent, who gained much practical experience there.

In World War II, despite the development of more lethal bombs, the major problem was accuracy. Techniques were developed, such as the use of radio beacons to fix targets and illuminating flares for night bombing. A recent improvement in accuracy is the use of lasers to guide the bomb, which enables pin-point targets to be hit with certainty. This system was successfully used in 1971 by the United States in Vietnam.

Bombs that carry their own aiming devices—such as infrared or magnetic seekers—have also been developed, with an emphasis on maximizing stability, range, and accuracy.

Bomb design

A bomb comprises four main parts: a body or case filled with the payload, a fin assembly to stabilize the bomb in flight, one or more fuses, and an assembly to arm the bomb at the moment of release. Arming a bomb is similar to releasing a safety catch. A parachute may also be included to stabilize or retard the bomb's fall to earth. The body usually has an aerodynamically streamlined shape, which tapers to a point, or ogive, at the nose, and a wall thickness that depends on the effect required on bursting. The stabilizing-fin assembly attached to the tail is often made of sheet metal, and it varies from a simple arrange-

▲ Top: British soldiers found these leaking napalm bombs, left behind by routed Argentinian forces after the 1983 Falklands War, strewn around a sabotaged Pucará ground-attack aircraft. Above: The U.S.A.F. A-10, the first jet designed specifically to strike ground targets, can carry about 15,000 lbs. (7,000 kg) of bombs and missiles, as well as 1,350 rounds of ammunition.

ment for normal trajectories to a complex design with offset airfoil surfaces to spin the bomb during its fall.

The fuse must include safety devices for handling and transhipment and yet must be capable of setting off a large quantity of explosive when the bomb strikes the target or after a predetermined delay. A substantial intermediary charge between the fuse and the main filling is incorporated to transmit the shock wave of detonation and produce the maximum explosive effect. Two fuses are sometimes used to ensure detonation at the target and to provide alternative ways of bombing. They must be fitted in the nose, tail, or body center. Once the bombs are installed in the aircraft, by means of lugs on the body, a wire arming system is attached. This arming wire may be released with the bomb, allowing the bomb to drop safely, or it may be retained by the aircraft, arming the bomb's fuse mechanism as it is released.

Terminal ballistics is the study of damage caused by a bomb. From this study a bomb can be designed to have a specific effect, depending on whether it is to explode on contact or penetrate the target. Detonation waves can travel through explosive materials as fast as 4 miles per sec. (6.3 km/s), followed by gaseous products from the explosive at pressures of 50,000 bar and temperatures up to 9000°F (5000°C). When the wave hits a solid material, it transmits a mechanical impulse that causes the material to fragment. By varying the design of the outer bomb casing, for example, by corrugating or otherwise shaping the surface, it is possible to control the shape, size, mass, and velocities of the fragments.

Types of bomb

The shape of the bomb often depends on the bombing technique employed. For instance, a streamlined 500 lbs. (230 kg) bomb dropped from

▼ Bombs used in a computerized aiming system have a cylindrical mount into which the bomb pivots. As the attitude of the aircraft changes, the system angles the bomb to keep it accurately on target.

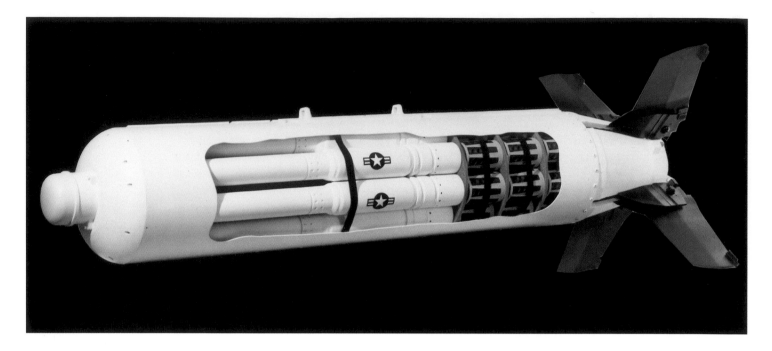

a high altitude, say 10,000 ft. (3,000 m), reaches a terminal velocity—at which air resistance prevents it from speeding up further—of about 1,000 ft. per sec. (300 m/s) and strikes at an angle within 20 degrees to the vertical. Providing the case is strong enough to withstand impact, the bomb could penetrate several floors of a normal building or some 20 ft. (6 m) of earth before coming to rest, causing a lot of damage before it detonates. An incendiary bomb, however, does not need to penetrate before ignition, and a lightweight body of poor ballistic shape is used because it has the advantage of restricting terminal velocity to less than 300 ft. per sec. (90 m/s). Wings and other control surfaces can also be fitted to give certain effects, as in an ingenious bomb designed by Dr. Barnes Wallis in Britain during World War II to destroy dams. When dropped from a specific height and speed, the bomb rotated and skipped along the surface of the water, as a flat stone does on a pond, until it came to the dam wall and sank to the bottom, where it exploded.

Depth charges, which are large high-capacity bombs with light cases, are designed for underwater demolition work. They are hydrostatically activated when the right depth is reached and also have a nose fuse for use against surface targets. Their main purpose is attacking submarines, which can be severely damaged by blast pressure. The bombs are cylindrical, with a flat nose to prevent ricochet. They have an explosive content of about 75 percent by weight and range in total weight from 300 to 700 lbs. (140–320 kg).

Armor-piercing bombs are designed to penetrate heavy armor and concrete-reinforced structures. They have a high-strength steel case, weigh about 1,000 lbs. (450 kg), are very stream-lined with a solid, pointed nose, and have a low (5–15 percent) explosive content. The fusing system has a delay to allow deep penetration of the target.

Cluster bombs are really cases that carry a number of bomblets to a target. A single carrier bomb may contain hundreds of bomblets, and these may be fused to explode at intervals over a matter of days, particularly when they are designed to deny an enemy use of a vital area such as an airfield. There are also submunitions under development that can guide themselves to specific targets.

Flying bombs were invented by the Germans in World War II. The V1 contained 1,870 lbs. (850 kg) of explosive in the body of an impulse-jet powered pilotless aircraft. The aircraft fell to earth when the fuel ran out and exploded.

Atomic bombs use energy released from the nuclei of atoms having the explosive force of thousands or even millions of tons of TNT. Early atomic bombs used nuclear fission; hydrogen bombs work by nuclear fusion. Only fission bombs have been used in war, and only twice, to devastating effect.

Chemical bombs include those filled with toxic gases, smoke producers, and incendiary materials. Gas-generating bombs can contain lung irritants, blistering gases, tear gases, irritant smokes, and nerve and blood poisons. Smoke bombs are filled with chemicals such as titanium tetrachloride, hexachlorethane, and zinc dust, while incendiaries use flammable oils such as napalm.

▲ A cluster bomb cut away to show a number of bomblets packed inside. These bomblets often have delayed fuses to cause damage some days after they have hit the target.

SEE ALSO:	AMMUNITION • BOMB-AIMING DEVICE • BOMB AND MINE DISPOSAL • EXPLOSIVE • MISSILE • NUCLEAR WEAPON

Bomb-Aiming Device

A bomb falling from an aircraft has four main forces acting on it: the downward force of gravity, the forward velocity of the aircraft, the air resistance acting against the bomb in the opposite direction to its travel, and the effect of the wind on the bomb during its fall—the drift. Initially, pilots judged by eye when to release a bomb, but it soon became obvious that there was a need for a bomb-aiming device.

Early bombsights, used during World War I, were no more than simple triangles with one side proportional to height and the other to airspeed, the longest side being the line of sight. These devices were sufficiently accurate at low altitudes and slow speeds, but as aircraft were forced to fly higher to avoid ground defenses and the blast of their own bombs, aiming became more difficult.

In effect, a bombsight was needed that could vary the speed and height sides of the bombing triangle to allow for the drift as the aircraft heading changed and for bombs of varying ballistics. The first of these bombsights, which came into use during the 1930s, were simple mechanical devices with hand settings, known as preset vector bombsights.

The next development, just before the start of World War II, was a bombsight with the speed, height, and drift adjusted automatically by a mechanical analog computer connected directly to the airspeed, height and heading systems of the aircraft. This was known as a continuously set vector bombsight.

Early sights, which used cross wires for aiming, had two disadvantages. The eye had difficulty focusing on both the wires and the target and the wires, being set in the horizontal plane of the aircraft, moved off the target whenever the aircraft banked. These problems were solved by a collimated sighting head.

During World War II, the tachometric bombsight was produced. With this, bomb aimers could allow for the one factor outside their control—the wind effect. The tachometric sight is based on the principle that, with the correct values set and with the crosshairs placed on the target, the sighting angle will change at the appropriate rate for the height and speed of the aircraft and the crosshairs will be synchronized, that is, remain on the target. If they drift off the target, then the wind settings are changed until there is synchronization. When the sighting angle, which is decreasing as the aircraft approaches the target, equals the computed bombing angle, the bomb is released automatically.

Another bombsight used in World War II was the angular velocity, or low-level, bombsight.

▲ Using the technique of toss-bombing, the airplane uses its speed to throw the bomb at the target, then climbs away from the blast.

Apparent direction of aircraft

Actual direction of aircraft after drift

Wind

Final trajectory
of dropped bomb

Target

This works on the principle that the apparent movement of a point on the ground is constantly changing, being fastest below the plane and slowest near the horizon. Any target in front of the aircraft therefore has a particular change of angle, or angular velocity, associated with it. A mechanism in the bombsight produces horizontal lines, superimposed on the ground, moving at a constant speed governed by the aircraft's speed and height and the ballistics of the bomb. At some point, these lines will appear to be stationary with respect to the ground. When this point crosses the target, the bomb is released.

An early blind-bombing system, devised during World War II, was OBOE. Two radio beacons were sited so that the aircraft could fly at a constant range from one beacon until a predetermined range from the other beacon was reached, when the bomb was released. The introduction of airborne radar that would map the ground resulted in the development of modern self-contained radar bombing systems.

Inertial navigation systems, which are used to guide spaceships to the Moon or intercontinental rockets to distant targets, can direct an aircraft from takeoff to a bomb-release point thousands of miles away. Modern "smart" bombs do not need to be aimed accurately at all. They are guided much as missiles are, carrying a TV camera or laser detector.

Inertial navigation systems are the basic aiming device of bombs that are delivered over medium or strategic ranges, such as nuclear warheads. This system is accurate enough for an attack on a town or a military base even over intercontinental distances but has to be complemented with a terminal guidance system (TGS) for the phenomenal precision necessary to destroy individual hardened missile silos. A typical TGS would be a bomb carrying a digital map display of its target and the surrounding area. A digital display uses a map divided into squares that are each given a numerical value according to some feature of their topography—perhaps the average height above sea level. The incoming bomb carries instruments that can read the altitude on the ground below, and this is translated into digital values to be compared with the on-board digital map. The computer can then generate signals to the bomb's fins or tail assembly so that it maneuvers to the desired position.

▲ A computer calculates the trajectory of the bomb, allowing for wind speed and direction.

SEE ALSO: AIRCRAFT DESIGN • BALLISTICS • BOMB • HEAD-UP DISPLAY • INERTIAL GUIDANCE • MISSILE • RADAR

Index